FIXING THE INDIES

★ ★ ★ ★ ★

NORM KAISER

To my wonderful wife Leslie, for putting up with all my crazy obsessions.

CONTENTS

★ ★ ★ ★ ★

The State of Affairs

"When you're in a hole, stop digging."
- *Denis Healey, British politician*

An all too familiar scene

It's Saturday night, and I'm sitting on a very uncomfortable folding steel chair. I'm in a community center gymnasium, and directly in front of me is a pro wrestling ring that looks so old and dilapidated, Gorgeous George himself may have taken a few bumps in it. The ring ropes are steel cable encased in an old garden hose and wrapped badly with duct tape. The ropes are droopy and sag in the middle; clearly the ring crew didn't bother to tighten up the turnbuckles. But in even worse shape than the ring ropes is the canvas. It's all ripped and torn and stained with blood, paint, grease, and whatever other grime it's accumulated over its 20 year lifespan, which is clearly 15 years too long. To prevent wrestlers from tripping on the rips and tears, the promoter has "fixed" the mat with – you guessed it – more duct tape.

I'm in this place with about 50 other people, so it doesn't take a mathematician to figure out that the guys behind the curtain nervously lacing up their boots (or, in many cases, old sneakers) aren't going to make much money tonight. I paid eight bucks to get in, and if my third grade multiplication skills serve me well, 50 times $8 equals a paltry $400 – barely enough to pay just for the building for the night. The boys behind that curtain? They'll be lucky to walk away with enough money to cover the cost of the gas they burned getting here.

It's 7:15. Bell time was supposed to be at 7:00. I'm getting antsy for the show to start. Finally a poor excuse for a ring announcer – a really sloppy guy in a t-shirt, jeans, and a baseball cap – makes his way to the ring and starts to announce the first match. Ah, but then a pudgy guy appears from behind the curtain, enters the ring, and grabs the microphone from the announcer. I take it from this guy's scuffed boots and faded trunks and the Metallica t-shirt intended to cover up the fact that he's never seen the inside of a gym that he's supposed to be a wrestler. I also quickly gather that he's a heel, based on how rudely he grabbed the microphone. That takes me all of five seconds to figure out.

So this guy starts out on some rant about how he got cheated last month out of this promotion's "world" title because the referee – who's in the ring now, dressed in blue jeans and a collarless, untucked, striped ref shirt and sporting a scraggily ponytail – counted slow. So tonight things are going to be different. Tonight the heel refuses to wrestle with that slow-counter officiating his match. He wants someone else. So the announcer takes back the mic, and with the look of a flight attendant asking over the plane's PA if any of the passengers onboard is a pilot, he wonders aloud if anyone in the audience is suitable to save the show and officiate the match. Sure enough, a "fan" is picked out of the audience, but wouldn't you know it? The "fan" is a seasoned mat veteran who allegedly used to kick a lot of butt around these parts and he just so happened to show up tonight to watch the show.

How convenient.

Eventually the sloppy guy in the baseball cap announces the babyface – a scrawny beanpole in tights that his mother made – and the match gets underway. They tie up. The baby takes the heel down with a poorly executed arm drag. The heel complains to the substitute referee that the baby pulled his hair. The ref refuses to believe him. Another tie up. Another takedown. The heel gets up and runs the ropes, charging at the baby with a clothesline. The baby throws a badly mistimed dropkick that misses by a mile. Confused, the heel decides just to sell the move anyway by tossing himself over the top rope. Surely you know where this is going – the heel loses the match and blames the guest referee. The guest referee stands his ground and, lo and behold, we have a new feud…

A bit later in the evening, another guy comes out dressed in what looks to me to be a leprechaun costume from last St. Patrick's Day parade. He's got the green felt derby with a four leaf clover sticking out of the band, a sequined green vest, a bright neon green boa, and – randomly enough – about 500 Mardi Gras beads hanging around his neck. Adding to the leprechaun image is that the guy is about 5' 6" and weighs about 180 pounds – most of which is pasty baby fat. He grabs the microphone (as all heels in the indies are wont to do), and speaks in that laughable phony inner city smack talk used by white guys who are desperately trying to be black. Consequently, I can't really tell what he's trying to tell us, as his pronunciation and enunciation are both very poor, but it's the standard heel shtick – the people in the audience are bumpkins, this town sucks, we should pay him more respect, we should shut up while he's talking, blah, blah, blah...

Finally his opponent for the evening comes out to his entrance music, which is some obscure rap song with explicit lyrics being blasted over a fluttering PA speaker. I notice as mothers quickly try to cover their five-year-olds' ears. The guy coming out to this awful "music" is about 6' 2", weighs all of 150 pounds, and looks like his day job is changing oil at the local Jiffy Lube. Somehow this guy is supposed to be both the promotion's champion and a babyface. How do I know he's a babyface? Because the leprechaun is a heel. And how do I know the Jiffy Lube guy's the champion? Because he's got a toy replica WWE title belt thrown over his right shoulder.

I'm not making this up.

So I'll spare you the boring details of their boring, uninspired botchy match and skip ahead to the finish. I forgot to mention that the leprechaun has a manager of sorts who looks more like the 60 year-old guy who hangs out all day at the dog track. He got all dressed up for the event – he's wearing black work jeans and a black t-shirt that says "Al's Towing" on it. I assume he's Al. He looks like an Al. He's the kind of guy who still combs his sparse hair straight back and holds it in place with gobs of Brylcreem. You know the type of guy I'm talking about. He's old. He's got a massive beer gut. And he serves no purpose at all other than to stand at ringside and block my view of the match. Until, that is, the finish, when he grabs the leprechaun's candy striped cane and cracks the Jiffy Lube champion over the head (gingerly, of course) while, conveniently, the ponytailed ref isn't looking. One, two, three, and the match is over. The leprechaun is handed the plastic toy belt and he's now the champ.

But it's not over yet! The leprechaun and Al go behind the curtain, only to reemerge seconds later with a briefcase and a piece of paper. The piece of paper looks suspiciously like an old flyer from last month's show, but according to the leprechaun, it's the contract that Jiffy Lube tech signed for this match. In the "fine print" of this one-page document is a clause that a) bars Jiffy Lube tech from ever challenging the leprechaun for the championship again and b) makes Jiffy Lube tech an indentured servant to the leprechaun.

Like a broken record

What I just described is repeating itself in bingo halls, VFWs, and community center gymnasiums all across the country. If you're an independent pro wrestler, promoter, booker, or just a fan, the scenario I just described is surely very familiar to you. It must be, because just about every indie wrestling promotion runs shows very much like this one. And I certainly hope the message I'm trying to convey by relating this show to you is perfectly crystal clear. If it's not, let me give it to you in black-and-white: This type of show is *awful*. Yes, *awful*. There's no other word that can sum it up or describe it any better.

Awful!

And what's really sad (and funny at the same time) is at the end of the night, the guys who've just risked life and limb and are covered with welts, bruises, and mat burns are all wondering why the turnout was so bad. Now, you may be reading this and feel a bit offended or defensive because you've been involved in shows like this. Heck, you might be a booker or promoter who books shows like this all the time and think you're a booking genius. Feeling offended, defensive, or a bit bruised by what I've said is OK. In fact it's expected. If you've been doing something for a long time and someone comes along and starts telling you it's crap, well, that's tough to stomach, and the natural response is to get ticked off. Even so, I ask that you read this book cover to cover with an open mind.

Albert Einstein once said that insanity is doing the same thing over and over again and expecting different results. If that's true, the world of independent pro wrestling is a certifiable basket case.

Doing the same thing over and over and over again, failing miserably, and then doing it all over again is standard operating procedure for independent pro wrestling. Worse, pro wrestlers and wrestling promoters are all a bunch of copycatters. So not only is one outfit doing the same stupid things over and over, other startup promotions see it and decide for some reason to do the same stupid things, too.

That's what this book is all about: Breaking this mindset – this curse – of insanity and stupidity. If you're a pro wrestler, manager, booker, promoter, or whatever, I'm glad you've decided to come along with me on this journey. But be warned – I don't pull any punches. After being involved in the spectacular and bizarre world of pro wrestling for almost 25 years, I've seen quite a lot, and I'm here to speak the unabashed truth. What you're about to read in the pages of this book is oftentimes controversial and may even make you a bit angry.

But it's what you need to hear. For the sake of the sport and spectacle of pro wrestling, it's what we all need to hear.

How we got here

So how did we get here, anyway? How did we arrive at a place and time where shows that sell 200 tickets is considered a good gate and anybody with a set of knee pads can climb into the ring? It wasn't always this way. Really, it wasn't. Talk to any old-timer and he'll tell you that during the territory days of wrestling – before Vince McMahon and WWE took over the world – local pro wrestling shows in many cities routinely sold tens of thousands of tickets *each and every week*. There was a time when pro wrestling was red hot and promoters just about printed money. But something happened along the way. The WWE cornered the market, forcing all the viable competition to fold their tents, and all that was left were a few penny ante promoters who ran shows on the side as a hobby.

Then along came the Internet, and almost overnight, pro wrestling's secrets were laid bare for the entire world to see. Teenagers all over the country were able to learn the basics of a standing suplex just by trawling newsgroups and message boards, and soon, backyard wrestling promotions were cropping up all over the place. Any kid who ever watched an episode of *Raw* now suddenly decided he wanted to try his hand at wrestling. It was like magician David Copperfield's best tricks had been exposed on the Internet and now kids everywhere were making Lear Jets disappear in their own backyards.

And since pro wrestling territories had vanished, a lot of pro wrestlers were left without work. So they figured it would be a good idea to start their own promotions, too. And to supplement their income, why not open up a pro wrestling school to stock their new promotions with "talent" that would work for cheap – or in many cases, for free? It didn't take long for these guys to realize that they could make more money by training kids with little athletic ability how to be wrestlers than they could by actually running shows. So in effect, shows took a back seat to the schools. Schools were where the money was at, so that's where the focus was put. But then who wants to pay to attend a wrestling school that doesn't run shows? Yeah, sure, you might learn how to wrestle, but what good is that if you don't ever get to appear before any screaming fans? So as part of the training "program," most of these two-bit schools ran shows on the side. But like any school, continued profits rely on recruiting new students. Accordingly, admission standards were set at an all-time low. Meanwhile, other retired or fired pro wrestlers saw the money being made by these schools, so they decided they wanted a piece of the action. Soon there were pro wrestling schools – and the second-rate shows they run – cropping up in backyards, warehouses, and strip malls all over the place.

It was (and still is) the perfect storm. Wrestling schools were a fine money-making racket, but to be viewed as "legit" you had to run shows. And to keep the money flowing, you constantly had to be on the lookout for the next kid who's dreaming he's the next Hulk Hogan. The result? Lots of crappy shows and lots and lots and lots of under-qualified, poorly trained "wrestlers" looking to get booked.

The Dream

Just about every indie pro wrestler knows *The Dream*. *The Dream* is the hope, the desire, the wish that someday, he'll make it to the big time – WWE, TNA, or maybe ROH. He has visions of his name in lights and screaming fans clamoring for his autograph dancing through his head. And it all seems so attainable. After all, if an average looking guy like Jeff Hardy can make it big, why can't anyone? *The Dream,* unfortunately, is what keeps indie pro wrestling going. It's all driven by young guys' hopes that they'll somehow get discovered in a dingy American Legion hall and get called up to the big leagues.

The chances are about 1 in 10 million. It's all a really, really long shot. And when you think about it, WWE and TNA already have development promotions that they recruit their talent from. If you're not in one of those gigs, chances are good you'll never even get looked at. That's just the reality of the situation. You can try to get into one of the feeder leagues, but considering how many people try out for them, it's hard to even get to talk to anyone.

Even so, thousands of young guys all over North America continue to pursue *The Dream.* They accept any booking they can get anywhere they can, even if the "purse" is a crumpled $20 bill. It's all worth it if it means a shot at realizing *The Dream.* Town to town, week to week, guys in the indies give it their all in front crowds of 50 toothless screaming people in middle school gymnasiums, Freemason halls, and strip mall parking lots. Some shows pay out more; some shows, you get stiffed. Either way, the "pay" is nothing to speak of, and you have to hold down a regular day job to make the rent. It's all OK, though – just keep chasing *The Dream.*

And then let's suppose you do get called up. *The Dream* has come true! What then? Well, if you're like 99% of the other guys who've gotten called up, your career will go something like this: You'll get the call. You'll be sent to one of the development territories to hone your skills. This is where most guys wash out. They fail to get over with the fans there and get dropped like a hot potato. But let's suppose you're not one of those guys. Let's say you get over with the fans and you show some awesome ring ability. So you get sent up to WWE, where you wrestle a few dark matches. Let's say the bigwigs there like you, so they decide to give you some TV time. On TV, fans take a liking to you, so the bigwigs decide to give you a push. What then? I'll tell you what then – they give you a silly gimmick and have you read promos off a teleprompter. You don't much care for the gimmick, but that's OK because you're giddy with the excitement of being on national TV. You give it your all because you want to be a team player and don't want to blow your big shot.

So you do the gimmick the way they tell you to, and it goes OK for a little bit, but then you notice the bigwigs start telling you that you can't do certain of your favorite signature moves. You can't do that superkick that you practiced for years because the superkick is Shawn Michaels' move. You can't do that tombstone piledriver, either, because, well, that's the Undertaker's. And that fantastic senton bomb you've been practicing off the diving board at the local public pool? Forget it – that belongs to Jeff Hardy. Thus limited, you notice the fans aren't popping for you the way you had hoped. This is the beginning of the end. Once the fans stop cheering, there's only one way to go – down. Your push ends. Soon you notice other new, fresh guys coming in to make their debuts. They're the next big thing; you, on the other hand, are yesterday's news. You get the word that you're going to have to do a few jobs for these guys to, you know, help get them over.

You have time remaining on your one year contract, so they job you out. *The Dream* is coming to a close. You hope that somehow you'll be reinvented and get another push, but in your heart you know it ain't gonna happen. The pro wrestling rotating door is always full of new guys, all chomping at the bit to get their shot, and you're in the way. Eventually, the dreaded day comes – you're released. So you go back to the only place you can go back to…

The indies. Granted, now you have some credibility, some star power, having been to the big leagues. Instead of getting $20 a show, maybe you can demand $100. Of course, few promoters can afford to pay you that (or at least that's what they say), so sometimes you have to agree to work for less. But even if you do get the $100 you expect, that's nowhere near enough to make ends meet. Even if you wrestle eight times a month, which is a stretch, that's only $800 per month, or $9,600 per year. Heck, you can do much better than that selling big screen TVs and

Blu-ray players at Best Buy, and you don't have to deal with bruised ribs, mat burns, or broken bones.

Think this isn't the case? Think it ain't so? Think it can't possibly be this bad? It is, trust me. If you don't believe me, just ask guys like Kid Kash, Colt Cabana, Justin Credible, Gangrel, or Jon Heidenreich – guys who've been there – and they'll tell you. The big leagues are a dog-eat-dog world, and to make it there is hard enough; to stay there, you either need to be a monster like the Big Show, John Cena, or Batista, or your father (or father-in-law) has to be a former WWF wrestler or WWE executive (a la Cody Rhodes, Ted DiBiase Jr., Triple H, and Randy Orton).

Forging our own dream

I have a dream. My dream is that the gatekeepers of *The Dream* someday won't just be Vince McMahon and Jeff Jarrett. What do I mean by that? I mean if we all share *The Dream*, why don't we pursue it on our own? Really, why do we need two big shots to determine whether or not we realize our ambitions?

Think of it this way. Mary Kay is a cosmetics company that sells its product line through an "independent sales force." In other words, it's makeup that housewives sell to other housewives door-to-door. The big promise is that you can become independently wealthy by selling cosmetic products to your friends, family, and coworkers. But the way to make big bucks, they say, is by recruiting other women into the business. You make a cut of whatever your recruits sell. And if your recruits recruit new people into the business, you get a cut of whatever they sell, too.

The big draw to this is a pink Cadillac. Yep, you read that right – a pink Cadillac. That's because the very top sellers in the Mary Kay company get to drive a pink Cadillac company car around town. They're the bigwigs, the hotshots. That pink Cadillac just screams, "Hey, look at me! I'm somebody! I'm driving a Caddy! And not only am I driving a Caddy, it's a pink Caddy!"

But here's the deal: If you want a pink Cadillac – if that's your goal – you don't have to sell lipstick and mascara door-to-door to get one. You can get a job or start your own business, save up enough money, go down to the Caddy dealer, and buy one off the lot! Sure it wouldn't be easy. You'd have to work hard and save your nickels and dimes, but I bet it would be easier to get your pink Cadillac that way than by selling stuff door-to-door and trying to con your friends into selling the stuff, too.

The point is you don't have to follow someone else's roadmap to reach your dreams. You can march to the beat of your own drummer. If you have a dream, you have to *make it happen!* Don't let someone else dictate to you how or when you can do something.

We don't need this guy: We all have a dream. We all have just one life to live. Why let this guy dictate to us whether or not we live our dreams?

How does this apply to pro wrestling? Easy – if we reinvent our sport, if we shatter our paradigms and reexamine how we sell ourselves and our product, *independent pro wrestling can become very profitable.*

We can realize *The Dream* on our own.

Laissez-faire

Make no mistake; I'm a big, big supporter of the free market system. Bobby Heenan once said, "If you own a gas station and don't like the idea of someone else opening up a gas station across the street, move to Cuba!"

He's right. Competition is ordinarily what keeps the wheels of capitalism turning, but in the case of pro wrestling, the ease of one's ability to either become a wrestler or a promoter is really, really hurting the business' credibility. It's just too easy to rent a building and a ring, hire a couple of 19-year-olds fresh out of a wrestling "school" or a backyard fed, and call yourself a promoter. Anybody can do it. And these days, just about anybody is. The result is a slew of poorly organized, poorly promoted shows with very poor production values that turn potential fans off: "Oh for crying out loud, look at that," they think. "Those pro wrestlers have a guy in a gorilla costume, a guy in a Spiderman getup, and a guy dressed up as a transvestite. Why does anyone go to that?" And that's before they even see all the botched spots, the befuddled match pacing, the nonsensical storylines, the lousy acting, or the 400 pound tub-of-lard in spandex.

We can't change the easy entry nature of the pro wrestling business – not unless we get government involved to "regulate" it, which just means you'd have to pay a tax or buy a license to run a show. That just cuts into indie pro wrestling's already meager profit margin. So regulation is not the answer. Some promotions that run shows in states that have athletic commissions may disagree about that, but that's just because they like the lack of competition that regulation engenders. So while we can't block unqualified newcomers from entering the business, we *can* raise our expectations. As fans, performers, and promoters, we all need to raise our expectations of ourselves, of the business, and of each other.

That, essentially, is the core principle of this book – that we all need to raise our expectations. Fans need to expect more from shows, from individual matches, and from individual performances. Promoters need to expect more from the pro wrestlers they hire. They need to expect wrestlers to be in proper shape, to have the proper gear, to present the proper appearance, and to have the proper training. Pro wrestlers need to look at themselves hard in the mirror and ask themselves, "Why am I doing this?" If the reason is to make it big, then you must set your goals high and develop a real plan to achieve them. You can't be half-ass and expect to make it anywhere. Nobody has gotten anywhere with a half-ass effort.

Cutting Corners

One of the biggest problems in indie wrestling today is too many guys are cutting corners. Now before I get into this point I need to make something perfectly clear because many guys I talk with get this concept confused: There is a major difference between being frugal and being cheap. To be frugal is to spend money wisely. A frugal person recognizes that certain things cost money – there's no way around it – but when it comes time to buy something, they always look for the best deal to stretch their dollar as far as possible. To be cheap, on the other hand, is to try not to spend money at all – even when it's required for something to be successful. For example, a new wrestler who buys a pair of used wrestling boots that are in perfect condition on e-Bay is being *frugal*. In contrast, a new wrestler who doesn't buy boots at all and instead wrestles in his sneakers is being *cheap*. Another example: A promoter who repairs his still functional ring ropes by neatly re-taping them with ring rope tape himself instead of buying new ropes is being *frugal*. A promoter who leaves his ropes ratty or repairs them with duct tape from Walmart is being *cheap*.

CHRIS YOUNG

First rate advertising: I bet this sign really packed the house that night. It looks like the promoter hired an ax murderer to paint it for him – in blood. I mean, really?

We need to stop being so *cheap* in indie pro wrestling!

You may be laughing at the examples I just gave, but you shouldn't because they're real! I see this type of stuff in just about every single indie show I attend. While I understand most indie promotions are shoestring operations, they're still businesses, and there are certain expenses that must be paid when running any business. Extreme attention to detail is critical to success, yet so few people in pro wrestling observe it. And that's where we've gone wrong. We're cutting corners to be cheap and avoid spending money. We're not paying attention to detail because we rationalize that "good enough is good enough" or because if we pay attention to detail, we'll spot so many things wrong that need to be fixed. If we ignore what's broken, it'll fix itself, right? The fan that shows up and sits in the front row won't see the tears in the mat because they're too busy watching the action, right? The fans won't notice that I'm fat and out of shape if I wear a t-shirt to cover up, right? After all, if I can do some really awesome high spots, it doesn't matter if I'm fat, right?

Wrong. People *do* notice the details. People pay attention. What we would like to go unnoticed is normally the thing fans (our customers) notice *first*.

To understand this lesson better, let's look at the US military. The United States has the finest, most professional, most unbeatable military in the world, and it's all because our military leaders instill the importance of extreme attention to detail in our young military men and women. When I joined the Air Force twenty years ago, I wondered why my drill sergeant would bust my chops about the condition of my foot locker. Everything had to be positioned precisely in an exact configuration. My underwear had to be folded into perfect six inch squares. My socks had to be folded individually. Every button on every pair of pants and every shirt had to be buttoned as they hung in my wall closet. For the longest time I didn't understand why. It all seemed like unnecessary harassment to me. Finally one day – I don't know why – I summoned the courage to ask my drill sergeant why he was such a stickler about such trivialities. To my surprise, he didn't glower or shout at me as I expected. Instead he dropped the drill sergeant act for a moment and said, "Well you see, son, we have no idea what you'll actually be doing in the Air Force once you finish boot camp. You might be working on jet engines or you might be working on nuclear missiles. I don't know. But I do know that's precision stuff. People's lives depend on that stuff working correctly. We can't afford sloppy work. We can't afford to allow young guys to do a half-ass job. This foot locker? To me it represents that jet engine you'll be working on. If you can't keep a foot locker up to snuff, you sure as hell can't keep a jet engine running right."

Clearly what we do at indie shows isn't on the scale of a jet fighter engine or a nuclear missile, but there's a clear lesson to be taken from what my drill sergeant told me – success or failure lies in the details. As such, if you want to improve your indie shows or your matches, you must stop cutting corners. You must stop being cheap. If you're a wrestler, you must get fully trained and be constantly working to improve your craft. You need to get in tiptop shape and you must have proper wrestling gear. If you're a promoter, you need to make sure your show presentation is topnotch. You need to recruit only the best performers who conform to what I wrote just a few sentences previously. And you need to realize that there are certain unavoidable costs associated with running a pro wrestling show.

It's time to stop cutting corners.

Pro wrestling schools

From what I wrote in the section about how we got here, you may have concluded that I'm down on pro wrestling schools. That's not true – I'm down on bad pro wrestling schools. As I alluded to earlier, anybody with a ring and a building can open a pro wrestling school, whether they know how to teach pro wrestlers or not. And the sad part is, just about every kid who watches "Raw" every Monday wants to be a pro wrestler. It's like "American Idol." When "American Idol" holds their tryouts in any given city, the line of hopefuls wraps around the building. Thousands upon thousands of people want to be stars. Thousands upon thousands of people want to be rich and famous. Thousands upon thousands of people have dreams of someday being a big name singer like Jessica Simpson or Britney Spears. But the problem is, only a very small percentage of those thousands of thousands of people actually have the talent to be a star. In fact, as evidenced by the hilarious outtakes from the "Idol" tryouts, many of the people in that line that wraps around the building can't carry a tune in a bucket.

Pro wrestling is a lot like that. Thousands upon thousands of young people dream of being a star, of having their name in lights, of having throngs of screaming fans, of riding in limousines and flying on private luxury jets, but the reality is, the vast majority of them simply are not equipped to be successful pro wrestlers. But where "American Idol" and pro wrestling differ is that "Idol" had Simon Cowell who told the untalented hopefuls that they suck. In pro wrestling, on the other hand, pro wrestling schools will accept just about anybody so long as they have the cash to pay the tuition. The school is

The master: Not all pro wrestling instructors are bad. Some like Rusty Brooks and Tom Howard (pictured above with actor Jack Black) are consummate professionals.

the money maker and running shows is just a side attraction, an inconvenient requirement.

As I mentioned earlier, the consequence of pro wrestling schools popping up all over the place like weeds is that there is a massive glut of undertrained, unqualified guys out there who call themselves pro wrestlers. This results in a condition that economists refer to as a *surplus of labor*. A surplus of labor occurs whenever there are more workers than there are jobs. In short, because pro wrestling schools rely on new recruits to make their money and because they'll accept virtually anyone so long as they can afford the tuition, quite logically we end up with more pro wrestlers than we need to fill a card!

Today the situation has hit a boiling point. Because there are so many guys out there who call themselves wrestlers and so few spots on cards, new wrestlers, in a desperate attempt to get noticed, often agree to work for nothing. Many promoters, thinking they're shrewd businessmen, recognize this situation and decide to cash in. After all, a wrestling show's greatest expense is typically paying the talent. If you can sign talent and pay them next to nothing, you can pocket a bigger profit – in theory, that is.

This is a mentality of greed that pro wrestling promoters need to break. While they may think they're cashing in, the truth is, they're only hurting themselves and the viability of pro wrestling in the long run. Poor quality shows will break anyone, even a big promotion with extremely loyal fans (just look at WCW). It's just a matter of time. Of course the problem is, it's all a vicious circle: A promoter buys a ring and goes into the wrestling business. Trying to make a quick buck, he signs inexpensive wrestlers from the local wrestling school. He runs a few shows and is mildly successful at first because his product is "new." But soon enough, fans realize that his shows are junk and they stop going. So he sells his ring to the next guy, who repeats the process.

Make no mistake: Not all pro wrestling schools are bad. There are many fine schools that train wrestlers very well and thoroughly and will not put a guy on a show until he's fully ready to go. Further, this is another area where we need to raise our expectations. As wrestlers, we should look for those schools with reputable trainers. As promoters, we should only sign guys who have received proper training from a reputable trainer.

It's worth repeating – we need to all collectively *raise our expectations!*

Wrestler & promoter: The uneasy alliance

In the previous section I talked about how many promoters, in an effort to be shrewd, book wrestlers who, in a desperate effort to get noticed, are willing to work for next to nothing. Further, it's fairly well accepted that some promoters, unfortunately, tend to shortchange their workers. This stems from a longstanding business practice in pro wrestling where a promoter promises the wrestlers a percentage of the gate. As the theory goes, if the turnout is good, the wrestlers get paid well. If turnout is bad, well, the wrestlers get next to nothing. Promoters justify this practice by contending that if the wrestlers are worth their salt, they'll draw. And if they draw, they deserve to get paid. If they suck, they won't draw, and accordingly deserve to get nothing. It seems fair enough – pro wrestling is a business, after all. But there are two problems that arise from this arrangement. One, some promoters abuse the agreement by lying about the gate, and two, it's brought about an independent contractor mentality among wrestlers. Let's talk about each of these problems individually.

It's no secret that there is a great deal of mistrust felt by wrestlers toward promoters. Veteran wrestlers tend to sleep with one eye open around promoters because it's not uncommon for promoters to try to cheat the workers out of their fair share of a show's proceeds. Some of the things promoters have done in the past are just downright thievery. I recently heard a story about a promoter who, right in the middle of a show that hadn't drawn as well as he had expected, slipped out the backdoor and went home, leaving the wrestlers in the lurch to finish the show without any hope at all that they'd be paid. This story is particularly amusing because once the show was over, the wrestlers teamed up and drove to the promoter's house, where, sure enough, there he was, sitting in his boxer shorts, watching TV and drinking a beer! Now I'm no rocket scientist or genetic engineer, but isn't it kind of stupid to skip out on a bunch of angry, hulking dudes and then go to the very place that they're going to look to find you?

This kind of underhandedness is what has bred so much mistrust. Certainly not every promoter is so low down, but a few bad apples tend to ruin it for the entire bunch. In addition to the fact that many wrestlers distrust promoters, the overabundance of wrestlers in most areas creates a climate of extreme competition amongst the boys to secure a spot on a card. This leads to a work-wherever-you-can attitude, which has brought about a general sentiment among workers that they are independent contractors. Many workers have little loyalty to any given promoter or promotion, and who could blame them?

What's an independent contractor, you ask? Simple. An independent contractor is a person who is not on the regular payroll whom you hire to come in, do a very specific job, and get out. Say you own a sub shop. Say you have four guys who make the sandwiches and serve your customers. They're your regular employees. They have a vested interest in your business succeeding because if your business fails, they're out of work and can't pay the rent. Now suppose you have a leak in the roof of your sub shop. So you hire a guy to come in and fix the leak. This guy is an independent contractor. You hire him to fix the leak, and once the job's done, he's on to do a job for someone else. He couldn't care less about your sub shop, you, or whether your business succeeds or fails. All he cares about is that you pay his bill once the roof is fixed. Once the bill is paid, if your business fails, he doesn't care because there are thousands of other leaky roofs in town that need repairing. This is precisely where we are in indie pro wrestling. Wrestlers are hired to work a show, they show up, do their match, get paid, and go home. Then they're on to the next promotion to do work there.

This is where our problems really begin to snowball. As I stated earlier, it's really easy nowadays for a guy to buy a ring and call himself a promoter. It's even easier for a kid to sign up with a wrestling school and call himself a wrestler. Promoters try to save a buck by booking kids who'll work for cheap. Wrestlers, in turn, distrust promoters and, because there are so many wrestlers in the business today, they try to find work wherever and whenever they can with the attitude of an independent contractor. As such they have no loyalties to any one promotion and really no true vested interest in the success of any one promotion. Sure, they wish any promotion they work for success, but they have no real skin in the game. If a promotion they work for fails, well, that sucks, but there will be another that takes its place soon enough.

So my question to you is this: If wrestlers distrust promoters and if they have no real vested interest in any particular promotion, who's left to promote the promotion? There's one answer – the promoter and, if he's lucky, his booker (if he has one). And I'll tell you straight away that that's one tall order. What typically ends up happening to "promote" an indie show this way is, the promoter whips up a crappy flyer in Microsoft Word (complete with lots of misspellings and grammatical errors), runs down to the local Kinkos, prints off a couple thousand black-and-white copies, and then he and his son or his wife hand them out in the Walmart parking lot and post them in the windows of local tire shops.

And then he wonders why only 50 people show up.

And then the wrestlers he books for the show complain about not getting paid.

It's a lose-lose situation. Ideally the situation should be a win for both sides, but because of how wrestling professionals have allowed the situation to run its course unguided (kind of like hopping into the backseat and letting a car drive itself), independent pro wrestling has become, by and large, and entirely unprofitable endeavor.

Hurray for Hollywood

So now let's compare and contrast the production and promotion of independent pro wrestling shows to the production and promotion of Hollywood movies. Granted, pro wrestling promoters have nowhere near the resources of big movie studios, but the comparison is still worthwhile. Consider what a movie studio does when it's completed filming a new movie and is gearing up to release it. The first thing they do is issue a press release so that the media is aware of the new movie. Then they make up promotional materials and start an advertising campaign. Then – and this part is critical to the point I'm trying to make – the *actors* in the movie embark on a promotional tour to promote the new movie. When Paramount Pictures was preparing for the release of *Mission Impossible III*, Tom Cruise appeared on every late night talk show and every daytime news variety show and dozens of radio shows to promote the movie. He gave interviews to anyone with press credentials, made scores of red carpet appearances, and signed autographs for fans on the street. Why? Because he wanted the movie to succeed. And why did he want his movie to succeed? Because the more successful the movie is, the more money he makes.

The point is, when it comes to promoting a movie, it's a coordinated *team effort*. Everybody does their part. And in the case of *Mission Impossible III* (or any movie, really), Tom Cruise wasn't the only one making talk show appearances; Michelle Monaghan, Laurence Fishburne, and Jonathan Rhys Meyers were all making the circuit, too. Hollywood knows the power of publicity. It also knows the power of picking a message, keeping it simple, and then saying it over and over and over again. That's why so many actors from the same movie make so many appearances.

The power of publicity is not only in who conveys the message but how often the message is repeated. The more people you can get to repeat the message, the better. Think about it. If you hear some annoying jingle on the radio for, say, a windshield replacement company called *Glass Masters*, the first time you hear it, it doesn't even register in your consciousness. Neither does the second time. The third time you're thinking, "There's that annoying commercial again." The fourth time you're thinking, "I really hate that commercial." The fifth time you're thinking, "For crying out loud! How many times are they going to run that stupid commercial?!" Then a rock hits your windshield and where do you take your car to get it replaced? That's right – *Glass Masters.*

And now don't try to tell me, "Well, actually, Norm, I wouldn't take my car to *Glass Masters* if they had an annoying commercial. I'd deliberately take it somewhere else to spite them," because you know it's not true. Nine times out of ten, you're giving your business to the company that has a message that they repeat over and over again, especially if the message is annoying. That's why Hollywood does it. That's why big companies like Coca-Cola and Frito Lay do it.

So how does all this apply to indie pro wrestling? Simple: The production and promotion of an indie show should be a *team effort* by everyone involved. You know those cheesy motivational pictures companies put up in the hallways that have some picture of a lion or an elephant or a guy throwing a javelin and underneath it it's got a motivational word like, "Integrity," or "Persistence," or "Leadership," or something like that and then underneath that there's some cliché? Ordinarily I'm not crazy about those things, but the one that says "Team: *Together Everyone Achieves More*" is appropriate here. It's true in this case. If everybody involved in the show – from the promoter to the wrestlers to the managers to the booker to the guys slinging the ring to the guys working security – worked *together* to promote the show and make the very best show possible, the show would be much, much more successful. Think about it – instead of the promoter and his son handing out flyers at Walmart, you have 18 or 20 guys plastering the city with flyers. And instead of just a poster in the window of the tire store, you have a poster in the tire store, the sub shop, the hardware store, the video arcade, and the movie theater because you divide and conquer. That way, a potential fan might see the poster once at the tire store and forget about it, but he'll see it again and again when he runs his errands elsewhere around town. Eventually the light bulb will go on over his head and he'll say to himself, "Hmmm…maybe I should go to that show."

Now before you flood my email inbox with a slew of hate mail and claims that you're an indie wrestler who's done this or that to help promote a show, set up and broken down rings, loaded trucks and trailers, handed out flyers, begged your mom and uncle to come to your shows, blah, blah, blah, granted – there are admittedly plenty of indie pro wrestlers who go the extra mile to help the show be successful. But before you click the *Send* button on that hate message you're about to send me, ask yourself very honestly, do you do *everything* you possibly can to promote a show? Do you really throw yourself out there and make the commitment to do whatever it takes for the show to be a success?

I didn't think so.

Learn from used car salesmen

If you're a promoter you might be saying to yourself, "Yeah, right. Wrestlers aren't going to help promote a show. They say that's my job. They just show up, work a match, and then stick their hand out for a payday." Under the current operating conditions, that's probably true. But that's the paradigm we need to break. Wrestlers typically don't help promote a show because a) you haven't bothered asking b) because they feel they have no loyalties to you or your promotion or c) they're lazy. Now before we consider anything else, if the answer is c), the guy's not someone you want working for you anyway, so get rid of him. So that leaves you with options a) and b), and actually the answer is probably both. Your wrestlers don't help you promote shows because you've never bothered to ask them to help and because they really don't feel any sense of loyalty to you. So let's fix that. Suppose you ask one of your workers to help promote the next upcoming show. Don't be surprised if his answer is, "Why should I?" because it's a perfectly valid question.

You ever wonder why car salesmen are so pushy? The answer can be summed up with one word: Commission. For every car a salesman sells he gets a commission – a cut of the sale. In fact, many car salesmen work for what's called a *straight commission*, meaning the guy doesn't get any hourly wage. If he doesn't sell any cars on a given day, he takes zero dollars home that day. This creates a sort of shark feeding frenzy among the salesmen and explains why 15 of them come running at you as soon as you walk through the door.

Did you ever wonder why car dealers pay their salesmen this way? Why not pay them an hourly wage? I'll tell you why – because they sell more cars by paying their salesmen on a commission. If the salesmen were paid by the hour, they wouldn't bother trying so hard because they make the same amount whether they sell a car or not. So paying the salesmen on commission forms a symbiotic relationship for the salesmen and the dealership. The more cars a salesman sells, the more money he makes. There's a direct motivation to work hard. And the more cars the salesman sells the more money the dealership makes overall. It's win-win.

This is the same type of relationship promoters should forge with wrestlers. Quite simply, more tickets sold equals bigger payday. Period. By doing this, the wrestler now has a direct motivation to help make the show a success. Instead of the wrestler thinking, "I should hand out flyers to next month's show because it's the right thing to do," the wrestler thinks, "Man, I should really hand out lots of flyers so the building will be packed and I'll make more money." By fostering this type of model, the promoter and the wrestler form a symbiotic, win-win relationship.

Again, it all comes back to the notion that indie pro wrestling should be a *team effort,* not an *independent contractor effort.* How do you do that? By fostering a win-win environment. Promoters should pay wrestlers *honestly* based on the gate and pro wrestlers should do everything they can to help the promoter promote the show. With that said, however, promoters should agree to pay their wrestlers a minimum appearance fee in the event the show does poorly. That way, wrestlers won't feel like they're getting gypped. More on this later.

Summing Up

All right, so let's sum up the current state of the business of independent pro wrestling and how we got here:

1. Entry into the business of promoting pro wrestling is extremely easy – all one needs is to rent or own a ring, rent a building, and secure event insurance, if required by the owner of the rented building.

2. Because it's easy to become a promoter, show quality oftentimes stinks. Everybody and his brother think they can be a promoter or a booker. This results in poorly organized shows and silly storylines that are either just ripped off from old episodes of *Monday Night Raw* or entirely improbable or nonsensical – like silly contract clauses inserted by the heel (why would a promotion allow a wrestler to insert his own clauses into their contracts, anyway?) that state that if the babyface loses, he has to be the heel's slave or something stupid like that. Oh, and let's not forget that for that to happen, the babyface either must be illiterate or too stupid to read what he's signing before signing it.

3. Becoming a pro wrestler is also somewhat easy, especially if you're willing to work for next to nothing. All you have to do is plop down your money at a local wrestling school, and voila! You're a pro wrestler, regardless of whether or not you have any talent, conditioning, charisma, or athletic ability.

4. There is a surplus of pro wrestlers because pro wrestling schools are constantly recruiting and churning out new wrestlers to maintain their primary source of income. Admission standards are low because who's going to turn away a paying customer? As a consequence, there's a feeding frenzy among wrestlers – qualified or not – in many areas to get on a card to get noticed. Many wrestlers agree to work for peanuts.

5. Many indie promotions are simply underfunded. They don't have the money to buy the essentials – like clean wrestling canvasses without tears in them, title belts, or turnbuckle pads – so they improvise or go without. This lowers the production standards of shows in general and hurts fans' perception of independent pro wrestling overall.

6. Many promoters are *cheap*. They refuse to buy things like those mentioned above even though they have the funds to. Again, this tarnishes the image of independent pro wrestling very, very badly.

7. Many pro wrestlers are *cheap*. They refuse to buy boots, trunks, and matching knee pads, and they won't shell out $10 to get a haircut. Instead they wrestle in dirty sneakers and jean shorts, arguing that they're trying to be like John Cena.

8. Many pro wrestlers are improperly trained because *anybody* can open up a pro wrestling school. All you need is a ring and a building. Heck, you don't even need a building; your backyard will do fine, so long as the neighbors don't complain. Improper training results in botchy matches, missed spots, poor pacing, confusion, disorganization…pretty much a complete cluster eff.

9. Many pro wrestlers are *lazy* (Let the hate mail fly!). They refuse to get in the gym five times a week and follow a disciplined workout plan the way other competitive athletes like linebackers, boxers, MMA fighters, rugby players, or halfbacks do. So we end up with droves of scrawny and flabby guys climbing into rings in bingo halls and rec centers all over the country.

10. Because of the feeding frenzy among pro wrestlers trying to get booked, a lot of guys resort to cheesy gimmicks and copycat acts to try to get noticed. The indies are just rife with clowns, Ultimate Warrior wannabes, vampires, mummies, zombies, witches, devil worshippers, death row inmates, hillbillies, insane asylum escapees, televangelists, gangstas, construction workers,

angels of death, transvestites, flamers…I could go on forever…

11. Pro wrestlers get away with being lazy because promoters let them since, well, they're cheap. Instead of committing to booking only those guys who take the sport seriously and take pride in themselves by being in shape, having gear in great condition, and being at the top of their wrestling game, they decide to save a few bucks by hiring the bottom feeders who are willing to work for next to nothing. As a result, the guys in the ring look no different than the marks in the audience.

12. Because there are so many promotions popping up all over the place and because wrestlers feel no loyalty to any particular promotion (and vice versa), wrestlers have developed an independent contractor's attitude towards work. That is, "I show up, I wrestle the match, I get paid, I go home."

13. Because so many indie pro wrestlers have developed an independent contractor's attitude, independent wrestling shows are under-promoted because most of the work of promoting a show is left up to the promoter and wrestlers seldom help out.

So what do we have? Silly gimmicks, poorly trained wrestlers, out of shape wrestlers, wrestlers without gear, rusting rings, sagging ropes, duct taped canvasses, botchy matches, mass confusion, disorganization, fluttery PA systems, crappy storylines, ponytailed referees, plastic championship title belts, copycatting, cheap costumes, dangerous spots, cheesy characters, overall sloppy wrestling, and lots and lots of empty seats. Put it all together and what does it spell?

Low rent!

It's a wonder anyone shows up at all anymore. You either have to be a really hardcore fan with wrestling in your blood who's willing to stomach a lot of crap in hopes of maybe seeing a good double underhook suplex, or you're a fan with just really, really low standards. But the mainstream, average Joe potential fans? They stay away like the building has been contaminated by the swine flu.

So how do we fix it? Well, that's what this book is all about. Read on…

Appearances Are Everything

"Polished brass will pass upon more people than rough gold."
- Lord Chesterfield, man of letters

Never judge a book by its cover

But everybody does.

It was a wise man who told us that we should never judge a book by its cover; it was perhaps an even wiser man who told us that even though we should never judge a book by its cover, everyone does. Think about it. You're in a bookstore or newsstand, looking for a paperback to stave off the boredom of the 500 mile ride to next week's show in Boondocks, USA. You're faced with literally hundreds of choices. What do you do? You scan the covers for one that catches your eye. Then when you see one that looks kind of snazzy, you pick it up, flip it over, and read the back. If the synopsis sounds pretty good, boom, you walk up to the counter and fork out $10.

Ka-ching!

Believe it or not, the average bookstore patron or Amazon browser (like you) isn't the only one who does this. Bookstores, book dealers, book distributors, and book wholesalers do the same exact thing. When they sit down to choose which books they're going to carry or distribute, they choose from a printout of book *covers* from the publisher. They don't even bother to look at the book itself at all. The cover tells them everything they need to know. Just by looking at the cover, they know whether or not a book will sell and make them money.

Virtually every company that sells consumer products knows all about this. Every year, companies spend over $100 billion on packaging *design*. We're not talking about the paper, plastic, Styrofoam, or cellophane that the product actually gets wrapped in – we're talking about the *design* of the packaging, how it *looks*. Why? Because it's no secret that people largely base their purchasing decisions on how a product looks.

In the early 1990s, for example, the Wrigley Company – the makers of Hubba Bubba and Juicy Fruit chewing gum – made a fortune by simply taking some cheap bubble gum, jamming it into a pink tape dispenser package, and calling it *Bubble Tape*. Kids flocked to stores and shelled out their hard earned allowances hand-over-fist to buy six feet of cheap bubble gum for five times the amount it would have cost them to buy the same exact bubble gum if it had been wrapped in paper instead of that gimmicky pink dispenser.

Kids aren't the only ones who are susceptible to slick packaging. In 1993, a guy by the name of Michael Boehm was considering giving up on his dream. He had just spent over a year trying to find a company – any company – that would team up with him to manufacture a new portable indoor grill he had invented. It was a novel concept – a simple electric grill that resembled a waffle iron – that he felt certain would be a hit. But he couldn't find anyone to go in with him on his idea. No matter how many juicy, delicious steaks, burgers, or pork chops he cooked up in demos to prospective investors, he got no takers. Then it hit him – his problem wasn't his product; it was his packaging. He realized he needed some big-name appeal. He needed to tap into someone else's fame. Right about that time, former heavyweight boxing champion of the world George Foreman had successfully catapulted himself back into the limelight by challenging for boxing's heavyweight title again at the tender age of 44. So Boehm approached Foreman with his grill, and the rest, as they say, is history. Once Foreman signed on and agreed to lend his name to the gizmo, Salton, Inc., a manufacturer of household appliances, immediately agreed to make and market it. They slapped Foreman's chubby smiling face on the box, and voila! An instant phenomenon. To date, over 100 million George Foreman Grills have been sold, making the victim of the infamous rope-a-dope a genuine mega-millionaire.[1]

So why am I belaboring the importance of packaging so much? Because appearances count. In fact, appearances are *everything*. Let me say that again: Appearances are *everything!*

Nowhere is this truer than in the world of pro wrestling. In the furiously fickle, dog-eat-dog world of pro wrestling, appearances can very easily spell the difference between success and failure. Yet it really surprises me how so many people in the pro wrestling business – especially in the indies – seem completely oblivious to this fact. Just take a look around the next time you're at an indie show and you'll see what I'm talking about. It's all stuff I've touched on already – flabby guts, pallid skin, torn ring canvases, peeling tape, jean shorts instead of trunks, dirty sneakers instead of boots, tattooed faces…

To make independent pro wrestling a successful business enterprise, we need to examine what big, successful businesses do. We need to learn what they know so well about the importance of appearances and packaging. We need to learn from Random House how they sell millions of paperback books every year by making slick, attractive book covers. We need to learn from the Wrigley Company how they made a fortune from *Bubble Tape* by slapping ordinary pink bubble gum into a new, snazzy tape dispenser. We need to learn from George Foreman how he hawked millions of electric grills by slapping his picture on the box. In short, we need to improve our packaging. If we improve our packaging, I guarantee you, more people will buy our product.

You never get a second chance

Just about every person on earth's mother has told them, "You never get a second chance to make a first impression." Mothers tell that to their children because they want their children to be independent and successful. Just as a mother wolf wants her cubs to grow up and be able to hunt for themselves, human mothers want their children to grow up and

---

[1] According to a story Hulk Hogan told on his reality show "Hogan Knows Best," the George Foreman Grill could have been the Hulk Hogan Grill, but he passed up on the offer, opting instead to market a Hulk Hogan blender.

be able to land a job that covers rent and groceries. Most human mothers, anyway. I guess there are plenty of human mothers who really don't care and just sit around smoking cigarettes and watching the "Maury Povich Show," but for those human mothers who do care about their children's future, the you-never-get-a-second-chance thing is pretty much a lecture she's required to give her children at some point in their development.

But even though it's kind of cliché, it's still very, very true. Anytime you meet a person, you will only meet him for the first time once. You'll surely meet him again and again in the future, but the first meeting only comes once. And the first impression is always the most important. Why? Because it's a natural human response – it's part of our evolutionary makeup – to size up a person from top to bottom the very first moment you meet them. Whether you realize you're doing it or not, you do it. Everyone does. Anytime you meet someone new, immediately the wheels in your head start turning. *Do I like this guy? Is this guy cool? Does he seem honest? Those sandals he's wearing are kind of gay. What's up with that hoop earring in his nose?*

That's why employment experts always advise job seekers to look sharp for an interview. That's why they always insist that job seekers should wear a conservative suit with a white dress shirt, get a conservative businesslike haircut, shave all facial hair (if you're a dude), and take your sunglasses off the top of your head. Now you might be one of those people with a bit of an attitude who says, "All of that is so shallow. People shouldn't judge me by how I dress. How I dress is how I express my individuality. People should judge me by the quality of my work, not by whether or not I have a suit on. And besides, people who dress up like that are so fake. They're followers. I'm an individual. That's what businesses need more of – individuals. In fact, if I come to the interview dressed the way I normally dress day-to-day, I bet I'll get extra points for being down-to-earth!"

Yeah, right. Keep on thinking that. Oh, and by the way, have fun in the unemployment line. If that's your attitude, you're going to have a very hard time in life.

Success in life often requires that a person prepare for the worst possible scenario. If you don't, if you go through life just expecting that people will think the way you do or judge things the way you judge them, you're bound for failure because whether you like it or not, people will not always agree with you. The best strategy for success is to anticipate what people might *possibly* think and then plan and act accordingly. The most successful salesmen are experts at this. They anticipate their potential customers' objections before ever talking to them and then prepare ready comebacks for those objections.

For example, suppose you're an appliance salesman and you're trying to sell a Whirlpool refrigerator to a customer. Suppose you're showing the customer the fridge and the customer says to you, "This is a Whirlpool. I only buy Maytag appliances. You got a Maytag?" For the sake of the discussion, let's suppose your store only carries Whirlpool. If you're the average Joe Blow salesman, your answer would be, "No, sorry. We only carry Whirlpool," and the customer would walk out, taking a nice, fat commission with him. And then you'd have to call your wife and tell her that you won't be able to afford to pay the cable bill this month. And then she leaves you for the mailman because at least he brings home a decent paycheck.

Now, on the other hand, if you had anticipated every possible objection a customer could have that you can think of, in lieu of the knucklehead "We only carry Whirlpool" answer, you might instead answer, "No, we don't carry Maytag here, but did you know that according to *Consumer Reports*, this particular model outscored the equivalent Maytag model in overall quality, value, and reliability? Here, look, I have a copy of the article right here…"

See the difference? In the first case, the salesman didn't bother to stop and think about what a customer's objections might be. He was *unprepared.* So when the customer said he only buys Maytag, it's end of discussion…see you later. Bye-bye, commission. Bye-bye, hot wife. In the second case, the salesman anticipated that the customer might prefer Whirlpool's biggest competitor, so he had a comeback already prepared. By showing the customer the *Consumer Reports* article, the discussion is still alive and maybe, just maybe, the customer might be persuaded to buy the Whirlpool.

Going back to the example I used earlier about dressing professionally for a job interview, the guy who scoffs at that notion, thinking, "I should be judged by my work, not my appearance," is clearly failing to anticipate all foreseeable outcomes. Sure, some job interviewers don't really care if you don't show up in a suit and tie. Some are perfectly OK with it if you show up in khaki pants and a golf shirt. But you know what? Many aren't. Many think, "This guy's resume looks pretty good, but for crying out loud, he's wearing a Polo shirt! What, the guy couldn't be bothered to iron a dress shirt and put on a suit?" And you know what happens next? Your resume winds up in the trashcan.

But now let's flip the scenario back around to the interviewer who's OK with you showing up in casual clothes. If he's OK with you wearing casual clothes, he'll certainly have no objection to you wearing a suit. So you can't lose by wearing the suit, right?

So you see how this works? You anticipate the *worst* thing that might happen and then you prepare yourself *as if that's going to happen.* I do this every day. Every day, I wear a tie to work at my day job. I'm not required to, but I do anyway. A lot of people ask me, "Norm, why do you wear a tie on the days you don't have a meeting or have to give a presentation?" The reason is because I *anticipate* that I might meet someone I'm not planning on meeting on any given day, and I know that I only have one chance to make a good first impression with that person. If I'm wearing jeans and a Polo because I don't have any meetings and I think I'll be at my desk all day, but then I get introduced to someone I've never met – someone very important, maybe a potential customer – I may have just blown it. That person's going to very possibly walk away thinking, "That guy's not very professional. He's wearing jeans at work!" And who knows what opportunities I just missed? It's better for me to wear the tie all day at my desk and interact with no one than to dress down to be comfortable and then bump into a potential customer I've never met before and they get the wrong impression of me.

All right, so how does all of this relate to pro wrestling, you ask? Simple: That fan sitting in the front row? He's our *customer.* And just as people pick which book to buy at the bookstore based on how good the cover looks, that fan – that *customer* – is judging you as a wrestler, as a ref, as a promoter, as a manager, or as a valet *based on how you look.* The very second you step through that curtain, every fan in attendance – whether he's in the front row or in the nosebleed seats – is looking you up and down and assessing you. He's immediately passing judgment.

He's looking at your trunks, your tights, your physique, your hair, your boots. Granted, *some* fans might not care if you've got skinny arms or a spare tire around your middle. But it's just like how some job interviewers are OK with interviewees showing up in khakis and a golf shirt. Some fans may be OK with you wrestling in a t-shirt, but many other fans will not. And remember, you want to anticipate the worst and then act accordingly. If some fans are OK with the t-shirt but others are not OK with it, get rid of the t-shirt!

In short, it is absolutely critical that your appearance be absolutely beyond reproach, because whether you realize it or not, as a pro wrestling professional *you are selling yourself. You* are the product. Think about it. Why do car dealerships wax a car to hard, sparkling shine, put Armor All on its tires, and spritz its interior with that New Car Smell spray? Because buyers get dazzled by shiny new cars. The car's engine could be a complete lemon, but if the exterior looks really shiny and sharp, people will buy it. On the other hand, a car might be extremely well designed, reliable, and durable, but if the paint is faded and the wheels are dirty, people will turn their noses up at it. People buy what looks good.

So, regardless of what else you do, be absolutely sure you look good.

The total package

Lex Luger called himself "The Total Package" because, allegedly, he had all the essential ingredients for a world champion pro wrestler – the looks, the brains, the physique, the strength, the in-ring ability. Well, that's what he said, anyway. I was personally never much of a Lex Luger fan (too much baby/heel flip flopping), but his moniker really should be the guiding principle in independent pro wrestling. That is, to be successful, an independent pro wrestling promotion has to deliver the total package. What do I mean by that? Simple: Every aspect of the promotion – from the wrestlers to the production to the ring to the banners with the promotion's logo on them – must be topnotch. You have to get *everything* right. You can't pay extreme attention to certain details but then ignore or skimp on others. It's like a wooden ship with lots of holes in its hull. You can't just fix some of the holes. You have to fix them all or the ship will sink. The same thing holds true for a pro wrestling promotion. You need to pay attention to all the details: The ref, the ring, the ring announcer, and, of course, the wrestlers. Remember, appearances are everything. So let's take a look at each of these facets individually.

The ref

Referees are often the overlooked unsung heroes of a pro wrestling show. How they look and what they do in the ring is a reflection of the promotion. In fact, to many fans, the referee *is* the promotion – or at least the promotion's official ambassador. So if your referee is sharp and looks professional, your promotion looks professional. If your referee is sloppy and wears cheap jeans in the ring, your promotion looks cheap. This is common sense, really, but many promotions evidently don't get it. If I had a dime for every time I saw an indie pro wrestling referee in ratty jeans or a faded, worn out referee shirt, I wouldn't have to be writing this book right now because I'd be a rich man. A lot of these guys look like the only time they wear a shirt at all is when they're refereeing a match. A lot of them look like the guy who walks into the convenience store wearing a pair of dirty Dickie's work pants, paint splattered work boots, no shirt, and a filthy baseball cap with the words, "I'll do it tomorrow...I've already made too many mistakes today," printed on it. You know the guy I'm talking about. He's skinny, always half drunk, and could stink up the Superdome. By day he installs lawn pumps...by night he's a professional sports official. And more often than not, he's got a real long, thin ponytail. It's thin because he's losing his hair and he thinks growing a ponytail makes up for it.

And then there's the guy who, for fun, eats so much at Golden Corral he's asked to leave. He's the guy whose pants are too small for him, so he's constantly at risk of having them fall down around his ankles. He's the guy whose referee shirt is too short for him, so it rides up his gut, revealing his enormous belly button. When he bends over to ask a guy in a side headlock if he wants to give it up, he moons the crowd with his plumber's crack.

Let's not forget tattoos and facial piercings. We have to throw a bunch of those into the mix, too. Some indie refs have more tattoos than tattoo artists and pirates. And why not toss in a few lip and eyebrow piercings while we're at it? Now mind you, I understand that the tattoo and piercing phenomenon is pretty hot right now and all sorts of people from all walks of life have jumped on the bandwagon. What started as a sort of statement of individuality and sexuality among college-aged kids has become a craze that even middle aged dads are smitten by. It's not uncommon to see 40 year-old dudes with tribal armbands and lower back tattoos. I guess they think they make them look hip or cool...or maybe younger. Heck, I've seen grannies with lower back and ankle tattoos. I guess these people think that the "coolness" of their tats masks their wrinkles and gray hair.

Anyway, more on tattoos in just a bit, but for now, let's stay focused on referees. As I said already, the referee is the strongest representation of the promotion. If your referee looks sloppy, your promotion looks sloppy. If he looks professional, your promotion looks that much more professional. It's a simple fact. Don't agree? Then let's look at what the big boys do. Look at the NFL as an example. Tune into any game and look at the officials on the field. Take notes. Look at guys like Mike Carey or Ed Hochuli.

Setting the standard: The NFL knows all about professional appearances. NFL referees are always the sharpest looking bunch in all of professional sports.

These guys just scream professional. They are fit and trim. Their uniforms are form fitted and pressed. Their white pants are gleaming and their black stripes are jet. Their hair is cut almost military style. Their shirts are tightly tucked in, and they carry themselves with poise and confidence.

To many NFL fans, that guy who blows the whistle, throws the yellow flag, calls the game right down the middle, maintains law and order, and announces, "Roughing the passer...number 91 on the defense...fifteen yard penalty...first down!" *is* the league, even though really all they do is get paid to enforce the league's rules, which are made up by the league's team owners. But fans don't see it that way. When an NFL official makes an unpopular call that's in the rulebook, fans boo and throw garbage at him – even though that official is just being fair, doing his job, and has nothing to do with the rule other than enforcing it. But, again, fans don't see it that way. Many fans see it as if the officials make up the rules. It's just like how many ordinary people think that the police make traffic laws or that the police *are* the government. Again, it's not true – they're just hired to enforce the law – but cops are, in the eyes of the vast majority, *the* law.

Accordingly, a ref is "the law" in a promotion. As such, if you are a referee, you need to make sure your appearance is perfectly polished. If you're a promoter and you have a referee that looks like one of the guys I just described, you either need to clean him up or fire him and find someone new.

Equally important as a referee's appearance is a referee's behavior. Too often these days you see referees who serve very little purpose in the match other than to count a pinfall. Other than that, they just kind of stand around and watch. I remember back in the middle 90s, a buddy and I were watching ECW on the local sports network (this is going way back) and I noticed a referee in the ring who was just kind of standing there while the wrestlers busted fluorescent light tubes over each other's head and shot each other with staple guns. I asked my buddy, "What's that referee for?" and he answered, "Yeah, you're right. Dude, buy a ticket!" His response was so appropriate. The ref in that match was totally pointless. Since he was just watching the match, he should have just bought a ticket and watched it from the comfort of a seat. Instead, he was "specteree" (spectator + referee).

Independent pro wrestling needs a lot less "specterees" and a lot more guys who know their role. Again, going back to the NFL example, Ed Hochuli has a very professional, commanding, authoritative presence on the field. So should pro wrestling referees. To see a real pro in action –

especially if you're under the age of 40 – I highly recommend you go to YouTube and search for NWA matches from the 1980s where Tommy Young is the referee. Trained by the great Lou Thesz, Tommy Young was a consummate professional. Tommy Young understood that even though he was "just" the referee, he still had a critical supporting role to play. Jeff Goldblum had a supporting role in "Jurassic Park," but that doesn't mean he just blended into the background and tried not to be noticed.

The same holds true for pro wrestling referees – *get in there!* Get in the action! Get *noticed!* Pull your shoulders back, hold your head high, and move confidently around the ring. If a heel blatantly cheats right in front of you, let's say he pokes the baby in the eye, get in his face. Block him from advancing toward the injured baby – and yell, "Hey!" Show an angry expression and shake your finger at him in warning. Show him you mean business.

Actually, I like this particular scenario, so let's walk through it in detail. Let's say the match has gone back and forth. Both men are sweating and breathing heavily. Suddenly, the baby gets the upper hand and starts laying in some heavy punches. The heel is sent reeling. In desperation, he reaches up and pokes the baby in the eye Ric Flair style. The baby sells it to the hilt. He turns his back to the heel, drops to one knee, and puts his hands over his injured eye. The referee sees the whole thing. He's outraged by the heel's blatant disregard for the rules and the audacity of committing such a flagrant foul right in front of him. The heel, meanwhile, senses blood in the water and starts to advance toward the baby to capitalize on the injury, but right then, the referee boldly jumps in his path, directly in front of him.

"Hey!" the ref shouts, as he points his finger in the heel's face.

Momentarily taken aback, the heel sheepishly says, "What?" But then he realizes that he's bigger than the ref (and, well, he's a bad guy), so he puffs up his chest and shouts, "Get out of the way!"

The ref remains unfazed. "That's your first warning!" he yells. "Do it again and it'll cost you the match!"

Now realizing that the referee has called his bluff and isn't going to be bullied, the heel does what all bullies do when confronted – he backs down. He does this subtly, though. He deflates his chest and takes a tiny step backwards. Meanwhile, the baby has mostly recovered from the eye poke and is ready to retaliate.

You see how this dynamic works? The referee lays down the law. By laying down the law, the referee *strengthens* the heel's character. After all, in a lawless society, there are no criminals. Think about it. Before the days of Prohibition (the period in the United States when alcohol was illegal), making and selling alcohol was perfectly legal and no one really thought ill of anyone for doing it. Then in 1920, the Eighteenth Amendment was enacted and alcohol became illegal throughout the country. The result? Mobsters like "Scarface" Al Capone entered the picture and started bootlegging booze. A brutal and bloody turf war ensued, and the police and the mob locked horns in an epic battle to undo the other. Celebrated good guy Elliot Ness and his band of upstanding, incorruptible, "untouchable" lawmen rose to prominence by battling the bootleggers. Thus, the legendary Ness/Capone feud was born.

All of this came about because of a *law*. And the stricter the law was enforced, the more dramatic the events became. In the eyes of the public at large, the mobsters became arch villains...for brewing and selling beer! The cops and the feds became larger-than-life heroes because they were trying to stop the villains from...brewing and selling beer! This feud was so hot, it became the subject of a bestselling book written by Ness titled *The Untouchables* (a great read, by the way) and blockbuster movie starring Kevin Costner by the same title. Interestingly, in 1933, the Eighteenth Amendment was repealed, and alcohol became legal again. What happened? The mob faded back into the shadows and went back to running the rackets it ran before Prohibition, and Elliot Ness eventually left police work all together and became a businessman.

The lesson to take from this little history lesson is this: Strict rules and laws make great villains. Weak rules and weak rules enforcement make weak villains because there are so few rules to break. And the bigger deal you make about the rules and about the travesty of them being broken, the more hated a villain becomes. And the more hated the villain is, the better the story is, the more heat you get, and the more butts you put in seats. Bad guys sell.

Just look at JR Ewing from "Dallas." Larry Hagman played the nefarious JR character so well, he made "Dallas" the highest rated show on television for five seasons. The writers of "Dallas" knew the importance of the villain. The importance of villains is so great that I devote an entire chapter of this book to the subject, but what you need to understand is that you can't have these strong villains without a strong referee.

A roll of dimes

Still not convinced? Let me relate another story. This one is a classic pro wrestling angle that is still talked about today and it all revolves around, believe it or not, a simple roll of dimes. It was 1987 and Curt Hennig was chasing Nick Bockwinkle for the AWA World Championship. The two had met at least once before in a thrilling match that went to a 60 minute draw. Meanwhile, Larry Zybszko was feuding with Bockwinkle because, according to Zybszko, Bockwinkle refused to grant him a title shot. Frustrated, Zybszko decided it was time for a new champion, someone who *would* grant him a shot. That person, he decided, was Hennig. So on the night of the big match, Zybszko was sitting at ringside. At a perfectly opportune moment, Zybszko slipped Hennig a roll of dimes. The exchange was never clearly shown to the fans. The exchange looked fishy, but they were very careful not to let the fans actually see the roll of dimes. Hennig then hit Bockwinkle with the dimes in his fist, knocking him out. Hennig secured the pinfall and won the title.

A huge controversy ensued that lasted for months. *Pro Wrestling Illustrated* even did a little gig where they did a "frame-by-frame analysis" of the replay footage to "determine" if they could spot the roll of dimes and get to the bottom of the issue. Hennig and Zybszko played the whole thing up beautifully, successfully flipping Hennig from a beloved "young kid" babyface to a despised heel character that he later ported to the WWF as Mr. Perfect. Years later, when Zybszko returned to the AWA after a stint in Jim Crockett's NWA, the AWA picked up the story right where it left off, with the AWA's front man Larry Nelson still grilling Zybszko on whether or not the accusations of the roll of dimes were true.

So here we have a very successful angle that lasted *years*. How did the AWA do it? Simple – they had very strict rules and very strong referees (Gary DeRusha in particular). As such, it was very uncommon for outside interference to occur. So when it did, it was a huge ordeal. It stuck out. Nowadays, outside interference happens in just about every single match, and in half those instances the interference happens right in front of the referee! And I'm not talking about just the indies, here, either. I see this happening all the time on WWE and TNA TV shows. A guy will reach down and grab some weapon from his manager or buddy at ringside and clobber his opponent with it. The referee does absolutely nothing except – maybe – say, "Hey now...come on. Get that out of the ring. You know you're not allowed to have that." And then the heel makes the cover and the referee makes the three count.

It doesn't take a rocket scientist to figure out that this doesn't make any sense at all and is nothing but plain stupid. Not only does it not make any sense for the heel to use a weapon right in front of the referee who then doesn't disqualify the guy, but allowing outside interference to happen so frequently completely ruins the whole concept of interference. Interference is cheating, and cheating is supposed to be an outrage. But because bookers are doing this so often – over and over and over again – fans have just become callous to it. The effect is entirely diminished. What should be outrageous has become really, really commonplace and fans respond to it with little more than a yawn.

Bottom line: Have a referee with authority. Enforce the rules. Don't let heels blatantly cheat in front of the ref and get away with it.

Summing up the referee

All right, so let's sum up everything we discussed concerning referees. Here's a comprehensive list:

1. Referees should present a clean, professional, business-like image. No facial piercings and no visible tattoos. A referee should have a proper, almost military style haircut and no facial hair (except, maybe, a mustache).

2. *No ponytails!*

3. A referee's uniform should always be first rate, sharp, clean, and pressed. The shirt should be collared and reasonably new, not worn out or faded. The shirt should also be properly fitted, not baggy or too tight. Pants should be jet black, not faded to where they look sort of gray. Buy polyester pants, not cotton. Cotton fades quickly. Pants should be flat front, not pleated. You can buy good flat front black pants at Walmart for cheap.

4. Pants should be fitted correctly. No high waters! And no pants that are so long that you step on the hem or that get all bunched up at the ankles. That's very, very sloppy. When pants are the proper length, the back of the hem ends just at the top of the heel of your shoe.

5. Do *not* "sag" your pants! This is a bizarre and annoying fad where dudes wear their pants below their waist to expose their underwear. It's something done by losers who are desperate for attention and/or desperate to look cool because they're dorks who can't get chicks. It really annoys me and many, many other people. And the even more bizarre trend is the "formal sag." This is the idiotic trend where dudes sag their pants in formal situations, like at work and weddings. For example, they're at work and their boss yells at them (appropriately) for having their underwear showing. So they leave their pants sagged down low but then buy an extra-long shirt to cover up their underwear and tuck the shirt in. You may think this is cool but it's not. It's sloppy, unprofessional, and stupid. Pull your pants up.

6. For crying out loud, *no jeans!*

7. Wear a plain black leather belt with a plain, simple buckle. Do not, repeat, do *not* go beltless! That holds true always. The only time it's OK not to wear a belt is when you're in the shower or when you're escaping from a POW camp. Again, $5 at Walmart.

8. Wear plain black shoes with soft rubber soles. Walmart sells shoes that look like plain dress shoes but they have soft rubber soles. Get a pair. No sneakers!

9. Wear plain black socks. No white socks!

10. Wear a black undershirt under your striped referee shirt.

11. Carry yourself with cool confidence in the ring. Focus like a laser on the match. Project yourself as a competent professional, not a bumbling Keystone Cop.

12. Get involved! Don't just stand around and let the heel do whatever he wants. Stand up to him. Threaten to disqualify him. Be assertive. You're part of the show!

13. When the wrestlers are in a rest hold, position yourself between them and the fans so that the fans can't see the wrestlers discussing the next spot.

14. Project your voice authoritatively so that the fans can hear you. Don't be shy. When the wrestlers roll out to the floor, count loudly.

15. When you admonish a heel, do that loudly, too! Let those fans hear you!

16. When the wrestlers are out on the floor, if they don't get back in the ring, count them out! Do *not*, again, *do not* feebly give up and just restart the count because they're not getting back in the ring on time. Either count them out or jump to the floor and tell one of the wrestlers to roll back in for a second to break the count so you can restart it legally.

17. When counting a pinfall, if the guy doesn't kick out in time, count his ass out! Even if he's supposed to win, if he doesn't kick

out in time, count him out. It looks really, really bad when a referee does the old, 1…2…holding up my hand, holding up my hand, come on, kick out, come on…

18. If you have to take a bump because you're being taken out (which I advise against…we'll talk about that), do it right and convincingly. Don't swoon and melt melodramatically to the mat. Take the hit and do a front face bump. Done.

The Ring

So we just took an in-depth look at how referees in the indies should look and behave. Now let's take a good hard look at the ring. Remember, a pro wrestling show is a total package. Everything counts. Success or failure is in the details. If your product is good but your packaging is poor, you will fail. And probably the very largest, most noticeable part of your packaging is your ring.

The ring is the very first thing fans see when they walk through the door to your show. So going back to the concept of, "You never get a second chance to make a first impression," the ring is going to make that first impression for any promotion. Think about it. Most fans show up early to shows to make sure they get a good seat. That means they're sitting in their seats idly, waiting for bell time. What do they do? They take a good look around at their surroundings. And to any pro wrestling fan, a real pro wrestling ring is an awesome sight. You know it's true. Think back to before you got into the business, when you were just a fan going to indie shows. Whether you said it out loud or not, when you first laid eyes on that ring sitting just feet away from you, your reaction was, "Wow!" You were probably tempted to go look under the ring skirt or squeeze a turnbuckle pad or feel the padding under the mat. Even fans who have been watching live pro wrestling events for decades are drawn to the sight of the ring. It's just such an awesome, imposing visual.

So it's only basic common sense that the ring has to look sharp. This is a lesson not lost on WWE or TNA. Their rings always look topnotch. Compare a typical WWE ring to the ring at the last indie show you worked. I'm willing to bet the difference is like night and day. It's like the difference between a traveling carnival ride and a ride at Walt Disney World. A ride at your typical carnival is beat up, old, and half the light bulbs on its sign are burned out and won't be replaced anytime in the next ten years. A ride at Disney World, on the other hand, always looks as good as it did on opening day. You will *never* see a burned out light bulb at Disney World. Don't believe me? Next time you're there, take a walk down Main Street in the Magic Kingdom and see if you can spot a single burned out

Definitely not WWE: Here's an example of what your ring should *not* look like. Notice the badly taped ropes, the duct taped turnbuckle pads, and the chipped paint on the ring post.

bulb anywhere. You won't. Why? Because the folks at Walt Disney World understand the importance of appearances.

And so do WWE and TNA. That's why their rings always look brand new. They pay close attention to the details. For the indies to be more successful, we need to do the same. Next time you're watching *Raw,* take a good hard look at the ring. Take stock of a few details. First, take a look at the ropes. Notice how tight and elastic they are. Notice that the ropes are all perfectly taped. There are no bare spots, none of the tape is peeling off, and there is certainly no silver duct tape filling in any missing gaps. Next, look at the turnbuckle pads. Notice that they are firmly affixed to the turnbuckle and not drooping. Next, the ring posts. Notice how each post is impeccably painted. There is no chipped paint or rust. Next, the ring skirts. Notice how tight they are. They don't sag in the middle. Next, the mat. WWE ring mats are never torn, frayed, stained, or patched up with duct tape. (What's up with the duct tape in the indies, anyway?)

Not only is the ring the first thing that fans see when they walk through the door, it's the stage for your show and your promotion. It's critical, then, that it be ready to frame the show in the most favorable light. Specifically, not only should the ring be in excellent condition, its colors should reflect the branding of your promotion. For example, Ring of Honor's colors are black and red. Accordingly, all its rings are black and red – black and red canvasses, red turnbuckle covers, and black ropes. If your company colors are red, white, and blue, it would be logical to use red ropes, blue skirts, and blue turnbuckle covers. Using a color scheme that doesn't match your branding is both confusing and projects a less-than-professional image.

Again, take a page from the NFL. If you ever go to Sun Life Stadium in Miami, there will be no doubt in your mind that it's home to the Miami Dolphins. Everything – from the bleacher seats to the scoreboard to the handrails to the stadium walls – everything, *everything* is aqua or orange. So if you already own a ring, make your company colors match the colors

Sun Life Stadium: The Miami Dolphins know all about branding. If this picture were in color, you'd be blinded by a sea of aqua and orange. You'll have to use your imagination.

you already have! Branding is a very powerful way to market your product and it must be entirely consistent. We'll talk about branding in depth when we discuss marketing, but for now, just know that you must keep your ring colors and your company logo colors consistent.

Another consideration is ring size. Wrestling rings typically come in three sizes: 16 foot, 18 foot, and 20 foot. Personally I believe 18 foot is the perfect size for indie promotions. Sixteen foot rings are too small – too small for the action and too small in appearance – and 20 foot rings are oftentimes too big for some venues. So if you're looking to rent a ring or buy one new, I recommend looking for an 18 foot ring.

Regardless of the size, here are the commandments for a professional-looking ring:

1. Keep the ropes in good repair. Keep them properly taped. Do not patch gaps with duct tape. And keep tape even. Don't just tape over tape over tape.

2. Keep the ropes tight. Saggy, loose ropes are both sloppy and very dangerous. They also spoil the illusion when guys run them. When a guy hits the ropes, he's supposed to dramatically ricochet

off of them, like he's hitting a tight rubber band. When the ropes are loose, they look more like wet spaghetti.

3. Invest in professional turnbuckle pads and covers. A great place to buy them is www.HighSpots.com. Remember, your turnbuckles should match the color scheme of your promotion's logo and should contrast with your ropes. So if your promotion's colors are blue and red, don't use red turnbuckles on red ropes. Make either the ropes or the turnbuckles red and the other blue.

4. Invest in a new ring canvas. Do *not* use a canvas that is stained, ripped, or has holes in it! Also, don't try to save some money by using a polyethylene tarp instead of a proper canvas.

5. Your ring skirts should also match your promotion's color scheme, like your ropes and turnbuckles.

6. When possible, use an 18 or 20 foot ring. A ring any smaller makes your show look "smallish."

The ring announcer

Another unsung hero of any pro wrestling promotion is the ring announcer. Like a referee, a ring announcer is a reflection of a promotion...actually, he goes beyond that – he's the *frontman* for a promotion. In the music industry, a frontman is the leader of a band or at least the person who does most of the talking for the band. He's usually the lead singer. Gene Simmons is the frontman for KISS. Kurt Cobain was the frontman for Nirvana.

Interestingly, while the frontman is the face of a band, oftentimes he's not the most talented member of the group. And typically, a band can survive the loss of few members – a drummer, a bassist, even a lead guitarist – but it cannot survive the loss of its frontman. Once the frontman goes, fans' connection to the band is lost. The band loses its identity. There are a few exceptions to that rule (e.g., Van Halen), but not many.

Nothing illustrates the importance of a strong frontman than the old hit show *M*A*S*H*. While *M*A*S*H* was a TV show and not a band, it still had a clear frontman – Alan Alda as Hawkeye Pierce. Just about every character on that show was replaced at some point – except Hawkeye. The Frank Burns character was replaced with Charles Winchester. Colonel Henry Blake was replaced with Colonel Sherman T. Potter. Radar was replaced with Klinger. Trapper John was replaced with BJ Hunnicutt. With all these changes to the cast, one might have expected that ratings would tank. On the contrary – ratings skyrocketed! In 1975, the show weighed in at an impressive #15 overall. By 1980, the show had climbed to the #4 top show on television! Why? Well, lots of reasons – better writing, characters with more "human-like" qualities, more dramatic storylines, less slapstick comedy – but one of the biggest reasons is because the frontman remained the same. Had Alan Alda been one of those actors on that show to call it quits, the show would have most certainly bombed. But because the frontman remained in place and provided the continuity that any show needs to succeed, the new actors were able to develop their characters into ones that exceeded their predecessors.

A pro wrestling promotion needs a frontman, too. During the 80s and 90s, the WWF had Gene Okerlund. Today, TNA *Impact!* has Mike Tenay and *Raw* has Jerry Lawler. The frontman is the face of continuity in an ever changing environment, and nowhere is this more critical than in indie wrestling, where the environment changes more often than Liberace changed clothes during a performance. Due to the extremely transitory nature of pro wrestlers, you never know who's going to be around next month. You might have a guy and plan big things for him, but at the last minute he might get a better offer and go somewhere else. You might have another guy who seems promising but the rigors of traveling and the meager pay lead him to quit. You might have another guy who gets in an argument with the booker over having to go under, so he's fired. It's all, at best, organized chaos. A promotion needs a beacon in this storm – and that beacon should be the ring announcer.

As such, be sure to pick a guy that fits the bill. He should be, beyond anything else, 100% loyal and dependable. You need to have the same guy calling the matches and firing up the crowd month after month after month. He's part of your branding. So you don't want to pick a guy out of expedience who might get bored and just stop showing up. If that happens, you'll have to throw someone else in there, and your loyal longtime fans will be thinking, "Who the hell is this guy?" And that's a terrible situation. Losing the frontman typically spells failure. Like when the guys who played Bo and Luke Duke on *The Dukes of Hazzard* walked off the set and the show's producers replaced them with lookalikes. What happened? Ratings completely tanked. Even though the show continued to follow its simple formula and the roles of the two leading guys weren't really all that difficult to play, fans despised the new guys. Why? Because they weren't the originals. They were different. They weren't what the audience was used to. Losing a ring announcer isn't nearly as devastating as losing your two leading men in a TV show, but it's a tough blow all the same.

So the first thing you look for in a ring announcer is dependability. The second thing is his voice. This should be a no brainer, but I'm still surprised by how many times I go to a show and some guy with a quavering weasel voice gets in the ring and starts doing ring introductions. No, no, no, *no!* Your ring announcer has to have a deep, clear, radio-quality voice, not one that's nasally, high pitched, or bland. Further, he has to be able to inflect emotion and energy in his delivery.

Learning to inflect emotion and energy

Inflecting emotion and energy is something that can be learned. It takes practice, but it's not extremely difficult once you know how to do it. Many years ago I learned a lot about inflection through a very old book I bought used from a secondhand shop titled *How to Read the Bible.*[2] What was most interesting about this book was that it wasn't what I expected. I expected it to be a book that discussed how to read the Bible to understand it. I figured it would include study methods, useful passages, interpretations, historical facts, background information, and so on. But that wasn't really what the book was about at all.

The book was *literally* about how to read the Bible – out loud. It was written for ministers and lectors who read Bible passages out loud to

---

[2] Frederick C. Grant, *How to Read the Bible* (Morehouse-Gorham Co, 1956).

a church congregation. The book's purpose was to teach you how to read the Bible to make a dramatic impact on the listener. You know how you go to church and some guy gets up and starts reading out of the Bible like a droning robot? What happens to you? You drift into la-la land. This book teaches the reader how to read the Bible with emotion and energy and impact so that people don't drift off into la-la land and are actually moved by the passage being read.

The author's method was simple, really, and could be applied to any type of public speaking. It's particularly useful in the performing arts – which includes, conveniently, pro wrestling. His method was to look at the text to be read aloud and analyze it for power words, words that evoke emotion or rouse attention. Circle or highlight those power words. Then when it comes time to read the piece to your audience, you want to place dramatic emphasis on those power words. Take this particular passage as our example:

> "And the Lord said to Moses, See, I have made you a god to Pharaoh: and Aaron your brother shall be your prophet."

A dull, ineffectual reader would read that passage like this:

> "And...the...lord...said...to...moses...see...I...have...made... you...a...god...to...pharaoh...and...aaron...your...brother... shall...be...your...prophet."

Boooooooring! You know what runs through my mind when someone starts reading or speaking like this? I think, "I really need to get the timing belt on the wife's car replaced. I should probably get the tires rotated while I'm at it. Oh! I have to remember to go pick up another wide receiver for my fantasy football team..." My mind wanders because the guy up at the podium is reading like an automaton and just isn't capturing my attention.

So now let's go back to the original passage and pick out the power words and see how this can be made so much better:

"And the *Lord* said to Moses, *See*, I have made you a *god* to Pharaoh: and *Aaron* your brother shall be your *prophet*."

You can probably already tell where this is going. The italicized words are the power words. When you read the passage, you put heavy, dramatic emphasis on these words, almost as if you're shouting them. Plus, you want to draw the enunciation of these words out. Like this: "And the *Looooord* said..." Read the above passage out loud to yourself, placing heavy emphasis on the power words I chose and notice how much more striking and alive the passage sounds. Not only does it sound more dramatic, the meaning of the passage becomes plainly evident.

Now you can make this even more powerful by inserting dramatic pauses. You insert a dramatic pause anytime you see punctuation – a two count for commas and a three count for periods and exclamation points. Like this:

"And the *Lord* said to Moses [count one...two] *See* [count one...two] I have made you a *god* to Pharaoh [count one...two] and *Aaron* your brother shall be your *prophet*."

So how does this apply to pro wrestling? Let's look at a wrestling example. Say you're the ring announcer at a show and you're about to announce the guys about to wrestle. Here's what you would typically announce:

"This next match is scheduled for one fall with a fifteen minute time limit. Making his way to the ring, from Toledo, Ohio and weighing in at two hundred and forty five pounds, please welcome..."

Fair enough, right? So let's pick out some power words:

"This *next* match is scheduled for *one* fall with a *fifteen* minute time *limit*. Making his way to the ring, from *Toledo*, Ohio and weighing in at *two* hundred and forty five pounds, *please* welcome..."

51

And then throw in the dramatic pauses:

> "This *next* match is scheduled for *one* fall with a *fifteen* minute time *limit* [count one...two...three] Making his way to the ring [count one...two] from *Toledo*, Ohio and weighing in at *two* hundred and forty five pounds[count one...two] *please* welcome..."

You see the effect? Pro wrestling is supposed to be exciting, energetic, and dramatic. Thus your communication should be exciting, energetic, and dramatic. I put this subsection under the section covering ring announcers, but really it applies to anyone who picks up a microphone. There has to be emotion in what you say, regardless of whether you're a ring announcer, play-by-play guy, wrestler, or manager. Otherwise, people will trail off, start twirling their hair, and wonder where the bathrooms are. And if that happens, you're dead.

So practice this method. And if you're a promoter looking for a ring announcer, see how well your candidates are at this. If you find somebody with a good radio quality voice who isn't really good at this yet, you can teach it to him to perfect his delivery.

Remember, appearances are everything!

Appearances are everything and the ring announcer is a promotion's frontman. As such, he has to look professional and sharp. No one knows the importance of this more than Donald Trump, the colorful billionaire and casino mogul.

In the 1980s, when Trump was just starting to promote boxing matches in his casinos, he discovered Michael Buffer, the ring announcer who trademarked the catchphrase, "Let's get ready to rumble!" Right away Trump knew he had to have Buffer working for him. He knew that Buffer's professionalism, charisma, booming baritone voice, and onscreen presence would immediately deliver tremendous credibility to Trump's boxing cards. He told his people, "We've got to have him!"

And we've got to have ring announcers that lend credibility to our sport, too. Beyond the radio quality voice and the powerful, dynamic delivery that we talked about previously, a ring announcer has to look the part. I remember a show I went to a couple years back had a ring announcer who, as it turned out, was a fairly well-known local radio DJ. The show's promoter felt having this guy would lend some immediate name recognition to his promotion. There was only one problem – guys on the radio are only heard, not seen. As such, a lot of guys on the radio look nothing like you imagine they would. A lot of guys have a voice that sounds like the voice of some tall, debonair movie star like Charlton Heston, when, in reality, they're short, fat, bald, and sloppy. And that's exactly what this particular ring announcer at this show looked like. He weighed, seriously, close to 400 pounds. He was wearing a ratty old t-shirt, shorts, beat-up tennis shoes, and a ball cap turned backwards. It looked as if the real ring announcer didn't show up and the promoter just pulled this guy out of the audience. Granted, the guy did a pretty good job of announcing the matches, but the fans in attendance just couldn't get past his appearance.

Don't let this happen to you. It doesn't take much to make someone look the part. Mark Twain said two great things on this subject. I couldn't decide which one I like better, so I'm going to throw both at you: "The clothes make the man," and "Naked people have little or no influence on society." How right he was! Remember those two quotes – especially the second one – because I'll be referring back to them both often in this book. The point is, as I've already said previously, to make the right impact, the players have to perfect their image. The ring announcer should be dressed in either a suit or a tuxedo, and make sure it fits! Nothing looks more ridiculous than an ill-fitting suit or tux. Whether it's too tight and the buttons look like they're going to pop off at any second or it's so baggy the guy looks like he's wearing a moo-moo, nothing screams low rent louder than a suit or tux that doesn't fit. Go to a suit shop like the Mean's Wearhouse, find a sharp dark suit (navy or black), and get the thing fitted. They have suits for under $200, and they'll make sure it fits correctly before you walk out the door. Do *not* go to Walmart or Target and buy a suit off the rack that you fit yourself, because I'm pretty confident you probably don't know how a suit is supposed to properly fit and hang. It's nothing against you – I'm not calling you a rube or anything – it's just that very few men know how a suit is supposed to properly fit.

Next, you need a dress shirt and tie. You can't go wrong with a white shirt – that is, unless it doesn't fit. Again, nothing screams "no class" louder than a dude trying to look sharp and professional by wearing a dress shirt and tie but the shirt doesn't fit properly or the tie is tied wrong. I'm sure you know what I'm talking about. Either a skinny guy drowning in a shirt that's so big the tail of it hangs out of the back of his pants like a parachute, or a portly guy whose shirt is leftover from when he weighed 50 pounds less and he had to move the top button over an inch so he can still get the collar around his chubby neck. And we can't forget the guy who ties his tie so short that it ends halfway down his stomach. Ugh! I always wonder how these guys don't realize that this doesn't look good. And don't try to tell me you never learned, because it's not that hard. All you have to do is look at pictures of people who know how to dress professionally and then copy them. Or go to a website of a store that sells men's suits and look at the pictures. Does the suit, dress shirt, and tie you wear look like the guys in those pictures? No? Then you're doing something wrong!

Summing up the ring announcer

All right, just as we did with the referee, let's sum up the points to take away from this section:

1. The ring announcer is an indie promotion's frontman. Like the lead singer of a rock band, he's the face that the fans will associate with the promotion.

2. A ring announcer must have a deep, resonating, radio quality voice.

3. A ring announcer should speak in language that's both dramatic and dynamic. Use the power word method to perfect this.

4. The ring announcer should look the part! Suit or tuxedo, dress shirt, black dress shoes, and a power tie are requirements for the

job.

5. Once again, appearances are everything. Like a referee, a ring announcer should project a very professional and businesslike image. A clean shave and a fresh haircut are both musts. No earrings, facial piercings, long hair, or ponytails!

The Wrestlers

Here's where the rubber really hits the road. Up until now we've discussed the appearance of just about everything else – the ring, the referees, the ring announcer – but now it's time to discuss what matters most, the centerpiece of any pro wrestling show, the reason why people buy tickets at all, the pillars upon which an entire entertainment industry is built: The wrestlers. Here's where you put up or shut up. If the wrestlers in a show don't look the part, if they look like losers culled from the audience or kids who got called up from their mom's backyard, the promotion – any promotion – is doomed to fail. The wrestlers are what the fans pay to see. Everything else is secondary – important – but secondary nonetheless. That said, I am about to say something that is probably going to tick a lot of people off, but it's 100% true: The sorry appearance of today's independent pro wrestlers is the number one reason why independent pro wrestling is struggling so badly.

Granted, as I've already documented previously, there are plenty of other reasons to go along with that, but even so, the biggest reason why so few people pay to witness independent pro wrestling is because nine out of ten independent pro wrestlers today look like bums, slobs, crystal meth addicts, and nerds who spend lots of time at Star Trek conventions. Again, you may not like to read this. You might even be calling me a few names that are not fit to print here. That's OK. If that's what you need to do, fine. But if you're a pro wrestler reading these words, I have a challenge for you, and I'm dead serious about it.

Put this book down and go find a large mirror, preferably a full length mirror. Take off your shirt, put on some shorts, and take a good, hard, brutally honest look at yourself. What do you see? Be honest...what do you see? There's nobody else looking and there's no one else in the room, so you can be honest with yourself. Does the man looking back at you in the mirror look like an athlete to you? Does he look like a combat sports competitor? Be honest, now. If the answer is no, then what are you doing calling yourself a pro wrestler?

I can hear what you're thinking. You're thinking, "But I'm a superheavyweight like John Tenta or Dusty Rhodes!" or "I'm kind of skinny and don't have a lot of muscle, but I'm awesome in the ring and great on the stick!" or "Yeah, maybe I'm a bit flabby, but I wear a t-shirt in the ring like Bubba Ray! It's my gimmick!" or "I'm no Terrell Owens, but the day of the monster dudes like Hulk Hogan and the Ultimate Warrior are over!" or "Not everyone can look like Arnold Schwarzenegger!" or "But I'm a highflyer!"

Bullshit.

Every one of these excuses is just that – an excuse. A rationalization. A justification. A pretext. A lie you tell yourself to make you feel better about the fact that, in truth, you don't measure up. A lie you tell yourself to make you feel better about the fact that you're too lazy to get your butt in the gym and put in the long, hard hours needed to get into the kind of shape that makes pro wrestling look legit. Ask yourself this: How many times have you seen a skinny, flabby, or downright fat MMA fighter, professional boxer, NFL linebacker, or rugby player? You might be able to name one or two, like boxing's sideshow Butterbean, but by and large, the vast majority of guys in any of those sports is a chiseled, highly conditioned, world class athlete. Now let's flip it around. Take a look at the guys you see in the ring at your average indie wrestling show. Easily eight or nine out of ten of those guys is either scrawny, flabby with a beer gut, doughy, or just out-and-out fat. Don't believe me? Check for yourself. Pick a local indie show to go to, take along a notepad and pencil, and then each time a guy emerges from behind the curtain, make a checkmark if he's scrawny, doughy, flabby, or just generally out of shape. Do the same for every guy who's clearly in shape. At the end of the night, I'll bet you dollars to donuts you'll have eight or nine out of shape guys for every one guy who is in shape.

That means that between 80 and 90 percent of indie pro wrestlers are out of shape! Let's compare that to the sport of boxing. How many fat guys do you see in boxing? I can only think of one – Butterbean. So he's, what, one in 100,000? That's .001%! So less than 1% of pro boxers are out of shape but over 80% of indie pro wrestlers are?

So why is it that 99% of boxers are in shape, anyway? Simple: Because to compete in boxing, you have to be in shape. Getting in good shape is a natural byproduct of all the training boxers do to learn their sport and get ready for a fight. Spend the grueling hours that a boxer does jumping rope, hitting the heavy bag, sparring, working the speed bag, and doing duck and dodge drills, and I guarantee you, you'll be in tiptop condition. The same holds true for football linebackers. Whether you're in varsity high school, college, or the pros, there is simply no way you're going to make it onto the field without being in first class condition. The demands of the

UFC Fighter Marcus Davis: Here's a guy who's not tremendously big, but you can tell he's a highly conditioned athlete. You don't have to be a steroid monster to be legit.

game are too great. So are the rigors of the training field and the weight room. Again, do the things that linebackers do to get ready to tackle charging halfbacks and sack 6' 3" quarterbacks and you'll have no choice but to chisel out an awesome physique. If a guy's not in shape, he either won't be able to keep up, will miss tackles, or will just plain be run over.

So why are so many pro wrestlers out of shape? Because pro wrestling is fake. Now I realize that might rankle your feathers a bit, but it's absolutely true. Pro wrestlers aren't forced to be in shape because pro wrestling is a cooperative rather than a competitive event. Think about it. Why else would old timers like Kevin Nash and Scott Steiner, who both have bad joint and back problems, still be able to wrestle and win? Simple – because the bookers say so. The young guys are instructed to take it easy on them, and they're allowed to simply not have to perform certain moves – like bumping.

The same holds true in indie wrestling. If a guy is too fat, too scrawny, or too weak to do certain things in the ring, it's OK. The guy just asks his opponent to dial down the intensity and not attempt to do certain spots. You can't do that in any other sport, but for some reason you can in wrestling. Heck, you can't even do that in ballet! If you're a male ballet dancer, you need to be able to hoist those ballerinas into the air. If you can't, do you think you can go to the ballet director and say, "Hey, boss, listen. I'm kind of getting up there in the years, and I haven't been working out as much as I should, so how about not making me lift those ballerinas up so high? Let's just change the dance around so I won't have to do the lifts, OK? The girl can do more jumps or something…" If you tried this, you'd get shown the door and you'd be replaced by some younger, stronger understudy who's been chomping at the bit for his chance to be the center of the show.

I'm not sure why, but indie pro wrestling does not have this expectation of its performers – but it should. As we talked about in the first chapter of this book, in order to make indie pro wrestling more successful (and thus more profitable), we need to raise our expectations. Pro wrestlers are supposed to be combat sport athletes, not sport entertainers. We need to stop lowering the bar to allow underachievers and middling performers to play. Guys who are out of shape, guys who are so skinny they look like they were the kids on the schoolyard who got all the wedgies, and guys who are so doughy they look like they spend more time at Dunkin Donuts than they do at the gym *hurt the credibility of the sport.* The guys in the ring are supposed to look like downright bad asses, but instead they look like guys that can easily get their tails whipped by someone in the audience! And if I'm a fan who sees a guy and thinks, "*I* can beat that guy's ass," why would I shell out $10 to come and see him fight?

It's just like bush league baseball. Hardly anyone goes to bush league baseball games because no one wants to see a bunch of average Joes with no chance at all at making the big leagues stumble around and commit errors. If I can play the sport better than you can, I'm not going to pay money to come see you play it!

I hope I've made myself clear. Wrestlers of the world, stop making up excuses and get your fat ass in the gym. Promoters of the world, stop booking guys who don't belong in the ring, whether it's because they lack the training or because they aren't in proper shape.

Bookers of the world, stop making concessions for guys who can't do what they're supposed to be able to do in the ring.

You don't have to be The Hulkster

Sometimes when I talk with indie wrestlers about getting in shape, lifting weights, and developing a physique, I get the old, "Yeah, but the days of Hulk Hogan and the Ultimate Warrior are over! Guys don't have to look like that anymore." Well, yes, that's true. But then again, I never said anyone needs to look like Hulk Hogan or Warrior. All I'm saying is that wrestlers need to look like well-conditioned athletes. Look at guys like Evan Bourne, Chris Sabin, Cody Rhodes, Alex Shelley, or Eric Young. None of those guys is a massive hulk, yet they're all in great shape. They're lean, muscular, and chiseled. Guys in the indies should strive for the same look.

Get the gear

One of my biggest pet peeves is pro wrestlers who wrestle without proper gear: Boots, kneepads, and trunks. For some inexplicable reason, a strange phenomenon has struck indie wrestling across North America where indie wrestlers climb into the ring without proper boots on. They're either wearing sneakers or they're barefoot. Either way, it's unacceptable. If you don't have money to buy a proper set of professional wrestling boots, get a part time job for a week or two until you've saved up enough money to buy a pair. Meanwhile, don't you dare step through those ropes!

Be aware that you can often get an excellent deal on used wrestling boots on E-bay or Craig's List. There are tons of guys who get into pro wrestling and then for whatever reason, they quit. So they're stuck with a pair of boots in almost new condition that they want to dump fast. You may be able to find a decent pair of boots for half the price, or better, than you would pay for a new pair. Just make sure the seller shows you good pictures of them, that they're your size, and their color matches the rest of your gear. Otherwise, you can order a new pair of boots online and still get a good deal. A great source is *ProWrestlingBoots.com*. At the time of this book's printing, they sell classic leather boots in a wide assortment of colors for under $150. They also sell trunks, singlets, masks, and other gear as well.

Let's learn about color theory

While on the topic of shopping for gear, it's important to mention color theory. If you're a pro wrestler, one of the big decisions you need to make is what color you want your gear to be. Choosing colors is up to you, of course, but whatever you do, use a matching *color scheme!* A color scheme is a set of colors that complement each other well. A typical color scheme includes three colors: A primary color, a secondary color, and an accent color. Before we go any further, let me make one step easier for you – your accent color should always be white. Got it? OK, good. That leaves the primary and secondary colors for you to choose. These are up to you, but these two colors should always match. Matching colors is not difficult, but for some reason, it appears to me today young people – guys in particular – are challenged by this. It's actually very simple, really, once you know the trick: Just pick two colors on opposite sides of a *color wheel.*

What's a color wheel, you ask? A color wheel is a simple diagram for combining colors. It's shaped in a circle and is sliced up like a pie. Each pie slice has a color – blue, orange, yellow, green, etc. The two colors that are exactly opposite each other are called *complementary.* This is the color scheme you should use when putting your gear together. So one color on one side of the wheel is your primary color and the other color on the other side of the wheel is your secondary color. Unfortunately, this book is printed in grayscale, so I couldn't include a sample color wheel, but there's an easy solution to that problem: Google it. Just go to your computer and Google "color wheel" and click on the first or second listing. You'll see a perfect sample color wheel.

Notice the colors that are directly opposite each other: Blue and orange, purple and yellow, teal and orange, and blue and yellow. See anything familiar? If you're a pro football fan, I bet you do! Blue and orange are the colors of the Denver Broncos, purple and yellow are the colors of the Minnesota Vikings, teal and orange are the colors of the Miami Dolphins, and blue and yellow are the colors of the San Diego Chargers! The NFL clearly knows how to use the color wheel! In the case of the Minnesota Vikings, purple is the primary color, yellow is the secondary color, and white is the accent color. In the case of the San Diego chargers, blue is the primary color, yellow is the secondary color, and white is the accent color. See how this works? It's easy! Now, if you like gray, silver, or black, that's fine. Use that color as your primary and then choose another color as your secondary. For example, if you like gray, you might choose that as your primary and yellow as your secondary. If you like black, you might pick it as your secondary and, say, pink as your primary, a la Bret Hart.

So how does this translate to gear? Simple – your boots and trunks should be your primary color, your kneepads and elbow pads should be your secondary color, and any markings (like a stripe down the leg of your trunks) or accents should be either your secondary color or white.

Why am I going on about this? Why is this important? It's important because wearing stuff that doesn't match – whether it's in pro wrestling or the workplace – screams tacky, low rent, and unprofessional. I can't count how many times I see guys come out wearing something like green long trunks, white boots, and then a black t-shirt with flames all over it. Or guys who wear blue trunks, red kneepads, and yellow boots. Getups like that make you look like you either got your stuff at the local Salvation Army or you're a hobo. And trust me, people don't want to pay to see hobos wrestle. Again, the central idea is to look organized, professional, polished, and put together – not thrown together, mismatched, amateurish, and cheap.

Now you don't have to use three colors if you don't want to, but three is the maximum number of colors you should have. If you prefer the monochromatic look like Goldberg's black trunks, black boots, and black pads, that's cool. That look works very well for bad ass characters like Goldberg and Stone Cold. Just be sure if you decide to go with the monochromatic look that your colors are all actually the same shade. For example, don't buy dark blue trunks, dark blue boots, and then light blue knee pads. That looks like you couldn't afford the dark blue knee pads so you bought the light blue ones on sale, thinking no one would notice.

As I mentioned in the previous paragraph, these rules apply to street clothes, too. I see dorks all the time wearing light khaki Dockers pants and a beige shirt. Wrong! If you wear khaki pants, you want a dark colored shirt.

To sum up, if you choose more than one color for your gear, make sure they're complementary. And never go with any more than three colors.

What not to wear

Let's do a quick episode of that show "What Not to Wear" for the pro wrestling world. Here's a list of what *not* to wear in pro wrestling:

1. Superhero capes and masks. I shouldn't even have to write this, but oddly I still see guys coming to the ring looking like a very, very cheap rip-off of Owen Hart's Blue Blazer gimmick. Incidentally, did you know that rumor has it that Vince McMahon forced Hart to resume that character in 1999 as a punishment? It's probably true. So if Hart was embarrassed by that gimmick, why are guys in the indies copying him by voluntarily dressing up like caped crusaders?

2. T-shirts. I know I've made mention of this previously, but it really needs to be driven home: Do *not* wear a t-shirt while wrestling! The only reason why guys wear t-shirts is to cover up their gross, doughy bodies. So if you're tempted to put on a t-shirt, maybe it's time you go buy yourself a gym membership instead.

3. Robes or jackets with those hoods on them that cover up your face. What is that, anyway? Why are so many people doing it? Samoa Joe, Christopher Daniels, AJ Styles...all big name guys doing it. Who started it, anyway? I guess someone thought it was cool to come out all mysterious with your face all dramatically covered up. Of course now everyone and his brother in the indies are doing it. You know what I'm talking about – they're wearing this hood over their face like an evil wizard or something and then they do the dramatic "reveal" where they grab the back of the hood and pull it back suddenly, as if they're unveiling

themselves: "Oh, hey, look! It's Samoa Joe! I would have never guessed it was him under that hood. Never mind all his signature rolls of fat." Incidentally, someone must have stolen Samoa Joe's little hoody jacket or it doesn't fit anymore, because lately he's been coming out with a towel over his face instead of his hood. Even if this was cool at some point in time, it's being done so much over and over again today, it's now really burned out and kind of silly. Here's a tip that you should always remember – don't copycat other people, regardless of how famous they are. In fact, the more famous a person is in wrestling, the less you should copycat him. The more you copycat someone famous, the more the fans think you're just a desperate, cheap hack trying to rip off someone else's gimmick.

4. Necklaces. AJ Styles and Samoa Joe are again prime offenders of this fashion faux pas. This is another trend that I don't understand. I can't for the life of me figure out where it stems from. These necklaces are made out of puka beads, silver balls, seashells, bamboo, leather, or some other "earthy" material. I can describe these things with one simple word: Unmanly. Seriously, can you imagine legendary tough guys like Charles Bronson, Clint Eastwood, Stan Hansen, Arn Anderson, or John Wayne wearing these things? No? Then why are you? I mean, these things are a lot like three dollar bills, if you get my drift. Moreover, why would anyone involved in a competitive combat sport – which is how pro wrestling is supposed to be portrayed – wear a necklace? It's a hazard. It's like a guy who works on a paper shredder all day wearing a necktie. That guys are allowed to wear necklaces in what's supposed to be a combat sport just adds to pro wrestling looking phony. So stop it!

5. Silly headgear. Top hats, court jester caps, derbies, beanies, fake afros, stocking caps…it doesn't matter what type it is or what you call it – if you wear it on your head and you're trying to get a laugh from it, it doesn't belong in the ring. I mean, think about it. You're in the locker room, about to go toe-to-toe with another

dude who – in kayfabe – wants to smash your face in. You're stretching out, bouncing on your toes to warm up, psyching yourself up to pummel your opponent. Then you hear your name being called by the ring announcer and you and your entourage (yeah, right!) head for the curtain. You're about to step through when you freeze and say, "Oh wait! I forgot my Ivy cap!"

Stop trying to be funny. Stop resorting to silly sight gags for a few cheap laughs. You're just making a laughing stock of yourself and the sport, which already has enough image problems as it is. More on this topic below.

6. Costume party getups. Ahhh, yes – good old costume parties. Where people get dressed up in all sorts of outlandish, wacky, and colorful getups in hopes of either making someone laugh or winning a prize at the end. The whole idea is, the more creative, off the wall, or funny your costume is, the more the laughs and adulation you receive. You're the life of the party. And everyone wants to be the life of the party, right? It's just good old fashioned all American fun – which is perfectly fine for Halloween but not at all acceptable in the pro wrestling ring. Halloween is one big joke. You put on a silly outfit to look, well, silly. For some reason, though, a lot of pro wrestlers have decided it should work well in wrestling, too. Wrong. Dressing up like a clown, vampire, zombie, hatchet murderer, mummy, ninja, caveman, or

Double Offender: Buff Bagwell has a really silly hat *and* puka beads. Any wonder the guy never got a world title run?

transvestite and climbing into the ring does nothing but make you and pro wrestling look silly. And those people laughing in the stands? They're not laughing with you, they're laughing *at* you because you're making a damned fool out of yourself in public.

Tattoos and Piercings

Before I begin this section, I need you to put this book down, go to the fridge, pour yourself a nice, tall, ice cold beer and drink the entire thing. Then sit down in the lotus position and take a few deep cleansing breaths. Relax…relax…

Because this section is probably going to piss you off. I'm just saying it straight out. There's a very, very good chance this section is going to *really* piss you off (if you're not already). But before you throw this book against the wall or burn it up in your George Foreman Grill, I ask that you give it serious consideration. I ask that you ponder all the points I'm going to make very seriously and openly. Open your mind. Take it all to heart. Give it a lot of thought. Resist the urge to get defensive or immediately reject what I'm saying.

Ready? Here we go.

I realize that tattoos and body/facial piercings are all the rage right now. You see them everywhere. Everyone's got one or getting one. And those who have one are constantly tempted to get another. It's hip. It's trendy. It's fresh. It's young. It's cool. It's a statement. It's a form of self-expression. It's nonconformist. It's in your face. It's bad. It's deep. It's individualistic. It's sexy. It's in. It's what everyone is doing. It's a part of Generation Y. It's shocking. It's controversial. It's rebellious. It's countercultural…

It's bullshit.

Yeah, you heard me right: Bullshit.

It's a stupid fad that a bunch of sorry followers with low self-esteem and an even sorrier need for attention are falling victim to. Read that again. If you're about to go get a tribal armband tattoo or an eyebrow piercing, I ask you to ask yourself one simple question: "Why?" Because it's cool? No, it isn't. Because you're being an individual? No, you're not. It's actually quite the contrary. People who get tattoos and piercings are nothing but bootlickers and suckers who are just yearning for someone else's approval. They're trying desperately to impress somebody whom they secretly feel that they can't impress with their words, actions, God-given talent, or bodies alone.

It's become out of control. There are so many people in this sorry state that just about everyone and his brother is doing it because they're all desperately trying to jump on the "cool" bandwagon. They aren't cool, but they're trying to buy their way into the club by doing what they think cool people do. It's just like all these dorks nowadays riding Harley Davidson motorcycles. It's a desperate attempt to fit in, be accepted, and be admired. It's a lame attempt at hiding one's dorkiness.

Just for the sake of the argument, let's psychoanalyze why someone would pay hard earned money for a tattoo that will be out of style in five or ten years. I've talked to a few people who've gotten tattoos, and if you really dig deep, you'll find that the reasons why someone does this are pretty sad. Let's start with a girl I used to know named Jill. Jill went down to her local tattoo parlor and got a ladybug tattooed on her lower back. Another guy I knew named Tom got a hammer and sickle tattooed on his shoulder. In Jill's case, she claimed she got the ladybug because her deceased father used to call her his "little ladybug" when she was a small child, so she got the tattoo to "remember him by." Translation: She wants to advertise the fact that her father is dead and wants people to feel sorry for her. She's being melodramatic. After all, if you want to remember your dead father, getting a tattoo on your back, where you can't see it, is the worst way to do it. A much better way would be to put a picture of him up in your bedroom or tape a picture of him to your bathroom mirror. That way she'd see him every day and could think privately about him. But that's just it – remembering her father wasn't really her motivation. Her motivation was to get attention from people asking her about the stupid ladybug.

Tom's hammer and sickle is similar. He got it because his great uncle served in the Soviet army during World War II and was killed in action. Like Jill, he's desperate for attention and he figures people will think it's cool that his uncle was in World War II on the Russian side. So he gets a tattoo so people will see it and ask him why he had a Communist symbol permanently inked onto his arm. Talk about a pitiful attempt to get noticed!

You see where I'm going with this? People do these things out of a pathetic need for attention, a false sense of belonging, or because they think it makes them look cool. I hear people claim that doing things like this makes you an individual when just the opposite is true – people who get tattoos and facial piercings (or do anything faddish, actually) because they're "in" right now are *followers*. They're just following along, doing whatever everyone else is doing like mindless, spineless lemmings. They're trend followers, not trendsetters. And as a pro wrestler, you're supposed to be a trendsetter. You're supposed to be larger than life. You're supposed to be bigger than the people sitting in the stands. You're supposed to be the guy whose t-shirt everyone wants to buy and wear. When you get covered in a bunch of tattoos and get your lips pierced, you just look like the guy in the second row. And what's that look like?

Trashy. Yep, trashy. Like this guy below. Think about it. There is a clear reason why the Dallas Cowboy cheerleaders, Disney stage performers, Superman, corporate executives, and the President of the United States don't have tattoos – because tattoos are trashy. And that's exactly the image that indie pro wrestlers project when they come out covered from head to toe in "body art" – that pro wrestling is trashy and appeals only to low class, trashy people who hang out at the tattoo

Come on in: Welcome to the show, folks! Glad you brought the kids. You're in for a real special treat tonight. Fun for the whole family!

parlor all day. Granted, a single "tough guy" tattoo on your shoulder like Rick Rude's US Navy anchor or Road Warrior Animal's Tazmanian Devil or the one on Colby Godwin's arm in the picture on the cover of this book are acceptable, I suppose, but these hackneyed, unoriginal tribal armbands, lower back graffiti, neck designs, dream catchers, suns, stars, ankhs, barbed wire, or any of those other stencil designs just look so cheesy and cheap. I mean, they use a *stencil* for crying out loud! That means 800,000 other people have the same identical tattoo as you. And how does this make you an individual?

I hear what you're saying. You're saying, "But Norm, both Randy Orton and Batista have all sorts of tattoos all over them, and they're main event superstars!" Yeah, well, you're not a ripped monster like Randy Orton or Batista. They can get away with the tattoos because, well, they're huge. But by and large – especially in the indies – being covered in tattoos – especially these faddish ones – just smacks of trailer trash, low rent, and low class. It hurts the sport's image and reduces its appeal. Tattoos and piercings hurt your image, not improve it.

Just ask Carolina Panthers quarterback Cam Newton. Newton, Carolina's sensational gunslinger who can both pass and run, was drafted in the first round and signed to a $22 million dollar contract. When he first met team owner Jerry Richardson, the first thing Richardson asked him was, "Cam, you got any tattoos or piercings?" To which, Newton said no, he didn't. "Good," Richardson said. "Keep it that way."

So cut it out already! If NFL teams don't think tattoos or piercings are good for their image, why in the world should we think that they're good for ours?

Facial Hair

What do Tom Selleck, Geraldo Rivera, Hulk Hogan, and my brother Lance all have in common? They're all part of that 1% of the population who actually look good with facial hair. I mean, can you imagine Magnum P.I. without his mustache? Can you imagine Geraldo without his? I bet not. They would all look pretty goofy without their 'staches.

But just as you are not Randy Orton or Batista, you're not Tom Selleck or the Hulkster, either. Most guys just don't look good with facial hair, especially these newer partial beards like those little triangular patches of hair right underneath a guy's lip or those little rectangular strips on a guy's chin. You know, where the guy has a little, perfectly trimmed rectangular strip on his chin but no facial hair anywhere else.

Or how about the chin beard without a mustache. What dorks start these trends, anyway? Who dreams these things up? Virgins R Us? Seriously, if you really examine the dudes who wear facial hair like this, they're typically the guys who were nerds in school who are now desperately trying to look cool, just like so many of the guys with tribal armband tattoos. You know the guy I'm talking about – he's the guy who gets all dressed up in silky GQ clothes, douses himself in Axe body spray (because of those commercials), and then goes to a nightclub, only to stand in the corner with his fellow goober buddies, drinking Zimas and hoping that somehow the girls will come to *him.* Oh, and he has sunglasses on his head. At night.

I actually worked with a guy like this. Not surprisingly, he was entirely clueless as to why he didn't have a girlfriend. So he went to one of those matchmaker services. You know, one of those women who fix up her male clients up with their female clients in hopes that some romance will sprout. This is a true story – I'm not making this up. Anyway, this guy is one of those guys like the ones I just described, complete with the little rectangular chin beard. So the guy shows up for his appointment with the matchmaker, and what's the first thing she tells him he needs to do? Shave his stupid little chin beard off! It's so ironic it's funny – these guys buy into these nerdy gimmicks because they think they give them a stylish, cool look when in reality, they're chick repellents.

Anyway, so the guy reluctantly shaved his little beard off, took the sunglasses off the top of his head, and got normal clothes, and guess what? Girlfriend.

The moral of the story? Shave.

Summing up the wrestlers

So, as we've done previously for everything else, let's review all the most important things to take away about wrestlers' appearances:

1. Pro wrestlers are meant to be portrayed as combat sports athletes like boxers and MMA fighters; therefore, they should look like athletes. They should have a well-conditioned, muscular physique.

2. Wrestlers should not be chubby, scrawny, doughy, or flabby. An exception here or there for "super heavyweights" types like Dusty Rhodes, One Man Gang, or John Tenta might be made, but by and large, wrestlers should in prime condition. The ratio, at most, should be ten to one – for every 10 in-shape wresters you have, you can have one guy who's not.

3. All pro wrestlers *must* have appropriate gear – trunks, knee pads, and boots, at a minimum.

4. No pro wrestler should ever be permitted to wrestle in a t-shirt!

5. Gear should be color coordinated the same way NFL and Major League baseball team uniforms are. Use three colors – a primary, a secondary, and an accent.

6. Wrestlers should avoid cheesy or goofy accoutrements (necklaces, top hats, fake afros, Groucho Marx noses and glasses, those glasses with the eyeballs dangling from springs, and so on).

7. Wrestlers need to clean up their appearance – give it a rest on the tattoos, piercings, shaggy hair, and goober facial hair.

Storytelling: What Puts Butts in Seats

"If you start with a bang, you won't end with a whimper."
- TS Eliot, preeminent poet and playwright

Telling stories

A lot of guys in the pro wrestling business – guys who've been in it for a long time – will tell you that the action in the ring is what sells tickets. The better the action, the more tickets you sell. Thus, they say, study your craft and wrestle better than anyone. Others will tell you that it's shock and awe that sells tickets – hot chicks in bikinis, fluorescent tubes busted over heads, blood, action that spills to the floor, stiff action that leaves real cuts and bruises, etc.

They're full of it.

Let me be absolutely clear on this point, because it's critical: What sells tickets to pro wrestling is good, old fashioned, simple storytelling. Period. End of story. Anyone who tells you otherwise is full of it. Don't get me wrong – having excellent in-ring action plays a huge role in selling tickets and is an essential ingredient to delivering a good show, but what truly motivates a fan to exchange his hard-earned cash for a ticket to an indie wrestling event is a simple, logical, engaging story. The wrestling action has to be outstanding – no argument there – but wrestling action alone does not sell tickets in North America. It might in Japan, but in America, no way. You have to have both – excellent action spurred on by a damned good story.

What makes a story good? That's what this chapter is all about. It's about how to develop and then tell a good story that's very simple to understand and follow, yet engaging and believable. At the very top of the list of reasons why indie wrestling is struggling so badly nowadays is bookers' inability to weave a good story. Typically the stories indie bookers cook up nowadays are just silly, convoluted, cockamamie series of events and conditions that make little sense or are entirely unbelievable. Either that or they just use retreads of angles from "Raw" or angles that have already been done over and over and over and over again – like the babyface's-girlfriend-turns-against-him-and-sides-with-the-heel angle or the wrestler-wins-a-match-and-becomes-president-of-the-promotion angle. It's the same crap that really wasn't all that good to begin with but has been repeated over and over and over again. It's as if bookers have no originality of their own, so they use the same five or six story threads repeatedly.

And what does that get you? It gets you boring, predictable, corny matches that make up boring, predictable, corny shows that no one wants to go to. Do some YouTube surfing of indie shows. It doesn't matter which promotions you look at or where they're located. The videos can be from shows in New York or New Haven, Miami, Florida or Miami, Ohio, Toledo or Tupelo – it doesn't matter, because you'll see the same things: Cheesy angles and lots and lots of empty seats.

I'm serious – right now, put this book down and fire up YouTube. Find, say, a dozen videos of indie pro wrestling shows. As you watch them, take note of how many times you see one of those tired, recycled angles that you've seen dozens of times before and then take a good hard look at how many fans you see sitting in the chairs at ringside. I guarantee you won't see very many. That's a point I've already made many times in this book, but it's so worth repeating – attendance at pro wrestling events is in the toilet these days for a lot of reasons, and chief of among them is because the stories being told suck.

So get ready for a crash course in story development and storytelling in this chapter. If you pay close attention and faithfully apply the techniques I'm about to share with you, I guarantee you'll start seeing your gate grow from show to show.

The three essentials

Ask any junior high school English teacher and she'll tell you there are three main essentials to any good story: Conflict, climax, and resolution. My seventh grade teacher taught me this over 30 years ago. Her name was Miss Hooper, and I remember it as clearly as day. She said, "I don't care who wrote it or what it's about, a story always, *always* has a conflict, climax, and resolution." I was skeptical at the time. I had a problem with her use of the word "always." Always is just so…absolute. So I blew her off. Surely there was some short story, some novel, some piece of literature out there that did not follow this construct. All I had to do was find one example.

Well, I'm still looking.

Why? Because she's right – a story without a conflict, climax, and resolution is not a story at all.

Make no mistake – there are plenty of crappy manuscripts written by wannabe novelists that drone on and on about stupid, boring topics like family reunions, vacations, home remodels, and bachelor parties, but guess what? Those manuscripts never see the light of day because, well, they suck. They suck because those types of events are not interesting. Why are they not interesting? Because nothing happens. Sure, your high school reunion may have been a complete blast to *you*, but unless something totally unusual or bizarre happened at it, no one else outside of your high school class gives a crap. In short, the retelling of your high school reunion or your vacation to Rome are not stories; they're just rehashes of ho hum events that millions of people do every single day of the year. No one cares.

But now suppose, on the other hand, that during your high school reunion you had one drink too many, passed out, and then woke up in a totally different place – say an abandoned building – and you find that your ID has been stolen. Your wallet is there but your ID is gone. *Now* you have the makings of a story.

This is an example of what Miss Hooper taught me about – it's an example of a *conflict*. It's a problem that the main character of the story must resolve. The high school reunion is not the story; it's the just the *setting* and the *background* for the story. It sets the stage for the actual story that comes later. It's what makes the *conflict* possible. But it's not

73

the story itself. Again, a story without a conflict, climax, and resolution is not a story. Period.

That said, what, exactly is each of the three essentials – conflict, climax, and resolution? Let's take a look. First off, before we start the discussion about conflict, climax, and resolution, it's important to understand that every story has at least one main character that the reader (if the story's a book), listener (if the story is being told out loud), or viewer (if the story is a movie) identifies with. That main character is called the *protagonist.*

The protagonist is supposed to have qualities that the audience likes or can sympathize with. The audience is supposed to be *endeared* to the protagonist. Got it? Great. So the conflict, like I said in the previous paragraph, is the *problem* that the protagonist is faced with and must attempt to solve. His efforts to resolve the conflict snowball as the story progresses. That is, as the protagonist attempts to solve the conflict, the conflict actually gets worse, bigger, more intense, or more complicated. The story builds up and builds up and builds up until, at last, it gets to its breaking point. That's when something big happens. This is the *climax.* The climax is the main event – the big turning point that switches the story from the problem growing to the problem getting resolved. Boom! The climax occurs, and the conflict is resolved. This is the *resolution.*

Make sense? Let's look at an example. Let's look at a movie everyone's seen, the original "Star Wars" movie from 1977. You know, the one where Luke blows up the Death Star. *Conflict:* The galaxy has been taken over by an evil galactic empire that has developed a new ultimate weapon that can destroy a planet and makes the empire seemingly invincible. Luke Skywalker, the protagonist, and his companions realize that the Death Star must be destroyed before the evil empire unleashes its full power on the unsuspecting inhabitants of the galaxy. *Climax:* Luke is about to fire his torpedo down the Death Star's reactor exhaust shaft right at the very second the Death Star's gunners are about to fire its primary weapon on the rebel base and destroy the Rebellion once and for all. Darth Vader has Luke in his sights and is about to shoot him out of the sky and prevent him from firing the torpedo. *Resolution:* Han Solo and Chewbacca emerge from out of nowhere and shoot one of Darth Vader's wingmen, causing the other wingman to crash into Vader and send him tumbling end over end into space. Luke has a clear shot at the exhaust port and fires his torpedo. The Death Star explodes into a massive fireball.

Conflict, climax, resolution.

You can repeat this same exercise with any novel you've ever read or any movie you've ever seen, but how does it apply to pro wrestling? Simple – any angle you're going to invent for a show should involve a conflict, have a climax, and then end in a resolution, and it's best to define these from the perspective of the babyface because, after all, he's the protagonist. So let's say you're developing an angle where the babyface gets cheated out of a title shot by a heel when the heel deliberately injures, say, the babyface's shoulder in a match to knock him out of the title picture. So what's our conflict? Simple: The babyface gets deliberately injured by a heel in a match designed to determine the number one contender, thus spoiling his shot at the title. The babyface must now come back from the injury and somehow win back his title shot. So after a brief recovery period for the shoulder injury, the baby starts climbing his way back up the ladder. Not too bad, huh? You might already be thinking of using this angle at your next show! But we're not done. Let's suppose, to make it interesting, the heel who stole the baby's title shot actually went on to win the title after injuring the baby in their match to determine the top contender. So now our baby is not only trying to get his title shot back, he's trying to exact some revenge on the heel, too. What's our climax? How about the baby finally lands a title shot against the new champion, the guy who stole his title shot by injuring him in the first place! There they are, toe-to-toe in the center of the ring, ready to lock up. And the resolution? After a seesaw battle back and forth, the baby rallies and defeats the heel, thereby "righting" all that had been wronged.

You see how this works? I just plotted out six months' worth of a wrestling angle by simply identifying its conflict, a climax, and a resolution. I know exactly how the angle and the feud is going to start, how it's going to build up, and how it's going to end. After six months have elapsed and the babyface is crowned my new champion, the entire angle will have made perfect sense and will have followed perfect continuity because I mapped the entire story out ahead of time. Believe it or not, most bookers don't do this. They just slap an idea together, throw it into the ring, and then just make up the rest as they go along. And that is exactly what causes crappy angles, storylines with gaping plot holes, story inconsistencies, and events that are entirely improbable or that just don't logically follow. You see this happen in wrestling all the time. Just look at WCW in 2000 – 2001. That promotion was so bad there at the end, it was plainly obvious that no one with any sense was planning out the angles from conflict to climax to resolution. They were just haphazardly and desperately throwing any crazy idea against the wall and hoping something would stick. And if they tried something and got worried that it wouldn't stick, they'd just drop it and try some other dingdong (no pun intended) idea. That left fans confused, frustrated, and feeling betrayed because they'd get into an angle, only for it to suddenly be dropped. And what happened? The fans changed the channel.

Don't fall into the same trap. Remember – conflict, climax, and resolution. Do this for every angle for every show. It's best, in fact, to actually write this out on paper so that you have it formalized and documented. Stories that are conceived in advance, logical, and completely planned out are always light years better than stories that are just made up as you go along. In fact, this method serves as a good litmus test for whether or not an angle you're considering is any good. If you've got an idea for an angle and then sit down to write out the conflict, climax, and resolution and find that you can't, your angle either sucks or is incomplete. Either go back to the drawing board or think the idea all the way through to its conclusion.

Hook 'em early

Steven Spielberg knows a thing or two about making movies and telling stories. In "Raiders of the Lost Ark," one of his very best works, Indiana Jones, our hero, a treasure hunter and archaeologist, braves his way through the thick Peruvian jungle to an ancient underground temple, where he finds a long-lost Incan idol made of pure gold. Upon removing it from its pedestal, however, Indy suddenly discovers that he's accidentally triggered the temple's ancient alarm system and the entire temple begins to collapse upon itself. As the walls start to crumble and massive stone doors slowly start to slide closed, Indy must navigate a string of deadly booby traps, obstacles, and pitfalls. As he is just about to make his way out of the caves of the underground temple, suddenly a massive, perfectly round boulder is released and starts rolling toward him. If he's a second too slow, he'll be crushed. He barely escapes, only to be confronted by local Native Americans led by his arch enemy, who steels the idol from him and gloats in victory. Indy must then run from the Native Americans as they chase him and try to kill him with blow darts and arrows. He narrowly escapes death by swinging from a vine and landing in a river, where he swims to a seaplane waiting for him. He then flies off into the sunset, robbed of his treasure, but alive.

All of this happens in the first ten minutes of the movie!

This is a perfect example of how important it is for any storyteller to hook the audience early. Whenever you're telling a story, whether you're writing a book, booking a match, or just telling a bedtime story to your four-year-old, you want to grab the audience's attention immediately by having something big happen right at the outset. Then once you have their attention, don't let go. Need another example? Look at the original "Terminator" movie. James Cameron, another silver screen super genius, grabs the audience's attention right from the get-go by having the naked Terminator (Arnold Schwarzenegger) approach three hoodlums and demand that they give him their clothes. In response, they mock him and pull out a switchblade. The Terminator then kills two of them brutally with his bare hands. The third, upon seeing how quickly the Terminator dispatched his two friends, comically starts undressing as fast as he can. Again, all this happens in just the first few minutes of the film, very effectively letting the audience know straight away that this is going to be one bad ass movie. The audience is drawn to the edge of their seats from the start, thus opening them up to accept and be excited about the rest of the movie that will follow. It's like tilling soil and putting down fertilizer for crops – by preparing the environment early, you're setting yourself up for overall success.

We should do the same thing in pro wrestling. When booking a show or angle, always look for ways to hook the audience early. If you hook the audience and get them involved early, you pave the way for a hot crowd for the rest of your show. The goal is for every fan to walk away from the show thinking, "Man, that was awesome!" And the best way to do that is to get them into it the same way Steven Spielberg did by having Indiana Jones run for his life from that rolling boulder.

Let's put this into play by imagining the initial moments of a typical indie pro wrestling show. Before the opening bell, the crowd is sort of milling about, talking among themselves, munching on popcorn, maybe glancing at the stuff on your gimmick table. Then the bell rings and your ring announcer takes center stage. The fans find their seats and turn their attention to him.

This is a critical moment in the show.

The fans are all thinking to themselves, "Hmmm…I wonder how this show is going to be? Is it going to be good or is it going to suck?" Now a lot of shows bring out two crappy undercard guys for the first match, almost as if it's a sacred commandment in pro wrestling booking. But that thinking is just out and out wrong. Why? Because think of what happens: Botched moves, inexperienced match pacing, missed spots, and novice selling. And what do the fans do in response? They think to themselves, "This sucks." And *that's* the tone you set for the rest of your show. For the rest of your entire show you have to fight to overcome that perception.

It's just like what we discussed in the previous chapter about making a good first impression. The opening moments of any show is your opportunity to put your best foot forward and make a big impression. So let's flip the example around. Suppose instead of opening the show with two undercard guys muddling about and screwing up, you instead open the show with two of your top workers. It's not your main event, but it's close. So let's plug that idea into the example. Fans are milling about, the bell rings, and the announcer takes center stage. The fans think, "Hmmm…I wonder how this show is going to be?" And then you bring out two damned good guys and open fast and strong with some immediate, furious, hard-hitting heat where the heel's just a feeding machine. After exchanging dozens of stiff punches and chops back and forth, the baby turns the tables immediately and pegs the heel with arm drag after arm drag, dropkick after dropkick, and the heel is bumping like a monster, making every bump sound like a cannon blast. Then the baby tops it off with a big gorilla press and slam. The heel rolls to the floor for a breather and to slow it down.

Right out the gate, your fans are on their feet and screaming. Their question, "I wonder how this show is going to be?" is answered instantly with a huge, jarring smack to the face. Right away they're thinking, "Awwwwww, hell yes! This is going to kick ass!" You've made your big first impression. Your fans are thinking good thoughts. You've just tilled the soil and spread cow poop all over it. You're now ready for a huge harvest for the rest of the night.

Don't get me wrong – I'm not against having undercard matches. AWA promoter Verne Gagne used to always stress that a wrestling show is a story unto itself. And anyone who watched the AWA faithfully would attest to how exciting and engaging AWA shows always were. It's because Gagne fully understood that a wrestling show is supposed to have its own conflict, climax, and resolution. Each match on the card is buildup for the main event, the climax of the story. Every match can't be main event quality because then you wouldn't have a buildup to a huge, explosive climax. Your opening match, however, *should* be main event quality because it's the match that sets the tempo and the tone for the rest of the show. So open with a huge bang, get your fans pumped up, transition to your buildup matches, then close the show with an even bigger bang in your main event.

Take out the trash

As I've alluded to a lot already, it's high time indie pro wrestling takes out its trash, and by George, it's got a lot of it. What do I mean by trash? I mean anything that doesn't make sense or is silly, unrealistic, over-the-top, nonsensical, cartoonish, outlandish, supernatural, or just plain stupid. A lot of people I've spoken with disagree with me on this issue, claiming that pro wrestling needs its colorful characters and campy storylines and situations to be what it is. They say that pro wrestling wouldn't be pro wrestling without its far-out angles and goofy characters. Well, that's baloney. Let me make this as plain and straight if I haven't already: Goofy characters and juvenile storylines are killing indie pro wrestling. It all relates back to what I said earlier – today's bookers are incapable of telling good stories. They substitute good, well-constructed stories and believable characters with ridiculous, unrealistic angles and goofball wrestlers decked out in sequins, Halloween costumes, top hats, and feathery boas. Why is this a bad thing, you ask? What's wrong with a few campy elements like a wrestling clown, a wrestling policeman, or a wrestling vampire? A lot of people contend that there's nothing at all wrong with it, that we're supposed to, in their words, "Have a little something for everyone." Have something for everyone and you sell more tickets, right? What's so wrong about that?

I'll tell you what's wrong with it – you can't have it both ways. You can't have your cake and eat it, too. You can't be the class clown and expect to be taken seriously as a studious scholar at the same time. You can't star in cheesy, low budget B movies and expect to win an Academy Award. It's one or the other. In the case of telling stories, you can't be silly and cartoonish in one moment and sober and realistic in the next. It doesn't jive. And the best stories are the ones that are realistic, believable, logical, simple, and involve characters you can relate to. When you try to do a serious angle, like one guy getting badly injured and then having to fight his way back into contention, where you try to convince the audience that what's happening in the angle is real, you completely invalidate it by following up that match with a match that involves werewolves, wizards, clowns, midgets, pimps, escaped convicts, or the undead.

Let's look again at WCW as an example. In 1995, WCW was hurting bad. I mean *bad*. Ratings were in the tank and the WWF (WWE) was just clobbering it in every possible way, despite the fact that WCW had Hulk Hogan, Ric Flair, and Randy Savage at the time. The reason? Because it was awful. In a pitiful attempt to compete with the WWF, WCW tried to just carbon copy all the WWF's characters and angles, which at that time were oriented toward a very young audience. So WCW was running all sorts of inane, nonsensical, cartoonish story lines in hopes that little Bobby would watch their show on Saturday morning instead of "Power Rangers." The low point of this era was WCW's creation of a really embarrassing and imbecilic wrestling stable called the Dungeon of Doom. This whole angle was so bad, it's painful for me just to think back on it. Nevertheless, the Dungeon of Doom was comprised of a bunch of oddballs and misfits – Kamala, the Zodiac (Ed Leslie), the Giant (Big Show), Meng, and Shark (John Tenta) – and was led by "Taskmaster" Kevin Sullivan, who, in turn, was led by a mysterious fat guy known as simply the "Master," who did nothing but sit covered in dust and cobwebs on a throne of some sort and berate Sullivan about how he and his "warriors" should destroy Hulkamania. Ugh. Any angle that somehow involves "destroying Hulkamania" is bound to be bad. At any rate, the members of the Dungeon of Doom all lived in a secret cave in "Parts Unknown" that oddly resembled a really bad TV set made up to look like a cave. They lived off magical water that bubbled from a fountain that looked boiling hot but wasn't. No, I'm not making this up.

So the Dungeon of Doom hated Hulkamania and Hulk Hogan, but try as they might, they couldn't defeat him. So at the end of a pay-per-view match between the Hulkster and the Giant, the "Master" transformed himself into the "Yeti," a seven-foot-tall mummy. Don't ask me why WCW had a Yeti, which is supposed to be the bigfoot-like abominable snowman creature of legend, dress up as a mummy, but they did. So the undead Yeti came down to the ring and he and Giant proceeded to bear hug Hogan (?!).

Now I ask you to seriously consider this: Is it really any wonder WCW was doing so poorly in the ratings? Seriously, grown men with the power of a multibillionaire behind them somehow concocted *this* nonsense and then put it on national TV. You've got the power of a multibillionaire and a cable empire behind you, and this is the best you can do? Believe it or not, when "WCW Monday Nitro" aired later in 1995, the imbeciles in charge at WCW were *still* running this asinine angle! WCW continued to plod along with this crap until finally Eric Bischoff, WCW's new booker, had a stroke of genius. Instead of copycatting the WWF and their silly cartoon characters, he decided instead to make WCW focus on realism and characters and angles that blurred the line between fantasy and reality. Bischoff wanted the fans at home to ask themselves, "Is this real?" when watching "Nitro," but to do that he knew he had to get rid of the mummies, ninjas, human sharks, wizardly taskmasters, and Ugandan headhunters. Thus the nWo was born and the Dungeon of Doom was jettisoned. As a result, ratings skyrocketed immediately, and so began a golden age in pro wrestling, the great Monday Night Wars era, during which more people were watching wrestling on TV than ever before. What sparked it? Storylines that made sense. Characters that were believable. Characters that resembled real people and actually used their real names in the ring. Characters with realistic motivations. Stories that were engaging, logical, and easy to follow. *That's* what brought about the biggest revolution in the history of the business. Sure, going head-to-head with "Raw" played a big role, but "Nitro" would never have been able to compete had Bischoff not formulated such an excellent collection of storylines.

Effectively, WCW took out its trash. The big dogs there stopped just throwing random drivel at the audience and instead focused on making "Nitro" a real TV show. That is, they developed long term storylines, took care so everything made sense, developed characters that were realistic and believable, and drove angles from conflict to climax to resolution. By shedding its silly cartoon world and all its ridiculous denizens, where nothing made sense and *anything* could happen, WCW was able to start developing stories that were grounded in reality and thus allowed the audience to relate and commit to them.

And that's the brass ring – developing serial storylines that fans commit to, get excited about, and keep tuning in to watch from week-to-week and month-to-month. This is how any business succeeds in the long run – by generating repeat customers. Getting fans to come back for more at each and every show is a paramount goal of any pro wrestling promotion. Promoting one great indie wrestling show is good, but it's not success. Success is promoting good shows month after month, year after year. And to do that, we need to take out the trash.

Again, you may disagree with me. You might be passionately disagreeing with me as you read these words. What I'm saying may sound like heresy. You might be one of those guys who believes that, "We need to have a little something for everyone." You may believe that wrestling needs its colorful, funny characters and circuslike look and feel. Fair enough. I understand your perspective and please don't take this the wrong way – but you're wrong. Remember how I had you surf YouTube and look at videos of indie wrestling shows? Remember how I had you take note of how empty the venue was? Again, one of the big reasons for this is lousy storylines. And just as Eric Bischoff realized he couldn't turn his ratings around without taking out the trash, we as indie wrestling promoters and workers can't increase our attendance unless we, too, do the same.

Think about it.

When anything is possible, nothing is impossible

It must be very difficult writing Superman comic books. Why? Because it's so hard to create difficult situations for him to overcome (i.e., *conflicts!*). You can't have Lex Luthor capture him and lock him in an abandoned prison cell because Superman would just bend the bars and get out. You can't have Bizarro chain him to a boulder and throw him into the ocean because Superman will just break the chain and fly back to the surface. You can't have General Zod kill Lois Lane because Superman will just fly around the Earth a million times against its rotation and turn back time to right before Zod kills her.

This is what happens when you create fantastic situations or characters with superhuman powers. You're extremely restricted in creating conflict because conflict involves limitations. That is, a conflict is a conflict to a character because the character can't easily resolve it. It's a challenge. Audiences love situations where the hero is against all odds or knocked down or put behind the eight ball or has the deck stacked against him and yet in the end, he prevails. But you can't create these situations if you don't have characters with real-world vulnerabilities, fears, failings, and flaws. If your characters are superhuman or impervious to pain, how do you tell a dramatic story of injury or comeback?

What am I talking about? Think about it – indie pro wrestlers today so commonly portray themselves as superheroes. They may not realize it, but they do. One guy bashes another over the head with a steel chair, and what happens? The guy who took the shot sells it for all of three seconds, then snatches the chair away and hits the guy back! In reality, if I hit you with all my might over the head with a folding steel chair, I would either crack your skull open, break your neck, or kill you outright. Yet this crap happens at every show, in almost every match!

Or how about the classic piledriver? Back in the 1970s promoters sold the classic piledriver as such a devastating move, it was "banned" in many promotions. One guy would hit another with a piledriver and the play-by-play guy would start howling, "Oh my God! I think his neck is broken! I think his neck is broken! He may be paralyzed! We need a stretcher down here! Get a stretcher!" And sure enough, in would come the paramedics with a stretcher, and the guy who took the piledriver would be wheeled away with his head taped to a brace. The promotion would then run an angle about whether the guy would ever be able to wrestle again and how dastardly it was for the guy who gave the piledriver to do something so low. Thus the stage was set for an awesome comeback blowoff match that would sell thousands of tickets.

Nowadays, though, fans respond to a piledriver with a nice, big yawn. Why? Because pro wrestlers book themselves as supermen. One guy hits the other with a piledriver, the guy who took it sells it for a few seconds, the guy who gave it attempts a quick cover, and then the guy who took it kicks out and is back on his feet, no worse for the wear. So now in this environment where piledrivers are as common as arm drags and hip tosses, can you run the angle with the ambulance and the stretcher and the neck injury? No, of course not. Why? Because fans have been conditioned to believe that a piledriver is nothing. Having a guy get seriously hurt by a piledriver and wheeled away on a stretcher would be like writing a comic book where Lex Luthor locks Superman inside a vault and Superman can't get out. Fans would be like, "Huh? That doesn't make any sense! Guys get hit with a piledriver all the time and are never injured. Why was this one so devastating?"

This holds true for just about everything that pro wrestlers pull nowadays. In 1986, Doug Somers and Buddy Rose beat Scott Hall and Curt Hennig for the AWA tag team titles by, believe it or not, Rose ramming Hall's head into the ring post. The AWA wanted to sell this heavily, so Hall bladed deeply and really let the blood flow. Now I ask you, could you run this angle in the WWE, TNA, or just about any indie nowadays? No! Why? Because nowadays, ramming a guy's head into the ring post is about as common as a collar and elbow. It's done so commonly, it's filler, something a guy does while thinking about how to transition to his next high spot. And what happens? The guy who gets his head rammed kind of staggers around like Curly from the Three Stooges for a few seconds and then is ready to make his comeback. In the real world, if you had your head rammed into a solid steel post, you'd have to be rushed to the hospital and would be at risk of dying from hematoma.

Pro wrestling is supposed to be portrayed as a real combat sport. Let me stress the *combat sport* part. Combat sports are supposed to hurt. If guys don't get hurt, the portrayal is unrealistic and cheap. If you allow guys to take what would be devastating blows or moves in the real world and then bounce right back up again perfectly fine, you're creating a Superman world. You can't create realistic injury and comeback angles because it's almost impossible in this world to be hurt! Your wrestlers become like the Coyote from the Warner Brothers "Roadrunner" cartoons. They get crushed by an anvil, blown up by dynamite, dropped off a cliff, run over by a truck, and smashed into a cactus, but in the next scene, they're perfectly fine.

So how do we fix this? Simple – stop it! If you're a promoter or booker, impress on your workers that you won't tolerate this crap. Put a stop to all the spotfests. Apply the laws of gravity and physics. If you're a wrestler, stop trying to impress the world by stringing finisher after finisher after finisher. Apply common sense to selling injuries. Apply common sense to matches.

Seize control of the creation process

Imagine Quentin Tarantino sitting down to write the script for his next big blockbuster movie. He hopes that this will be his biggest movie ever. He fires up his word processor and starts to write. But instead of him having complete control over his story, the characters, and how it all ends, 20 random people send him an email describing a character they would like to see in the movie. What's more, each of the 20 people wants his character to be the leading character that wins the day and rides off into the sunset at the end. Now I ask you, how good a movie would that be?

Trick or Treat! Who needs good character development when you have great leftover Halloween costumes?

MARK SCOTT

It would be fricking terrible!

Considering that this method clearly makes absolutely no sense when writing a movie script, why in blazes is it the norm when booking pro wrestling shows? Think about it – the standard procedure for putting together an indie pro wrestling show is for the promoter or the booker to look around for talent he likes and can afford, call them up, and ask them if they'll work the show. Then the wrestlers show up with a premade gimmick and dictate to the booker what the gimmick is all about. Oh, and don't forget that these wrestlers use their same gimmicks at every single other promotion they work for – including the competition right there in the same town!

Anyway, so the booker does his best with the random gimmicks that show up and nine times out of ten, a terrible, nonsensical show ensues. In one match you've got a guy who's trying to be a Chuck Liddell UFC fighter taking on another guy dressed up as a transvestite. In the next match you've got a barefoot guy pretending he's a savage cannibal taking on another guy who pretends he's an undead zombie. Then in the third match, you've got a guy dressed up as a hillbilly in overalls taking on a guy dressed up as a super commando mercenary. In the end, the show looks more like a Halloween costume party gone really, really wrong than an athletic event. There's no rhyme or reason to it, no consistency, no continuity, no overall guiding vision – just a bunch of crap thrown incongruously together. The show isn't something you designed, but rather, what just happened to show up through the door that night.

Now you might be protesting. You might be saying, "But that's how indie wrestling is! Each worker is responsible for developing his own gimmick! You work with what you have!" Well, yes, that is how indie wrestling currently "works." But let me remind you – that's exactly why no one goes to indie pro wrestling shows! This is one of those longstanding paradigms we have to shatter. Just as with a movie, for a pro wrestling show to be successful, you need *one* guy with *one* vision who's the boss. He calls the shots. He decides what the stories are going to be and who the characters are going to be. Sure, he might have a couple guys help him with ideas here and there, but in the end, one guy needs to make the ultimate decision.

Think about it – nothing great was done by a committee. The Mona Lisa was not painted by a team of artists. Beethoven's Fifth Symphony was not composed by multiple composers. *To Kill a Mockingbird* was not written by a panel of writers. "Avatar" was not filmed by a team of directors.

But when you allow wrestlers to walk through the door and do their own gimmick, you're doing just that – you're allowing a random committee to put together your show. You're allowing them to take control of the story.

Developing characters

Ernest Hemingway, one of the greatest American novelists to ever live, once said, "When writing…a writer should create living people; people, not characters. A character is a caricature." How right he was. After all, who would be so stupid as to second guess a legend like Hemingway? Seriously, the point Hemingway was making when he said this was simple: Make the people in your stories as close to real as possible. Real, believable characters make real, believable stories. Too often pro wrestling – especially indie pro wrestling – concerns itself more with creating caricatures than with creating people.

Take John Tenta as an example. John Tenta, a member of the ill-conceived Dungeon of Doom we talked about earlier, spent just about his entire career portraying caricatures. When he arrived on the scene in the WWF, he was billed as "Earthquake," a big, fat guy whose finishing move was to run the ropes and then sit on his opponent. They built up a feud between Hulk Hogan and him for a few weeks; did a pay-per-view main event where, surprise, surprise, Hogan won; and then what? They kicked him to the midcard because he was just a silly gimmick character (that is, a caricature) whose gimmick had been all used up and now they had nothing to do with him. So he floundered about on the midcard for a while, did a stupid angle where he allegedly crushed and cooked up Jake "The Snake" Roberts' pet snake Damian, and then jumped ship for WCW. WCW renamed him "Avalanche," which was pretty much the same gimmick he had in the WWF. So he floundered about WCW's midcard for a while, not really interesting much of anyone, so WCW remade him again as "Shark," a wrestler who was billed as, well, a real shark – even though he was clearly human. Soon enough, WCW had nothing left for him to do, so he once again wallowed in the midcard, doing jobs for new guys getting a push.

John Tenta is the perfect example of what becomes of gimmick characters – their gimmick gets old really, really fast, fan interest wanes, and the promotion has nothing left for the guy to do. So the promotion has to dream up another silly gimmick for the guy, which lasts half as long as the first. Then they dream up another gimmick and that one lasts half as long as the previous. Eventually they just job the guy out because fans couldn't care less about him anymore.

Now compare John Tenta to, say, Dusty Rhodes, and you see two entirely different careers. While Tenta was a gimmick wrestler, Rhodes was a *character*. And unlike Tenta, Dusty Rhodes never had to change his identity. For his entire career he was, plainly and simply, Dusty Rhodes – with the one exception of the time he wrote himself into an angle where, in kayfabe, he was suspended by the NWA, so he donned a mask and called himself the Midnight Rider and continued wrestling while "suspended."

Dusty Rhodes never had to change his gimmick because the character he developed – a bad ass, tough Texan who always stood up for what was right – was so exciting and endearing to fans, he didn't need a gimmick. He was Dusty Rhodes…enough said. The same thing can be said about Ric Flair, Ricky Steamboat, Hulk Hogan, the Rock, and Steve Austin. Once they established a *character* for themselves – not a gimmick – that character endured forever and landed them all in pro wrestling's hall of fame.

Flip that around and look at guys who didn't do that, who instead relied on gimmicks like John Tenta did, guys like Ed Leslie, Barry Darsow, and Ray Traylor. Granted, they all were main eventers for a while, but their time at the top was short. They all got pushed to the top for one or two big events under whatever gimmick they were working at the time, but once that was resolved, the gimmick had run its course. There was no place for those guys to go but down – down to the midcard, and then from there, down to doing jobs for the new gimmick characters the WWF or WCW were cooking up at the time. Why is this always the case? Why do gimmick characters burn out faster than toilet paper doused in gasoline? Because gimmicks are not characters. A gimmick is just that – a silly caricature that's both unrealistic and shallow. If your gig is that you're an invincible death row escapee, once you get beat, well, guess what? You're no longer invincible. So your entire draw from being some bad ass death row guy evaporates into thin air. And then what? How do you reinvent yourself and branch off into a new storyline if you're a death row escapee? That *is* the storyline. There's nowhere to go from there because you're entire angle was one dimensional. The only thing you can do is invent another gimmick, which burns out even faster.

So why do characters endure the test of time while gimmicks fizzle out in the blink of an eye? Because characters lend themselves to storytelling that can evolve over a very long haul. The reason why a gimmick gets heat is because of the gimmick itself. That is, when a promotion introduces a new gimmick – say a seven-foot-tall, invincible mummy that calls himself the Yeti – the way the invincible mummy gets heat is by being an invincible mummy. He's pushed as some mysterious and possibly magical creature from another world that our superhero babyface champion can't possibly beat. So when the whole thing goes down and the mummy is finally beaten, fans think, "OK, so long, Yeti. You're not so unbeatable after all. What's next?"

In the case of a character, however, what draws heat is what the character *says and does*. Who could possibly forget Dusty Rhodes' legendary feuds with Harley Race, Ric Flair, Terry Funk, and Tully Blanchard? These longstanding wars ebbed and flowed, rose and fell over the years and were never quite resolved and never forgotten. Think of Dusty's sizzling hot feud with Ric Flair that started in 1981. That feud lasted for *eight years* and no one ever got tired of it! Why? Because both Rhodes and Flair projected themselves as believable, real people with realistic moral codes, motivations, resentments, strengths, weaknesses, jealousies, angers, and hatreds. Their feuds were over realistic issues – the coveted world title and *personal* vendettas.

This method should be embraced in the indies, too. That is, to make a conflict real and hot, make it *personal.* And the way to make things personal is to make the characters of your story *people,* just as Hemingway said. Instead of creating cheap, gimmicky angles where two outer space aliens battle over whose planet is superior or where two cowboys squabble over who has the better horse ranch or where two pimps scrap over each other's hos, develop rich storylines that involve real people with real emotions, real pains, real weaknesses, real fears, and real motivations. How do you do that? Let's examine that very topic in detail.

Really, really know your characters

Ask any successful novelist and he'll tell you that the best way to write a good story is by first getting to know your characters. This might sound crazy since characters in a book aren't real, living people, but believe it or not, bestselling writers work very hard to "get to know" the people that spring out of their imaginations and onto paper. By "knowing" their character well, by knowing every detail about them – where they went to school, what jobs they've held, who their spouse is, who their parents are, what their dreams are, etc. – the stories they spin about them are much fuller and more realistic.

The same should hold true in pro wrestling. After all, pro wrestling is about telling stories first and foremost, so as such, we should flesh out our characters deeply by getting to know them. Let's say you're developing a heel character that you're going to start portraying. It's not done very often, but ask yourself, why is this guy a bad guy? What made him bad? What made him such a jerk? Typically in pro wrestling these questions never get asked. A heel is a heel because he's a heel. But this isn't the way people turn bad in real life. I seriously doubt anyone has ever woken up one morning and said to himself, "You know what? From now on out, I think I'm going to be a jackass. Yeah…that's what I'll do – be a jackass and take advantage of everyone I meet."

That just doesn't happen. People don't just become self-centered, arrogant, haughty, selfish, or disloyal overnight or for no reason. There's always a reason why someone does something or acts a certain way. An arrogant person may have been ridiculed as a child and is now overcompensating. A narcissistic person may have had secret fears that he was ugly growing up and is now looking for people to validate his perception that he's actually very attractive. A selfish or self-centered person may have had bad parents who were themselves very selfish. A hostile or overly defensive person may have been abused or bullied. A bully might actually be insecure and bullies people weaker than him to make himself feel bigger or powerful or to impress his friends. Whatever the character flaw, there's always some reason why it exists.

The same can be said about babyfaces. If you're developing a babyface character, ask yourself, why is this guy a good guy? Why does he play by the rules? Why does he stick up for his friends? Why is he modest? Why does he stand by what he believes? A giving or caring person may have had a good Christian upbringing that taught him the value of others. A courageous person may have had a father who won the Silver Star in Vietnam who taught him what it meant to be brave. An appreciative person may have had to struggle in life to get to where he is. As with character flaws, any virtue has a reason why it exists.

So your mission when developing a character is to flesh these things out. What made your character who and what he is? What makes him good? What makes him an ass? What made him decide to become a wrestler or a manager or a valet? What type of athletic background does he have? Was he the quarterback of his high school varsity football team and well versed in organized sports or was he just a brawler on the mean streets of Brooklyn? Did he travel to Thailand to get schooled in Muay Thai or was he an amateur wrestler in college? What are his motivations in wrestling? Does he love the sport and dream of being its champion or does he just want to be the champion to get rich? Does he love the jet-flying, limousine-riding lifestyle or does he prefer to be low key and fly coach? Does he love the ladies or is he a family man? Does he trust his friends and partners or is he suspicious or jealous? What does he regret, resent, abhor, cherish, love, and hope for?

Asking and answering these questions will really breathe life and believability to your characters. And once you have the answers, it's a very good idea to write them down so that you don't forget them and can refer back to them as your character develops over time.

One thing that has always driven me crazy about pro wrestling is how it forgets its own history. Promoters will book some big angle that involves, say, a career threatening injury to the babyface's back or neck that takes him out of action for a few weeks. They'll even plug it as if the guy needed to undergo surgery to have the injury repaired. Then they'll run the angle through its paces, but then four or five months later, they'll never mention it again as if it never happened.

Ric Flair's feud with Terry Funk in 1989 is a perfect example. The feud started when Funk jumped Flair after Flair had just wrestled Ricky Steamboat in a thrilling match. Funk then piledrived Flair through a table (which was shocking at the time), badly injuring Flair's neck. The injury was in kayfabe, of course, but the promotion did a fantastic job of selling it as if it was real. They plugged away at it, selling it as career-threatening. They even brought in Flair's doctor for an interview and to ask him if Flair would ever wrestle again. A few weeks after the "injury" Flair and Funk faced off in an "I Quit" match that Flair ultimately won.

What happened next? The promotion never mentioned the "devastating" neck injury again. But conversely, the promotion mentioned Flair's real-world back injury he suffered in a plane crash at every opportunity. So to the fans who paid attention (and most do), it became very clear that the neck injury was fake and just a cheap story thread.

Don't make this mistake. As you develop your characters – from conception to their first appearance at a show to their ultimate run as the promotion's champion – write down everything that's happened to him along the way. Keep a journal. That way you'll know your character as if he's a close friend or a member of your family, which is the cornerstone of good storytelling.

The stuff of great stories – human emotions

In 1975, an unknown actor wrote a movie script about an obscure boxer who, by a stroke of sheer luck, gets a shot to challenge for the heavyweight boxing championship of the world. The script was made into a movie in 1976 with a budget of only $1.1 million. Upon release, it shocked the world and quickly went on to make over $117 million at the box office and won three Academy Awards, including Best Picture. The movie I'm talking about, of course, is "Rocky," and the unknown actor who wrote the script was one Sylvester Stallone. "Rocky" was a smash hit that earned a 10,000% return on the movie studio's initial investment and catapulted Stallone to superstardom overnight. It spawned five successful sequels and is today considered a treasured piece of classic Americana.

Sylvester Stallone was inspired to write the script for "Rocky" while watching a real heavyweight boxing match between a virtual unknown by the name of Chuck Wepner and the legendary Muhammad Ali. Going into that fight, no one gave Wepner a chance. Everyone expected Ali to make mincemeat of him and knock him out early. But Wepner had other plans. The fight went all the way to the fifteenth round, and Wepner actually even knocked Ali down in the ninth round with a heavy blow to Ali's chest. It wasn't until the very final twenty seconds of the fight that Wepner finally lowered his guard and Ali knocked him out. Stallone, watching the entire fight unfold live on TV, was struck by Wepner's steadfast determination to stay on his feet and slug away toe-to-toe against the greatest boxer to ever step through the ropes.

Sylvester Stallone poured all that raw emotion – and then some – into the script of "Rocky," and that's what made it such a tremendous success at the box office. It was a simple tale, but Stallone's effective portrayal of a poor prizefighter dreaming of and pursuing something bigger for himself captured the hearts of audiences. Who could forget the imagery of Rocky Balboa running up the steps of Philadelphia's Museum of Art, flanked by local children, all cheering him on? Who could forget the slow motion images of him jumping for joy with his arms held victoriously in the air upon conquering that flight of steps? Who could forget him shouting "Adrian!" as the announcer reads off the results of the split decision? Who could forget the heartwarming moment as the two profess their love for each other even as it's revealed that Rocky has lost the fight of his life?

Borrow this page from Sly Stallone's playbook. What makes stories really great, what connects the audience to the characters more than anything else is raw human emotion – joy, fear, hate, anger, jealousy, resentment, rage, and triumph. Think about it – why do so many people like those reality shows that pack a bunch of strangers into a house together? Because it's a sure bet that they'll become jealous, resentful, and angry with one another, which inevitably leads to arguments, confrontations, crazy outbursts, and fistfights. Whether they're willing to admit it or not, TV audiences love this stuff. It appeals to our shared morbid fascination that grabs our attention and prevents us from changing the channel, even though our consciences insist that we should.

Infuse your storylines with emotion. Direct your wrestlers to be passionate and emotional. When they give an interview after a big match, tell them to be excited or angry, depending on whether they won or lost. This is what pro wrestling has that boxing and MMA don't. Think about it. When MMA fighters are interviewed after a big fight, nine out of ten times, they're duds. They stand still, with their hands on their hips, breathing heavily and saying things like, "It was a great fight. I'm glad I won. He was a great opponent..." The loser, afterwards, says, "It was a great fight. I wish I had won. He was a great opponent..." Boring!

Contrast that with Stone Cold Steve Austin's taunting Jake "The Snake" Roberts, then portraying a Born-Again Christian, by saying, "You sit there, and you thump your Bible, and you say your prayers, and it didn't get you anywhere. Talk about your Psalms, talk about your John 3:16... Austin 3:16 says I just whooped your ass!" Or contrast that with Tommy "Wildfire" Rich's extremely natural exuberance upon upsetting Harley Race for the NWA world title. He was so surprised, overwhelmed, and excited when the referee handed him the title, he jumped for joy and accidentally tackled the ref in the process! The victory was so heartwarming and thrilling, the fans of Augusta, Georgia celebrated it for days afterwards.

Emotion rubs off on everyone around you. When you're happy, the people around you are happy. When you're depressed, people close to you become down, too. Energy is contagious. So if your babyfaces are overjoyed when they win big, your fans will be, too. But if they behave in a ho hum, business-as-usual manner, fans will be left unaffected and bored. Winning a title or a big match is a *huge,* earth shattering event for the victor, and wrestlers, as actors, should behave that way to communicate that message to the audience.

Don't base characters on professions

Vince McMahon once said in an interview granted to the magazine *Cigar Afficianado,* "We have no boundaries or limitations. We can go anywhere we want to. We're only limited by our imagination and creativity. We take the best of show biz and roll it all into one." Believe you me, when he said this, he was dead serious. This wasn't buzz or a sound bite. In the 1980s, he did exactly what he described – he discarded wrestling's Hippocratic Oath and told his staff, "Anything goes." He didn't care about believability, realism, sport, or kayfabe. He just cared about making money. If people would pay big bucks to see an elephant painted pink with wings strapped to its back, make no mistake, there would be a pink, winged pachyderm in the center of his ring in Madison Square Garden.

He and his staff went nuts in the 1980s and 90s with pulling out the stops. Anything they could dream up, they did. Pretty much their standard operating procedure was to take some blue collar profession and turn it into a wrestling gimmick. McMahon had wrestling prison guards, soldiers, policemen, clowns, repo men, Elvis impersonators, porn stars, barbers, dentists, and garbage men…to just name a few. And, of course, as pro wrestling is so wont to do, every other promotion large and small – and still to this day – started copycatting. Promoters everywhere starting thinking, "If Vince can make money doing it, why can't we?" And thus began the endless cavalcade of wrestling construction workers, prisoners, chefs, plumbers, farmers, truck drivers, cabbies, boat captains, lumberjacks, ninjas, and doctors…again, that's just to name a few. Effectively pro wrestling now looks more like the suburbs on Halloween night than a serious athletic competition.

I know this is a point I've harped on quite a bit, and again, you might be questioning me. You may well again be thinking, "Come on, now. What's so wrong with that? Fans *expect* colorful, whacky characters. You gotta give the fans what they expect." If you are, in fact, thinking this, my response to you would be to point out the huge difference between what fans *expect* and what fans *want*. You *expect* something to happen because you've become conditioned to it happening, but that doesn't necessarily mean that you *want* it to happen. For example, when I go to the dentist to have a tooth pulled, I *expect* that it's going to hurt; I don't *want* it to hurt.

The same thing holds true in this discussion of whacky characters based on professions in pro wrestling. Indeed, there have been so many of these characters in wrestling for so long, fans are conditioned to it.

To illustrate this point, let me tell you a little about a Russian scientist named Ivan Pavlov. Way back in 1901, Ivan Pavlov conducted a famous experiment on *reflexive conditioning*. He penned up a bunch of dogs and would ring a bell every time he fed them. After a while, every time he rang the bell, the dogs would start drooling, even though there was no food anywhere in sight. Though the experiment was conducted on dogs, people behave very similarly. Pavlov demonstrated how people frequently react reflexively to various situations based on conditioning, and wrestling fans *expecting* silly characters in wrestling is a perfect example of this in action. Pro wrestling is chock full of instances where one worker could say to another, "Hey, this doesn't really make much sense," or "Hey, you know, this is kind of stupid," but the other guy answers by saying, "Yeah, but we've been doing it forever, so shut up."

Pro wrestling, in effect, has become indoctrinated in stupidity.

And *that's* exactly what's wrong with basing characters on jobs – it's stupid. It's stupid, shallow, one dimensional, cheap, and unoriginal. Not to mention, it really doesn't make any sense, either. If a guy's a construction worker, trucker, or plumber, what's he doing wrestling? Are we telling our fans that pro wrestling is such a rinky-dink sport its participants have to stoop to mopping floors and emptying trashcans to feed themselves? Granted, many athletes work day jobs while they pursue their dream of making it big in their chosen sport. Many minor league baseball players, boxers, and MMA fighters work hard labor jobs to make ends meet while they work their way up in the ranks and try to make a name for themselves. But you know what? None of those guys really wants the world to know about his day job. No minor league baseball player who dreams of someday playing for the Major Leagues is proud of the fact that by day, he drives a beer truck. No amateur boxer who spends grueling hours in the gym each day to get ready for his first pro fight is crazy about the fact that he works as roofer to pay the rent. So if you don't see other up-and-coming pro athletes parading their day professions about, why do we see it so often in pro wrestling?

Simple: Because it's the easy way out. Instead of developing a realistic character with a full history, a deep personality, complex motivations and deep seated resentments and grievances, promoters instead just take a guy and stuff him into a prison jumper and call him "Death Row." Or they buy the guy a set of chaps, throw a cowboy hat on his head, and call him "Tex." Oh, and let's not forget that in the case of "Tex," we need to also buy him a whip or a bull rope so that at the end of his matches, he can take his opponent and hang him by his neck over the top rope. Oh, and let's also not forget the branding iron, either. Every cowboy in wrestling needs to carry around a branding iron. That way he can prop it up in the corner and use it on his opponent when the ref's conveniently not looking.

This is the kind of garbage we need to throw out. If you've been watching pro wrestling for any length of time, admit it – you've seen plenty of "Death Rows" and "Texs" over the years. And when I mentioned that bull rope and that branding iron, you knew *exactly* what I was talking about and *exactly* what I was getting at long before I described it. That should be all the evidence you need to realize how trite and predictable stuff like this is. It's high time we stop thinking so one-dimensionally and start working diligently on developing characters that mean something, are believable, and that fans can easily identify with. We need to think outside the box and strive to be genuinely creative and innovative. This is one of the essential keys to reversing the trends of dwindling gate and waning fan interest.

Howdy, Tex: Anybody working as a cowboy in pro wrestling needs three things: A vest, a cowboy hat, and a whip or bull rope.

Don't kowtow to the wants of a few

Before we go any further on the topic of good storytelling and developing rich characters, I want to warn you about the dangers of trying to appease the minority. What do I mean by that? Let me put it this way: If you were to take the argument I just made in the previous section and post it on a popular wrestling forum on the Internet, I *guarantee* you, you'd get lots responses from people who disagree with me. There's not a single doubt in my mind. Why? Because in just about any industry, no matter what you do, there are always going to be a few people who really, really like it. You could make a product that's complete crap, market it heavily, and believe you me, some people will love it…even though it's still crap.

Take the Chevy Vega as an example. *Time* magazine included it in its special feature on the worst 50 cars ever made. *US News and World Report* went even further – they ranked it as *the* worst car ever made. Even General Motors admitted that the thing was a lemon and that it very badly hurt the company's reputation. But despite all that, there are still people who to this day love their Chevy Vega. There are even a few Chevy Vega car clubs!

Let's look at even better example. South Beach – the southernmost chunk of Miami Beach – is one of the most hip, booming, hopping, popular, and commercially successful areas in the entire world. It's home to the hottest nightclubs, swankiest shops, ritziest boutiques, trendiest bars, and fanciest restaurants on the east side of the Mississippi River. It's a boomtown, a virtual goldmine. But believe it or not, it didn't always used to be that way. On the contrary, by the early 1980s, the South Beach area had become one of the seediest, most rundown areas in all of Miami. It had become, by and large, a retirement community, home to elderly people with very small fixed incomes. So many poor elderly folks had moved to South Beach to retire, people started referring to it as "God's Waiting Room." The place was so rundown, the hit show "Miami Vice" would frequently film episodes there whenever they had a scene that called for an abandoned building or seedy hotel room.

But then in the late 80s, a visionary developer named Tony Goldman saw South Beach as a real diamond in the rough. He decided to redevelop South Beach's art deco district and preserve it at the same time. He believed that if the classic, old hotels along the beach that had become retirement homes could be restored, South Beach would become extremely hot property. So he set out to do just that. A lot of people called it a lost cause. Others just laughed at him. Worst of all, many of the people who were then living in South Beach liked it just the way it was. They didn't want it redeveloped. They didn't want anything to change. They opposed Goldman tooth-and-nail. They wrote letters to the newspaper. They appeared on the local TV news broadcasts. They claimed Goldman was ruining Miami Beach. They claimed he was ruining its heritage, its history, and its ethnic roots. A lot of armchair quarterbacks and wannabe experts jumped in and said things like, "Yeah, that guy should listen to the people. They know the area. It's their home. Who does he think he is?"

Fortunately, Tony Goldman just ignored them all. He evicted the homeless people and the drug dealers from the crumbling old hotels and vacant apartment buildings he had bought and ran them out of town. He scraped away all the peeling paint from the art deco facades, gutted building interiors, widened sidewalks, and fixed the burned out neon lights that had lit the place in better times. Soon, other developers saw what was happening and bought in, too. Shops started opening, and fashion designers from Los Angeles and New York actually moved their offices there. Twenty some years later, and it now gives Beverly Hills a run for its money in being the swankiest, most fashionable, most extravagant places in America.

The moral of the story? Sometimes to make something great, you have to piss some people off. In order to turn the fortunes of a struggling endeavor around, you have to make drastic changes, changes that the old guard and the status quo won't like. Their numbers are small, but they'll scream very loudly. If you cave in to their demands, if you fail to be a visionary because a handful of people tell you they like something how it is, if you change your direction because you decide you need to "listen to the people," you will undoubtedly fail. Likewise, if you propose some of the ideas I've advanced in this book so far – like doing away with "colorful" wrestling characters based on professions – a few people will very vociferously contend that they hate the idea. But to move forward, we largely have to purge the old to bring in the new. We have to piss some old timers off.

So don't kowtow to the whims and demands of the old guard. Sparking a revolution requires bold, determined action. Many people just won't be able to see your vision until it's real. And then when it's real, trust me, they'll be jumping all over your bandwagon and calling you a genius. Listening to the gripes of these detractors – people who don't get it or who like things the way they are – will serve only to derail you.

Don't stoop to stereotypes

Rusty Brooks, the man who taught me how to wrestle and arguably the best trainer in the business to this day, really liked the British Bulldogs back in the 80s. He particularly liked the Dynamite Kid (Tom Billington). He liked the idea of a slightly undersized but well-conditioned wrestler who uses high risk, high flying moves like the diving headbutt to compensate for his lack of mass and brawn. He believed that wrestlers of his size could reinvent wrestling by infusing it with an entirely new, exciting style. Mind you, this was 1988, long before the term "cruiserweight" had ever been introduced to pro wrestling.

Turns out he was right.

Anyway, suffice it to say that when I first climbed into Rusty's training ring in 1988 to learn the craft from him, he had me pegged. I was 5' 10", weighed 190 pounds, and had been doing a lot of bodybuilding. My build was a far cry from Dynamite Kid's awesome, ultra shredded, chiseled physique, but I fit the bill perfectly to wrestle in that style. So once I had mastered the fundamentals of mat work and chain wrestling, it wasn't long before Rusty had me doing snap suplexes and diving headbutts. To be honest, I wasn't crazy about this, as back then to wrestle as a high flyer required that you had to be a babyface, and I had always wanted to wrestle as a heel. But not wanting to be difficult, and because I trusted Rusty's judgment way over mine, and because I was afraid he'd kick my ass if I refused, I took on the role in earnest and started studying tapes of the high flyers of the time, guys like Scott Steiner, the Great Muta, and, of course, Dynamite.

One of the things Dynamite's partner Davey Boy Smith did that Rusty also liked was how he used the headbutt as a strike, like a punch. Davey Boy would batter his opponent with a rapid succession of sudden, "snap" headbutts the way an average wrestler would use a closed fist. Rusty thought it was cool, so he told me to do it, too. So I started practicing doing headbutts against a manikin head that my girlfriend at the time had brought home from her beauty school class. After practicing against the manikin head for a while, I started doing it in the ring. One day I was practicing for a big upcoming match with an African-American opponent (whose name I can't remember...sorry). He and I traded blows back and forth a bit, and then I hit him with one of my headbutts. To my surprise, he didn't sell it.

"Why aren't you selling?" I asked him.

"Because I'm not supposed to," he answered. "You are."

What? This confounded me. I had given the headbutt, so why was he expecting me to sell it?

"But I gave it," I insisted.

"Yeah, but you're a white guy and I'm a black guy."

I blinked a few times, thinking the guy was pulling my leg or something.

"So?" I finally said.

"Don't you know?" he asked, now smiling big.

"Know what?"

"Any time a white guy head butts a black guy – whether he gave it or not – the white guy sells to the black guy."

"What?" I asked, not buying it.

"Yeah," he said. "In wrestling, black guys are billed as having harder heads than white guys. Oh, and Polynesian guys? Those guys have the hardest heads of all. Everyone sells to the Polynesian guys."

Convinced the guy was just putting me on, I turned to the boys who were standing at ringside, watching us practice. To my shock, they all nodded in agreement. There was an established "headbutt pecking order," and I was at the bottom of it! Much worse, this practice stemmed directly from blatant racism. It was sort of a racist, off color joke that subtly implied that black guys and Polynesian guys are more primitive or less evolved than white guys, thus their heads are harder. The really sad thing about it was, there was a full expectation that everyone in the audience would think it was perfectly funny. From that day forward, I refused to do a headbutt ever again because I didn't ever want to risk having to play along in such a blatantly racist sight gag.

This "headbutt pecking order" thing is a perfect example of a *racial stereotype*. Stereotypes, whether they're based on a person's race, nationality, religion, gender, or place of origin, are very bad things. At best, they're cheap and banal; at worst, they're racist, inflammatory, and divisive. Pro wrestling doesn't use stereotypes quite as much as it did in the 80s, but that's not saying much.

What, exactly, is a stereotype, you ask? According to the *American Heritage Dictionary,* a stereotype is a conventional, formulaic, and oversimplified conception, opinion, or image. Note the words "formulaic" and "oversimplified." "Formulaic" and "oversimplified" are two words you *never* want to hear used to describe a character you've written into a story or a plot that you've developed for that novel you've been working on…or, for that matter, an angle you've booked for your next big wrestling show.

Need some examples of stereotypes? If you watch pro wrestling, you don't have to look very far. The Polynesian guy who's barefoot and wears a grass skirt and lei to the ring? Stereotype. The Native American who wears a feathered headdress and moccasin boots and comes to the ring beating a Native American animal skin drum with a tomahawk? Stereotype. The African-American dressed up as a pimp, complete with a pimp hat and pimp cane? Stereotype. The redneck dressed in camouflage and a hunting camp who comes down to the ring chugging beer? Stereotype. The ditsy blonde who can't add and uses her sexuality to get her way? Stereotype. The cowboy from Texas who wears chaps and a ten gallon cowboy hat and carries a branding iron and/or whip to the ring? Stereotype. The Russian with the shaven head wearing a red singlet with "CCCP" and a hammer and sickle on it? Stereotype.

When you stereotype you pigeonhole people. You're effectively saying, "All people who are *X* do *Y*," when clearly, that isn't true. Very few real Native Americans wear feathered headdresses anymore. Most Russians aren't Communists anymore. Only about .00000001% of African-American males are actually pimps. And as I've already stressed, worse than pigeonholing, many of these stereotypes are downright insulting. You're tapping into what you assume is a deep-rooted prejudice shared by all members of your audience. For example, by creating a redneck who wears camouflage and guzzles beer, you're implying that everyone from the South is like that and you're expecting your audience to laugh because you believe that everyone in your audience sees Southern people that way, too. When you create a thug "gangsta" heel character, your attempting to tap into what you believe is the audience's silent contempt for young blacks. When you create a flamboyant homosexual character, you're trying to tap into the audience's homophobia to either get a cheap laugh if the guy's a baby or cheap heat if the guy's a heel.

Don't lower yourself to this. This sort of thing is both uncreative and usually offensive. Like creating gimmick characters based on professions, basing characters on stereotypes is taking the easy way out. Instead of doing the hard work of creating a character that has a personality and depth, you instead tap into tired, old stereotypes that misrepresent a people, a culture, or a heritage. And that's just plain trashy. Remember, we need to take out our trash if we're hoping to attract the general masses back to our shows.

The power of the villain

What do the movies "Star Wars," "The Terminator," "The Wizard of Oz," "Back to the Future," and "It's a Wonderful Life" all have in common besides being considered some of the very best movies ever made? Easy: They all had an iconic, powerful villain. The villain in each of these movies is so powerful, in fact, one could say the villain *made* the movie. Who could possibly forget the imposing black figure and ominous breathing apparatus of Darth Vader in "Star Wars"? Or who could forget the awesome, invincible Terminator with its red eyes and infrared vision? Or who could forget the scary, green witch of "The Wizard of Oz?" She really creeped me out as a child and still does to this day! Or how about the dimwitted but mean-spirited bully named Biff in "Back to the Future"? Or perhaps worst of all, Mr. Potter, the mean, miserly slumlord of "It's a Wonderful Life"?

Let me make one thing crystal clear right here and right now – in pro wrestling, heels *are* the show. You cannot have a pro wrestling show without heels. Period. They are the most important people in the building. They dictate the success or failure of the promotion. If you have good, strong heels, you'll have a successful promotion. If you have weak heels or too few heels, no one will come. This is absolutely critical. It's so important, in fact, that you should re-read this entire paragraph and memorize the point, "Heels *are* the show."

As I've already mentioned, heels are so important to the success of a pro wrestling show that I've dedicated an entire chapter of this book to them. I don't want to go into too much detail here on the subject since we'll have that entire chapter to discuss it, but I do want to pound home that heels are vital to your success. They provide the conflict of any angle (story) you develop. They provide the hurdles the protagonist (babyface) of the story must overcome. Thus, without them, you have nothing.

Perfect example: Fritz Von Erich's World Class Championship Wrestling (WCCW) promotion back in the 80s. In the middle of that decade, WCCW was on fire. Fritz's sons Kerry, Kevin, David, and Mike were all over like a grand slam homerun. Because WCCW was a member of the NWA at that time, the promotion benefited from visiting NWA talent, most notably the one and only Ric Flair. Since Ric Flair was such a monster heel then, the Von Erichs' feuds against him are the stuff of legend. Soon after that, however, the Von Erich cult of personality just got too big. The entire promotion revolved around the Von Erichs, and they ruled the roost the same way the Four Horsemen ruled Jim Crockett's NWA. But there was one major difference – the Four Horsemen were heels; the Von Erichs, conversely, were babyfaces. Thus the good guys were way on top in that promotion, and there were no real monster heels underneath them vying to knock them off their pedestal. So WCCW became like a western movie where everyone wears a white hat. In a word, it became *boring*. This was the beginning of an ultimately tragic end for that promotion.

The message I hope you take from this is that a show without great villains is boring. In fact, villains are so important, the stronger you make them, the better. They should rule the promotion and carry the titles most of the time. Remember, you want a villain who's on top and dominant. That creates a huge uphill battle for your babies to face and overcome. *This is what sells tickets!*

Essential characteristics of a babyface

Any good story needs a main character that the audience can identify with. He's the good guy, the guy the audience likes, the guy the audience hopes wins at the end of the story. He's the guy the audience roots for. Through him, the audience experiences the conflict and climax of the story. Through him the audience feels the thrill of victory once the struggle is resolved and the feud is settled once and for all.

The worst thing that can happen to any story – whether it's a book, movie, TV show, or pro wrestling main event – is the audience not caring about what happens to the good guy. This is the undoing of any story, and it's a fatal mistake made too frequently these days by Hollywood. Big movie makers rely on flashy computer generated special effects, big explosions, dazzling scenes, and "thrilling" car chases to sell a film without bothering much with character development. The end result? The audience is assaulted with all sorts of onscreen pomp and circumstance – spaceships and monsters and explosions – that really mean nothing at all and just leave the audience confused, numb, and bored.

Wrestling nowadays is falling into the same rut. Wrestlers attempt in vain to shock and dazzle the audience with spotfest matches, tightrope walking across the tops of cages, insane leaps from balconies, and bone jarring crashes through stacks of tables. It may have worked 15 years ago in ECW when it first started, but today, fans walk away yawning and unaffected. Wrestling would do much better by spending its time and energy developing realistic characters and booking matches involving traditional headlocks and armbars and lots of punching and kicking spurred on by lots and lots of bad blood.

That's what excites fans.

I wrestled as a babyface, and one thing I learned very early on was, if my opponent did his job well, my job was a piece of cake. If a heel is a good heel, fans will cheer for you, almost regardless of what you do. Why? Because an effective heel is so despised, fans don't want to see the good guy win, they want to see the bad guy lose. That said, some guys are better at being good guys than others. Hulk Hogan and Dusty Rhodes were both so good at it, they had crowds eating out of the palms of their hands. How did they do it? They had all the right essentials. What are those essentials? Let's take a look.

Courage

A babyface is always courageous, especially in the face of the longest odds or great danger. Think of how Dusty Rhodes stood up to the villainous threats of the Four Horsemen, or how Hulk Hogan faced down the biggest challenger to his title, Andre the Giant. In both instances, the promotion built up the heel and stacked up the odds against the baby. By stacking up the odds, the baby is afforded an opportunity to demonstrate great courage. This is what WCCW failed to do, as we talked about previously. The Von Erichs were not afforded opportunities to demonstrate their courage because they were always on top. They were pro wrestling's royal family, effectively shielded from the dastardly acts being committed by the heels underneath them. At worst, if a heel "acted up" too much and one of WCCW's other babies couldn't handle the matter, one of the Von Erich boys would be called upon to smack the heel down and put him back in his place. If anyone demonstrated any courage, it was the heels!

Don't make this mistake. As we've talked about repeatedly, stack the deck against your babyfaces, not the heels. Then throw your babyfaces to the wolves and let them shine. Everyone loves an underdog, especially when he's a good guy opposing a jackass that everyone hates.

Charm

A babyface needs to learn how to turn on the charm. Fortunately in pro wrestling, this isn't too hard. It's very simple: Smile.

A lot.

Whether you realize it or not, a pro wrestling ring elevates your status enormously in the eyes of the fans. As you walk down the aisle for your match, you may still feel inside like an "ordinary" guy. You may even feel a bit like an imposter. But that's not the way the fans see you. In their eyes, you're a celebrity. You're in a position of status. So when you stop, smile, and look into the eyes of a fan, that fan feels privileged, and that's very powerful. Don't underestimate the effects of this. When you meet a fan – whether it's while coming down the aisle to the ring, during an autograph session, or during an intermission – make eye contact and smile.

Turn on the charm. This is a mistake I made very early on in my career. I didn't know to turn on the charm. At one show very early on, I came out from behind the curtain and started down the aisle, but my mind was completely focused on the match I was about to work. It didn't enter my mind that I had to smile and engage with the crowd because I was so consumed with what I had to do in the ring. Consequently, fans had no idea who I was. They didn't know if they should cheer or boo. So they just sat there until my opponent, a veteran heel, emerged from behind the curtain with the most hateful scowl I'd ever seen. It was then that the crowd figured out our respective roles and started behaving more or less the way you would expect a pro wrestling crowd should. So fortunately my heel opponent saved the match for us.

Don't make this mistake. It can happen to the rookie or the veteran. In the case of the rookie, you might do what I did – just forget to turn on the charm. In the case of the veteran, it's easy to slide into complacency. That is, you believe you've established a well-known character and name for yourself and you slip into "coast" mode. That is, you don't work as hard as you once did to engage the fans and stoke the crowd. The fallout of doing this is precisely what I described – the fans don't know who you are and can't get behind you. They don't identify with you, and as a result, your match is a bore.

So if you're a babyface, always, always, always turn up the charm.

Humility

No one likes a braggart. In fact, the most hated people in the world are those people who are really, really good at something and let everyone know it. On the flip side, some of the most loved people in the world are those who are great at something but take little credit for it.

The best example I can think of is the great Barry Sanders, arguably the greatest running back to ever play in the NFL. In one game where his team, the Detroit Lions, faced the New England Patriots, he famously juked one of the Patriots' defenders clear out of his shoes. He turned the guy inside out. Later, an interviewer asked him how he did it. He replied: "I was just trying not to get tackled." People loved Barry Sanders not only because he was a phenomenal athlete, but because he was humble and down-to-earth about it.

Let's look at a pro wrestling example. Suppose your top babyface has just defeated your top heel to win the title. During the post-match interview, your ring announcer says to him, "What a match! How did you do it?" The babyface's response should be humble and gracious, like this:

Being humble: Pro wrestling needs a lot more of this and a lot less "attitude." This is the sort of message babyfaces need to send.

"I got lucky. He left an opening, and took advantage of the opportunity. I want to thank the fans and God for being behind me tonight."

Note that more and more athletes today are making religious references when they win or do well, like former Boston Red Sox pitcher Curt Schilling, who claimed after pitching a big game, "Tonight was God's work on the mound..." or quarterback Kurt Warner who shouted, "Thank you, Jesus!" after he won the Super Bowl. It might be a good idea to have one or two of your babies do the same. Almost everyone appreciates a devoutly religious person, and it wouldn't hurt pro wrestling to hear a message like this once in a while.

On the flip side of the gracious, humble sportsman would be someone like Muhammad Ali, probably the greatest boxer of all time. He was never humble about, well, anything. He bragged about himself and his ability in the ring at any given opportunity. And the result? He was universally despised. Everyone paid big bucks to watch Muhammad Ali fight because everyone hoped beyond hope that he would get beat and eat his words. Of course it rarely happened, which made people hate him even more.

An interesting fact about Muhammad Ali is that it was all an act. He wasn't the heel loudmouth he portrayed himself as. Believe it or not, he developed his character after watching Gorgeous George's act in pro wrestling! He realized that a loudmouth braggart would be hated by everyone, and that would motivate people to buy tickets to his fights.

So the lesson to take from this is simple. Guys who are good at a sport but humble about it are loved by the fans. Guys who are good at a sport and brag about it are hated. So when wrestling as a babyface, always show great humility.

Persistence

You may not know this, but Ted DiBiase – the former arch heel who wrestled as the Million Dollar Man in the WWF and tried to "buy" the world title away from Hulk Hogan – started out as a babyface. In fact, he was enormously over as a baby in Bill Watts' Midsouth promotion in Oklahoma in the 1980s. He was over because Watts was a master of booking. He knew what characteristics to give his babyfaces. And the characteristic he emphasized in DiBiase's character was persistence.

One match in particular stands out as a perfect demonstration of this. It was a match between a young Ted DiBiase and Ric Flair in his prime for the NWA World Title. The setup for the match was impeccable. Flair and DiBiase were in the ring before their match, waiting for the introductions. Unexpectedly, Dick Murdoch, who had earlier in the show confronted Flair and claimed that *he* was the rightful number one contender, showed up to demand that DiBiase step down and allow Murdoch to have his shot. As one would predict, DiBiase refused, so Murdoch sucker punched him. The two exchanged furious blows back and forth, with DiBiase eventually getting the best of

Murdoch. DiBiase knocked him out the ring and then stood over him in the ring, holding the top rope. Flair moved in and sneak attacked DiBiase from behind, knocking DiBiase out of the ring and down to the floor alongside Murdoch. Murdoch grabbed DiBiase and viciously rammed his face into the ring post. DiBiase bladed deep, releasing a gushing river of blood from his forehead. The camera crew cut to Bill Watts standing in the interview area. He explained to the fans that DiBiase's injury was grave, but that the kid wanted to go ahead and wrestle Flair for the title anyway. He said that the medical staff had applied a "pressure bandage" to DiBiase's head to stem the blood flow, but, he warned, that bandage may not hold. He warned fans that what they were about to see may be extremely graphic and they may not want to watch.

Brilliant!

Who in blazes would turn the channel? No one! In fact, I'm sure fans were calling friends to tell them, "Hey! Are you watching the wrestling? Turn it on! It's going to be bloody!" No one can resist their morbid curiosity. Sure enough the camera cut back to the ring, and there stood DiBiase with a bloody bandage wrapped around his head. The match got underway, and it turned out to be a veritable war. Back and forth it went. Sure enough, that bandage was ripped off DiBiase's head, and the blood really started to flow. Smartly, the broadcast team started marveling over how DiBiase was hanging tough after losing so much blood: "I don't know how this kid can continue! Talk about heart! Talk about intestinal fortitude! How is he still on his feet?" They were playing up how high the odds were stacked against DiBiase, yet he refused to give up.

He was persistent.

As the match approached its climax, DiBiase's blood was everywhere – all over DiBiase, all over Flair, and all over the mat. It had been a gory, grueling battle. DiBiase was set to win the match by slapping on the figure four in the middle of the ring, but right before Dibiase had the figure four locked in, Flair kicked DiBiase, sending him head-over-heels over the top rope. When he landed, he banged his head again on the guard rail and fell flat on his back. The referee counted him out, and Flair narrowly escaped with his title. Flair had won the match, but DiBiase had clearly secured a bigger moral victory.

It's hard to imagine a better booked match. It allowed Flair to keep the NWA title so he could continue "defending" it in other territories, but at the same time, it catapulted DiBiase to the top of the MidSouth promotion. Fans were deeply endeared to DiBiase because of his valiant persistence, his refusal to give up, his taking it to Flair despite how badly the odds were stacked against him. He had lost the match, but that was OK. It didn't bury him – it elevated him in fans' eyes.

If you've never seen this match, do yourself a favor and find it right now on YouTube. It should be mandatory viewing for anybody who calls himself a pro wrestler.

After you watch the match, I ask you, would it be possible to book a match like this in WWE, TNA, or your average indie promotion today? Not on your life. Why? Because of the very things I touched on in earlier in the section where we discussed how when anything is possible, nothing is impossible. In the DiBiase/Flair match, two things happened that have been completely devalued in modern pro wrestling: One, the promotion sold getting your head rammed into a ring post as being a devastating injury. And two, the promotion sold getting thrown out of the ring over the top rope as a devastating injury. Nowadays both those things happen all the time, and wrestlers bounce right back up after, say, a whole three seconds of selling, no worse for the wear and go on with the match as if nothing ever happened.

The point I'm driving at in this section is *persistence*. People love persistence. They love guys who don't give up. They love guys who get knocked down but get back up again. They love guys who are hurt but refuse to give in. They love Rocky Balboa. Unfortunately it's difficult to set up a situation like the one created by Bill Watts because, again, wrestlers bill themselves as indestructible. If we would reverse this trend, we could tell awesome stories of persistence again, stories that rally the fans and bring them to their feet in appreciation, stories that sell out the house and leave the crowd wanting more at the end of the night.

Good guys are persistent. Make sure yours are, too.

Types of heels

In the previous section we talked about the essential characteristics of babyfaces. Now I want to talk briefly about the essential characteristics of a heel. As I've said before, I've dedicated an entire chapter to heels, so I don't want to go into great detail here, but I do want to introduce the topic, since heels are the most important ingredient in storytelling. Heels are to storytelling what flour is to baking a cake – you can't have one without the other.

One of the biggest mistakes pro wrestlers and bookers make today is creating what I call "catchall heels." A catchall heel is a heel that exhibits every character flaw imaginable. He's a liar, traitor, coward, bully, hothead, cheater, opportunist, egoist, braggart, madman, manipulator, exploiter, thief, and bumbling buffoon all rolled into one. The result? Pretty much every heel in every show is a carbon copy of the other. They're all the same. And they're all 100% unrealistic. They more resemble Yosemite Sam from Bugs Bunny cartoons than they do real people. Bad people in the real world don't possess *all* these character flaws; they possess only a few...and in a lot of cases, only one! The world is full of people who, by all accounts, seem to be perfectly good people, but when put into just the right situation, they betray a friend. Or you might have a friend who's a very good friend to you, but then one day you learn that he's a thief who embezzled thousands of dollars from his employer.

A much better approach than the catchall heel is to take two of the heel types I listed above and combine them. For example, you could create a heel who's a traitor/hothead like Larry Zbyszko, an opportunist/egoist like Ric Flair, or a bully/madman like Randy Orton. By doing this you create fictional bad guys who more accurately resemble real world villains. If you do this correctly, you can create characters that fans will find themselves truly hating, even if they've already been smartened up and are perfectly well aware that the whole thing is an act. Remember, realism is the name of the game, and that extends to creating realistic bad guys, too.

Much more on this subject later.

Cool it already with heel/face turns!

Nothing is more overused and abused nowadays than the heel/face turn. These days, wrestlers flip flop back and forth between heel and babyface more often than they change their underwear. It's ridiculous, really. A guy will go from high-fiving fans one week to flipping them off the next and back to high-fiving them a week later. Come on! What are you, schizophrenic? This is a prime example of something that, because it generated tremendous heat many years ago, wrestlers and bookers have been repeating it over and over and over and over and over again. Pro wrestlers clearly have never learned the lesson about going to the well too many times. These days, heel/face turns are so overdone and devalued, fans actually *anticipate* when a guy will make a turn.

Check any Internet wrestling forum and sure enough you'll find someone saying something along the lines of, "AJ Styles has been a babyface for a while now. I think it's about time he makes a heel turn." What? "About time"? Fans nowadays have been so conditioned to bad booking, they've come to expect it! Instead of a heel/face turn driving a monster angle like when Larry Zbyszko turned on his mentor Bruno Sammartino, instead fans expect wrestlers to flip flop "just because." Fans think wrestlers should flip flop because they've "been a baby too long."

This is a terrible state of affairs bordering on complete catastrophe. If wrestling has become so predictable that fans are conditioned like Pavlov's dogs to expect something to happen, pro wrestling will lose what little appeal it has left. After all, who wants to go to a show where the audience knows exactly what's going to happen just based on repetitive patterns and angles? Things are so repeated, hackneyed, and overdone nowadays, nothing means anything anymore. Nothing is of any consequence. Think about it: Everyone remembers the classic heel/face turns of the 1980s – like when Curt Hennig turned on his tag team partner Greg Gagne in the AWA – but name me *one* famous heel/face turn from, say, 2004. You probably can't, because there were so many superfluous, meaningless heel/face turns that year, none of them made a mark in your memory. It was all in one ear and out the other.

A heel/face turn should be monumental. There should be a very good and thoroughly planned reason for it, not just because "it's time for a change."

Another great example of this besides the two I've already given in this section is when Andre the Giant turned heel to challenge Hulk Hogan for the WWF title. This is an example of a perfectly logical, perfectly executed heel turn. Andre the Giant, the big man with the undefeated record for so many years, finally grew tired of all the hype over Hulk Hogan and of not getting a title shot. Plus, the WWF tossed in the awesome story element of Bobby Heenan getting involved, "poisoning" Andre against Hogan by whispering dark suggestions in his ear. It made perfect sense. Andre was World Title caliber, and he knew it. But he wasn't getting a shot. According to the angle, Andre felt Hogan was snubbing him and hogging the spotlight. So his anger, resentment, and jealousy snowballed inside him until he snapped and turned to the dark side.

For every example of a good heel/face turn there are at least 1,000 bad ones. One that comes immediately to mind that most longtime fans will recall is Sgt Slaughter's heel turn in 1990. The whole angle was in poor taste and designed solely to capitalize on the First Persian Gulf War by having Slaughter, a guy who had built his career as an "American Soldier" who would hand out American flags to kids at ringside and even had a character on the popular GI Joe cartoon a few years earlier, did an inexplicable heel turn and became, of all things, an Iraqi sympathizer. He aligned himself with Adnan Al-Kaissie and the Iron Sheik to destroy the Ultimate Warrior and Hulk Hogan. For selling out and betraying his character, Vince McMahon rewarded the Sarge with a short-lived WWF title run. At the time, the world had totally overestimated Saddam Hussein's military, so the WWF's brain trust had expected that the angle would last at least a year. But when Saddam's military was crushed in less than a month, the WWF found itself in a bind – Sgt Slaughter was still the top heel, but he was still "aligned" with Iraq, which had been humiliated and soundly defeated, meaning Americans' contempt for Iraq started fading fast. So the WWF realized they needed to get the title off the Sarge and flip him back to babyface. So they shot a series of rushed, slapdash vignettes where Slaughter traveled to a few American monuments shouting, "I want my country back!"

At the end of the series we learned that viewing the monuments had somehow exorcised the evil Iraqi demon that had possessed the Sarge, and voila! We had our all-American hero back.

There are quite a few words that could be used to describe this angle. Inane, cheap, opportunistic, and tawdry are the ones that immediately come to my mind. Not only was it in poor taste, it made no sense. Why would Sgt Slaughter align himself with Iraqis, even if he was angry with America and was hungry for a title shot? And then, what, the audience is so stupid that after just a couple months, Sarge is back to normal again and all is forgiven? Cheap. Don't insult your audience's intelligence.

So here are the commandments for handling heel/face turns:

1. A heel/face turn should be extremely rare.

2. Have a damned good reason for the turn! Don't just turn a guy "just because," for cheap heat, or because the guy is getting a bit stale or bored.

3. Don't flip-flop! Flip-flopping back and forth between baby and heel is just phony baloney. Once a wrestler turns, 99% of the time, there's no going back. If a guy's a baby and he turns heel, you can't just flip him back to being a baby again. If a guy betrays his friends and fans, how can he go back? Unless there's some major repentance and request for forgiveness that's deliberately written into the storyline from the get-go, don't flip-flop!

4. Remember, *realism!* People don't flip-flop back and forth between being good and evil in real life. Hitler didn't flip from being Hitler to a saint and back to Hitler again, right? Then it shouldn't happen in wrestling, either. Sure, some good people go astray for a while and then come back "into the light," but it's very rare. It certainly shouldn't happen every single dadgum week. Enough already.

Oh, and by the way, the Iron Sheik is from Iran, not Iraq.

Keep it simple, stupid!

Quentin Tarantino's first movie was a low budget independent film called "Reservoir Dogs." The movie is a cult phenomenon and now considered a modern classic. *Empire* magazine even named it the "Greatest Independent Film of All Time." While a bit violent and gory like all Tarantino films, it's an exciting, engaging, funny, and engrossing motion picture.

Not bad for a movie filmed almost entirely in an abandoned warehouse.

Yep, if you've not seen it, "Reservoir Dogs" was shot almost entirely in an abandoned, empty warehouse. How did Tarantino make a movie lauded as the "Greatest Independent Film of All Time" by a major entertainment magazine in a warehouse? By focusing on three fundamentals: Awesome characters, lots of violent action, and, most importantly, a simple but engaging story. "Reservoir Dogs" is the ultimate testament to how keeping a story, setting, and conflict straightforward and simple can result in first rate entertainment. This lesson should be applied in spades to pro wrestling – to keep the audience engaged and coming back for more, keep the angles simple.

"Keep it simple, stupid," was the guiding principle of a brilliant man by the name of Kelly Johnson. Johnson was an aeronautical innovator, a designer of airplanes, who founded the legendary top secret "Skunk Works" research lab that designed some of the greatest aircraft of the US military. The "Skunk Works" lab was responsible for the historic U-2 spy plane and the legendary, supersonic SR-71 Blackbird reconnaissance jet. The engineers at the "Skunk Works" designed and built these extraordinary aircraft by always adhering to Johnson's "Keep it simple, stupid" or "KISS" principle. Anything that was overly or unnecessarily complex was always tossed out. Simplicity of design was the foundation for everything the "Skunk Works" ever did.

Since then, the "Keep it simple, stupid" principle has been embraced by countless businesses, organizations, and distinguished individuals. Bill Clinton used the principle masterfully in the 1992 presidential election against George HW Bush. Clinton realized that to defeat Bush, who had been very successful in foreign affairs, he needed to focus on a very simple message that resonated with everyday Americans. What did he come up with? Simple – the economy.

In 1990-1991, the country had sunk into a deep recession. People were losing jobs left and right. The price of gas had skyrocketed. Companies were going out of business. The stock market was plummeting. People, as they're wont to do, blamed the President. So Bill Clinton capitalized on that. He hung a sign in his election campaign headquarters in Little Rock, Arkansas that read, "It's the economy, stupid!" an obvious play on the KISS principle. Everywhere Clinton went, he harped on the economy and how he was going to make things better. He didn't talk about much else. He didn't talk much about Iraq, Russia, terrorists, nuclear energy, race relations, infrastructure, or even education. Instead, he hammered away at the economy. Economy, economy, economy. He kept it simple. He kept it focused.

And it worked. On November 4, 1992, William Jefferson Clinton was elected the forty-second president of the United States.

So if the KISS principle worked to win the Presidency of the United States, surely it can be extremely effective in putting asses in seats at independent pro wrestling events, right? How? How do we leverage the KISS principle? Let's take a look.

In 1999, Ric Flair's son David decided (or was conscripted, accounts vary) to be a wrestler. He joined his father in WCW, which, at the time, was losing ground fast to the WWF in the Monday Night Wars. The masterminds running WCW at the time thought it would be a good idea to bring David onboard, despite the fact that he had very little training as a wrestler and had the physique of a college football water boy. These were desperate times for WCW, seeing that they were getting pounded in the ratings consistently by at least a solid point, so they were trying just about anything to win some viewers back from Vince McMahon, who was then at the peak of his legendary feud with Stone Cold Steve Austin, one of the hottest angles in the history of pro wrestling.

Anyway, WCW decided that fans would at least be curious to see Ric Flair's son wrestle, so they rushed him into the mix, long before he was ready. Ric was feuding with Hulk Hogan and the nWo at the time, so initially David joined his father against Hogan and his cronies. That lasted, oh, about a couple weeks before WCW decided to have David turn heel and attack his dad with a cattle prod. Why would he do that, you ask? Because, you see, a hot chick named Torrie Wilson told him to. So David was now under Torrie's spell, and as a result of his son turning on him, Ric went kayfabe crazy. Literally. WCW shot vignettes of Flair in a mental ward, wearing nothing but a hospital gown and skivvies. Somehow Flair escaped and resumed his duties as President of WCW (!). As president, Flair then stripped Scott Steiner of the US Championship and gave it to David. Don't ask why or how that happened; it just did. Then one of WCW's referees started idolizing Ric, calling himself "Li'l Naytch," and started officiating matches in Ric's favor. Then to cap it all off, somehow Ric's old friend Roddy Piper joined the fray and became Ric's Vice President of WCW!

I really don't need to say how terrible this cockamamie, convoluted, hard-to-follow, outrageous, make-it-up-as-you-go-along storyline was – I can just let the ratings talk for me. During this angle, WCW experienced one of the worst drops in the ratings in its entire history. Previously, the WWF had been consistently beating WCW by anywhere between a half and a full ratings point; but then while this angle was playing out, the WWF started trouncing WCW by two solid points! That means the WWF was being watched by over two million more households than WCW. In television, ratings are the name of the game, and clearly WCW was getting beaten badly.

Now let's do a what-if. What if WCW had applied the KISS principle when it decided to recruit David Flair into the wrestling business? Instead of that crappy, nonsensical angle WCW slapped together, suppose they secretly had David train at the WCW Power Plant training facility for a full year. Also suppose that they put him on an intense bodybuilding program to bulk him up and get him in great shape. Then make Ric the World's champion. At this point, the audience has no idea David is about to debut. In fact, they don't even know that he even exists. Then Ric Flair, as champ with the Big Gold Belt around his waist, standing in the middle of the ring and flanked by Arn Anderson and the other Horsemen at the time, grabs a microphone and introduces his son to the world. David steps from behind the curtain and walks down the aisle to the shock and delight of the fans.

The next generation of Flairs has arrived.

David joins the Four Horsemen and is pushed to the moon. According to the storyline, Ric has brought his son into the sport to succeed him in a few years down the line. What he doesn't expect, however, is that David becomes an overnight sensation, like the way WCW pushed Goldberg. He's a prodigy and his rise to the top of the rankings is meteoric. Ric had expected his son to be great in four or five years; instead, David wins the US title in a matter of months. Now, suddenly, David is the number one contender to Ric's World title! Ric expects David to bide his time and stay content as the US champ, but David wants more – he wants his dad's title. So he respectfully and graciously requests a title match from Ric, but Ric refuses and flies into a rage. He rails about how David should be loyal and demands that he "wait his turn." Instead, David turns face, quits the Four Horsemen, and goes to the WCW commissioner to request his title shot.

Meanwhile, in the buildup to a match for the US title between David and convenient contender Arn Anderson, Flair instructs Anderson, his thug, to "teach David a lesson." That is, forget about winning the match and just beat the hell out of David. Anderson uses various dirty tricks to win the upper hand and starts beating David down, but David heroically turns the tables and gives Arn the beatdown instead and emerges victoriously. So now Ric's played every card he had. He's got nothing left up his sleeve. He has no choice but to wrestle his son for the World title. Thus we have the main event of Starcade '99 – Flair vs. Flair!

Now, compare the angle I just outlined above to the awful angle WCW actually ran. The angle I created is simple – it's a classic father/son rivalry where the protégé son rises up to take on his mentor father. It's believable. It makes sense. It involves a myriad of likely emotions and conflicts – jealousy, resentment, perceived betrayal, anger, family ties, love, loyalty, and disloyalty. It involves a long, slow buildup to the ultimate showdown match, sure to sell out the house and set a new record in pay-per-view buys. Seriously, what wrestling fan wouldn't want to see this?

But instead of an awesome, serious match between father and son, we got cattle prods and skanky girls, Ric Flair hanging from the ropes in his bikini underwear, a trip to the mental ward, Ric Flair for

President of WCW, an evil referee who idolizes Ric, and, believe it or not, Roddy Piper as Ric's Vice President!

Had WCW applied the KISS principle, the promotion could have had a red hot pay-per-view main event and an angle it could have milked for well over a year. Instead they had an entirely forgettable angle that lasted for maybe a couple months that did nothing for them other than drive ratings into the toilet.

Don't make this mistake! In fact, if you spend some time just reminiscing about past pro wrestling shows, I'm sure you can dredge up dozens of angles like this one that were ill-conceived, convoluted, full of plot holes and inconsistencies, and nearly impossible to follow. On the flip side, if you look at all the most exciting and biggest money-making angles of history, you'll find that the underpinning story was simple, logical, and straightforward.

So keep it simple, stupid! When developing an angle, always think of simple motivations for why your two guys or two tag teams are going to feud. And 99 times out 100, it should be about wrestling.

Plan it out

Former Secretary of Defense Donald Rumsfeld is a controversial guy. People either love him or hate him. But regardless of your opinion of the man, he said something once that I think is right on target when it comes to pro wrestling: "Think ahead. Don't let day-to-day operations drive out planning." As bookers, promoters, and workers, we all need to write this quote in bold letters on a piece of paper and tape it to our bathroom mirrors so that we see it every single day. No industry needs to pay attention to it more than pro wrestling. Why do I say that, you ask? Because pro wrestling is plagued by decisions, characters, and angles that very clearly were not planned out, and too often, bookers and promoters just "wing it" when it comes to booking. That is, they just make things up as they go along. They don't have an overarching plan for where the story is going to go. Instead they just set something in motion and then just play it by ear.

This is no way to tell a winning story. Think back to the Flair vs. Flair angle I conjured up in the previous section. To pull an angle like that off takes planning, lots and lots of planning. Think about it. You sit down with the rest of your creative team and say, "I have an idea. I want to run a feud between Ric Flair and his son David." But right away you realize that in order for this to work, you have serious work cut out for you. You have to get David in shape and get him ready to work in the ring. In order for the feud to be really meaningful, you want Ric to be at the top of the promotion. That means you have to put the strap on him and give him a long title run. That way David challenging him for it would give Ric something huge to lose. The angle would have to progress from David making his debut to him becoming a Horseman to him becoming a dominant player to him challenging his dad to him and his dad arguing over the matter to David wrestling Arn to, finally, their big pay-per-view matchup.

All this takes big-time *planning*. You can't pull something like this off by just winging it. If you just threw an angle like this together on the spot, large parts would be missing – David wouldn't be ready, fans wouldn't view David as a serious contender for the title, Ric wouldn't have the title to challenge for, etc. Making things up as you go along just doesn't work. That method results in sloppy storytelling that makes little sense. It's like writing a research paper at the last minute on the bus on the way to school. Remember how you would do that as a kid? You'd forget an assignment and then do a rush job on the way to school or during recess, and what did you wind up with?

Crap.

Don't do this. Do your homework long in advance!

Think Payday

I love big paydays. The concept of a big payday goes hand-in-hand with the importance of planning. What's a big payday? Simple – it's when you carefully and methodically build up an angle over time that culminates into a huge event that pays off big. The big payday is the brass ring of pro wrestling, an elusive goal that everyone strives for but few – especially of late – ever realize. Why is a big payday so elusive? Because so few people know how to build up a big payday. A big payday is not something you can just whip up at the last minute, just like you can't pull a term paper out of your ass on the bus ride to school. A big payday is like lifting weights – it takes a long time and lots of determination to get there, but once you do, the reward is tremendous. Too many guys in pro wrestling nowadays try to whip up a big payday out of thin air, typically by just haphazardly copying something that someone else did that paid off big.

Ole Anderson gave a great example of this in his tell-all book, *Inside Out.* He talked about how promoters and bookers would copy the things he did without ever bothering with any of the legwork or the buildup that needed to precede them. The example he gave was how he one time got way over as a face by smashing a guy over the head with a folding steel chair. Of course nowadays that sort of thing is received with a yawn, but somehow he got awesome heat from it. The promoters and bookers around Ole saw it and said to themselves, "Hey look! Ole got over by hitting a guy with a chair, so let's do it, too!" And sure enough, chairs were flying all over arenas from Portland, Oregon to Portland, Maine. But a very telling thing happened along the way – none of this drew any heat. Promoters and bookers would then scratch their heads and wonder, "How come Ole got over by doing that?" which made Ole laugh. He wouldn't tell them, but the answer why he got over and they didn't was *buildup.* Many weeks prior to busting a chair over that guy's head, Ole had his opponent repeatedly wrong him – bad mouth him in interviews, sucker punch him after a match, insult his mother, go after his wife, run over his dog, etc. All of that was the buildup. It was diesel fuel being poured over a pile of dry fertilizer, and that chair being smashed on the guy's head was the spark.

Kaboom!

Smashing the guy over the head with that steel chair was the *big payday.* When done correctly, this is absolutely thrilling, and fans will happily and eagerly pull all the money out of their wallets and hand it over to you to see more of it. A properly executed big payday has an awesome, long-lasting effect – it creates legions of fiercely loyal fans that rave about your product and spend their hard earned dollars on t-shirts, hats, bumper stickers, and posters with your logo on them. That is, they pay to advertise for *you!* What's more, they call up their friends and say, "Man, that show last night was awesome…awesome! You need to come to the next one!"

All this said, don't make the mistake of thinking that a big payday is always a big main event *match*. Nope. That's not always the case. Actually, if you go back and reread the first paragraph of this section, I said that a big payday is a huge *event* that pays off big. And when I say "event" I don't mean "show." I mean a "moment."

A moment is something that happens suddenly and unexpectedly. The moment itself lasts only a short time, but the memory and effects of it are enormously emotional, successful, and unforgettable, like when Hulk Hogan body slammed Andre the Giant at WrestleMania 3, when Ricky Steamboat arrived from nowhere in the NWA as "Mr. X" to challenge Ric Flair for the World title, or when Mick Foley defeated The Rock for the WWF title with the help of Stone Cold Steve Austin, who had been MIA for good while and completely off fans' radar screen. It's moments like these that pro wrestling fans live for. They're the reason why fans keep tuning in or buying tickets week-to-week; they're all hoping to witness the next *big payday*.

Work backwards

But as I've already stressed, a big payday requires long-term planning. You can't pull off a big payday without planning it all out, and the best way to do this is to work backwards. That is, you decide on what the big payday event is going to be and then make up the rest of the story in reverse, from finish to the very beginning. This is exactly how Margaret Mitchell, the esteemed American novelist, wrote *Gone with the Wind,* one of the greatest novels ever. She wrote the last chapter first and then worked backwards. This method is extremely effective in building up a big payday.

Let's suppose you're going to do a big David vs. Goliath angle. Your plan is to have a smaller but very popular underdog baby defeat a monster heel in a shocking title match. David vs. Goliath matches are very common in pro wrestling – especially the indies – but 99 times out of 100, they suck. Why? Because they're entirely predictable. You can see them coming from a mile away. Some indies are so dumb, they even advertise the match as a David vs. Goliath match in the pre-match hype and on their flyers! The only way a big payday works is a) when the event is built up gradually and logically over time and b) the event itself is a complete surprise. You want fans with their jaws on the floor, thinking, "Holy cow! I never saw that coming!"

So in the case of a David vs. Goliath, the fans should come into the match thinking that there's no way David is going to win. They should think the match is going to be your run-of-the-mill squash match, and the David wrestler is just going to do a job to make the Goliath look that much more invincible in preparation for some big match against another Goliath somewhere down the road.

Are you with me so far? OK, great. Let's keep going. Let's work backwards. We'll start by identifying our big payday event. Our big payday is when our David wrestler shocks the world by miraculously pinning Goliath. OK, got it. Now remember, we can't tip our hand to the audience and let them figure out that we're doing a David and Goliath match. If we do that, the entire surprise is spoiled and the big payday never happens. So we need to figure out how to make our David wrestler look like a David and Goliath look like Goliath without making it obvious that this is what we're setting up.

So we'll start with the Goliath wrestler, as he's pretty straightforward. You pick a guy who's, well, a giant. The bigger and more muscular, the better. Of course, you have to tell the guy what your plan is to make sure he's willing to go along with eventually doing a job for a smaller guy, but that shouldn't be a problem, since you're going to give him a run as your champion. So you push this guy to the moon. You bring him out and completely squash a bunch of opponents week-to-week. Have your play-by-play guy or your announcer sell the guy hard by saying things like, "This guy's a monster!" and "Will *anyone* be able to beat this guy?" Build up a very impressive unbeaten streak, like WCW did with Goldberg. Have him assume an attitude like that of Mike Tyson in the late 80s and early 90s – that he's so unbeatable, he "owns" the sport. Have him squash, squash, squash. Eventually, book him in a title match and have him win it. Then send him back to squashing jobbers left and right.

Meanwhile, let's develop our David character. For this role we need an extremely athletic young guy who's a bit undersized but still muscular and a legitimate heavyweight. We don't want a midget in this role, as that would be obvious that we're setting him up as a David and it would be pathetically cheap. We don't want this guy to win very much, because that would put him on the fans' radar as a viable contender. By the same token, we don't want the guy to be a jobber, either, because his beating the invincible giant would go over like a lead balloon with the fans. They'd feel ripped off, like how WCW inexplicably made Paul Roma – the perennial jobber tag team specialist – a Four Horseman in the 90s.

So how do we make him a respectable winner but not really a winner? Easy – make him a journeyman tag team wrestler. Have him team up with various jobbers – a different one each week – and have him always start the match. You could have him perform well at the beginning of the match, showing some flashes of greatness and some fireworks here and there. Then have him tag out and have his jobber partner lose the match. Thus fans see the guy as having some potential but still a nobody, just a guy getting paired up with random jobbers to get another tag team over.

All right, so you run this for a good long time. Your giant is running roughshod over all the competition, squashing everyone in sight, and being sold by your announcer and your promotional materials as a "monster" or a "one man wrecking crew" or something similar. Fans are completely taken in by the notion that your plan for this guy is to keep him on top. Incidentally, since this is indie wrestling, you would have to make sure that the wrestler you get to play your Goliath role agrees not to do jobs for other indie promotions! It wouldn't be very convincing if your guy wins every match in your show but loses at shows in the next town over!

All right, so the stage is set. Your Goliath has the belt on and is completely over with the fans as being "the man." He's unbeatable. He's 65 and 0. Meanwhile, your David is working matches well, showing his stuff, but still going down in the loss column week-to-week because his partners suck. We're ready for the big payday. At this show we announce that Goliath has a mandatory title defense and your David character has had the "misfortune" of getting his number drawn as his perfunctory opponent. He has to face the monster. On the surface, this looks like every other match your Goliath character has been wrestling for the past six months. It's totally routine, just a tune up match, an opportunity for

Goliath to showcase his awesomeness…like Mike Tyson's matchup against Buster Douglas in 1990.

The match gets underway. As usual, Goliath dominates from the get-go, punishing David and toying with him. David takes the punishment, covering up and taking long rests as Goliath gloats, yells at the fans, and casually walks about the ring in between moves with a completely blasé attitude. When he lifts David from the mat to set him up to showcase a big move – maybe a suplex or gorilla press – he's casual about it and in no hurry. He even takes time to look to the crowd and flex a bicep. This, to him, is no contest. It's his standard operating procedure. It's what the fans have watched him do in every other of his squash matches for the past six months. Fans are kind of bored, tuning out as they think they already know everything that's going to go down in this match because, from their perspective, they've seen it so many times before. Finally, after gloating and showing off enough, Goliath hits David with his big finisher and puts his foot on David's chest for the cover. One…two…

David kicks out.

This, folks, is your big payday moment.

Fans are shocked. What just happened? Was that a botch? Was he supposed to kick out? No one's ever kicked out from that before! What's happening? I wasn't expecting this? Who's this guy? I thought he was just a jobber!

Shocked and enraged, Goliath goes to grab David to punish him for having the audacity of kicking out, but David ducks and lands a huge punch to Goliath's stomach. Suddenly, the tables have been turned! Now the match becomes a match as both men engage in a brutal, seesaw battle where the upper hand is traded back and forth, back and forth. Fans are at a loss. They don't know what to think because they weren't expecting any of this to happen. They're taken completely by surprise. As the battle wages, every fan in the house is on his feet, completely drawn in to the match. The real world has melted away. They forget that they were ever smartened up. To them, for the moment at least, what's happening in the ring is real. Nothing to them matters at this instant other than how this match ends up.

Pro wrestling's brass ring.

The big payday.

Desperate now, Goliath makes frantic attempts to just knock David out with one big punch or move, but David dodges and defends against them. David stymies Goliath's every move and counterattacks tit-for-tat. Then, at last, at the match's climax, Goliath corners David and attempts to crush him with a big haymaker, but David ducks, slips behind the giant, and rolls him up with a quick crucifix. One, two, three, and it's over! New champion! Confusion and controversy set in as Goliath argues with the referee that the count was fast. Meanwhile, the ring announcer steps into the ring and makes it official. The belt is strapped onto David, and the crowd is stunned and delighted at the same time. They leave the show excited and happy, sure to call their friends and tell them, "You should have seen what happened..."

You get it? We *planned out* a long-term angle by first identifying the angle's end, the *big payday*. We then *worked backwards* from the big payday moment to the very start of the angle, filling in all the details along the way. With it all planned out, the only thing left to do is actually *do* it. You know exactly what you're going to do and how things are going to end up. Put simply, you've done your homework long in advance.

This is how you develop stories for pro wrestling.

Don't copycat

In the previous section I recounted a story Ole Anderson told in his excellent book *Inside Out* of how bookers and promoters copied his angle of hitting a guy with a steel chair because they saw him get over with it once and so they thought they would, too. That's just one of a zillion examples I could give of pro wrestling's number one vexation – copycatting.

They say imitation is the sincerest form of flattery, but for crying out loud, pro wrestling takes this way, way, way too far. If *anybody* does *anything* that gets the least bit over, sure enough, pro wrestling copycats will very quickly follow suit.

One of TNA's more recent angles was the insipid Main Event Mafia (which itself is a case of copycatting the nWo), where a bunch of has-been former main eventers unaccountably band together to…do something. Who knows what. It doesn't matter. The point is, because there were a bunch of well-known wrestlers in it, because they had cool mafia-esque intro music, and, most of all, because it was on TV, indie wrestlers all over America started forming their own "mafias." We had the Redneck Mafia, the Trailer Trash Mafia, the Gangsta Mafia, the Bad Boy Mafia, the Wrestling Mafia, the Maple Leaf Mafia, the Elite Mafia, the Mafia Mafia…

Enough already! Use your own imagination and make something up for yourself, for crying out loud. Be original. Stop copying what the big boys are doing.

Another famous example is the concession stand battle from Midsouth Wrestling back in the 80s. Midsouth shocked the wrestling world by having four guys battle their way from the ring to the concession stand and fight it out by using anything they could find – baking sheets, pots and pans, an old mop, a huge jug of mustard – as weapons. There was literally mustard and ketchup flying through the air, like an ECW version of a food fight. Frankly, I thought the whole thing was kind of dumb and boring, but the rest of the wrestling world ate it up. Why? Because it was fresh and new and no one had seen it before. People were raving about this angle for weeks after the show. So, sure enough, wrestling promotions the world over started doing their own versions of the concession stand fight. There are promotions *to this very day* that are still doing this gimmick, even though it's more worn out than a bald recapped tire.

Regardless of how much you like a particular angle you saw on "Raw" or "*Impact!*," resist the temptation to copycat it. Remember, the fans who attend your local shows are also regular viewers of the big wrestling network TV shows, so anything you've seen, they've seen, too, and they'll spot a copycatted angle or character from a mile away. That'll leave them thinking, "Oh, please. I saw that on 'Raw.' This is so rinky dink." And the last thing you want is for your fans to walk away thinking your show was rinky dink. On the contrary, as we talked about moments ago, you want fans walking away thinking your show was phenomenal so they'll a) come back and b) bring their friends next time.

There's nothing to be gained from copycatting. Avoid it at all costs. Copycatting will serve to do nothing but insult your audience and leave a bad taste in their mouths. You're better off not having an angle at all – that is, just telling your guys to go out and beat the hell out of each other in a straight up match – than you are copycatting something out of desperation.

A little bit of inspiration is OK

That said, don't mistake desperation for inspiration. That is, there's a huge difference between out-and-out copycatting and searching for genuine inspiration. Copycatting is cheap and wrong; looking for inspiration, however, is a natural part of the creative process.

Virtually all creative people look to the works and accomplishments of others for inspiration. The idea is to jog your own creativity by studying the creativity of others, not copy the creativity of others. The late Michael Jackson, the King of Pop and arguably the most commercially successful musician of all time, called the legendary James Brown his greatest inspiration. At James Brown's funeral, Jackson called Brown "The Master" and said that when he saw James Brown perform as a child, he knew from that very moment forward what he wanted to do with the rest of his life. He studied Brown's music, his singing style, and how he moved on stage. That said, he never *copied* James Brown. There was no mistaking a Michael Jackson performance for a James Brown performance!

As the head booker for Jim Crockett's NWA promotion, Dusty Rhodes would watch old western movies for inspiration. He found ideas for characters and angles by watching classic old films like "True Grit," "She Wore a Yellow Ribbon," and "The Man Who Shot Liberty Valance." While a lot of Dusty's booking was controversial – particularly his penchant for the infamous "Dusty Finish"[3] – it was still very original and exciting. Who could forget his Midnight Rider angle? Or how he

---

[3] A "Dusty Finish" is an ending to a match where it initially appears that the babyface has won, but then the result is reversed by the referee. Many wrestling fans assert that Dusty's booking was responsible for the bankruptcy of Jim Crockett's NWA promotion, but that just isn't true. Crockett went broke because he spent money frivolously and booked venues he couldn't fill.

orchestrated Barry Windham's heel turn and how Windham subsequently joined the Four Horsemen, which took the entire pro wrestling world by surprise? Or how in 1985 he took Ray Traylor, then a jobber, and repackaged him as Big Bubba Rogers, turning him into a star? Dusty Rhodes did great stuff (and, admittedly, a lot of not-so-great stuff) as a booker, and he did it by looking for inspiration.

So even though I condemn copycatting, I encourage you to look for inspiration to spark your imagination and creativity. Where should you search for inspiration? Let's take a look.

Art imitating art

The example I just gave of Dusty Rhodes watching old westerns for inspiration is a prime case in point of *art imitating art*. Dusty used a piece of art (a movie, which is an art form) for inspiration for the art that he would go on to create (wrestling angles, also an art form). You can do the same thing by looking for inspiration in any art you come in contact with – novels, TV shows, movies, video games, etc. If you keep your eyes open, you can find inspiration for wrestling characters and angles all over the place. Get into the habit of always being conscious of what you're watching and constantly asking yourself, "How could I turn this into a wrestling angle?" Remember, you want to keep the angles you create believable, realistic, and human, so if you're watching a movie like "Freddie vs. Jason" or "Plan 9 from Outer Space," you're probably not going to get very many good ideas. On the other hand, if you're watching a TV show or movie or reading a book that involves realistic people in realistic situations, you can find all sorts of inspiration – if you let your mind run free.

Here's an example – "Charlie's Angels," that classic but cheesy TV show from the 70s about three hot chicks who solve mysteries. On the surface you might be thinking, "Come on, Norm. That show was nothing but Jiggle TV. People watched it to see the girls in tight jeans and low cut shirts, not for the stories." Well, that might be true, but there's still a potentially very good pro wrestling angle that can be lifted from it.

Take the show's premise – three girls graduate from the police academy but are assigned crappy jobs like directing traffic and working the telephone switchboard. A rich guy named Charlie, who owns a profitable private investigation agency, hires them away from the police department to work for him as private detectives.

Stop right there. That's all I need to whip up a decent angle. Let's say you have three young jobbers. They're all new to the sport and thus very green. They all show flashes of promise – sometimes taking their opponents to the limit – but in the end, they all lose their matches. They put up game fights but lose at the very end. Are you with me? Three jobbers with some potential. Next, you introduce a new character to your promotion, a manager along the vein of Bobby Heenan or JJ Dillon who dresses in fancy business suits and constantly does "business" on a Blackberry. You give him a big, ritzy, rich guy name like "Thurston Rodham" and have him appear in interviews, brashly saying, "I'm here to recruit the next champions of this promotion. I can bring any athlete to his fullest potential. I can bring out the best in any wrestler, and I'm going to prove it." Whom does he recruit? You guessed it – our three young jobbers.

He doesn't waste his time on the established names in the promotion; he goes for the young bucks whom he can mold and manipulate. You then start pushing the three guys to the moon – slowly at first, but steadily. Eventually you have one of the three capture the singles title and the other two guys capture the tag titles. They're now red hot. True to his boasts, Thurston Rodham was right. He said he could take any wrestler to the top, and he did. Eventually you could do a swerve by having one of the three turn on the manager and break away from the group. Thurston Rodham could then become outraged, saying, "I'm the one who got you where you are now, and I can put you back where you came from!"

Simple, isn't it? I took the "Charlie's Angels" premise and asked myself how I could turn it into an angle. And what I came up with is perfectly realistic and believable. It's art imitating art.

Notice, however, that in my angle I didn't have the rich guy come in and turn the three jobbers into private detectives who uncover crimes and other wrongdoings committed by the promotion's top heels! I also didn't have the rich manager guy hide behind the curtain and communicate invisibly with the three wrestlers/private eyes by speaker phone like Charlie character did on the TV show! Doing that would be a) copycatting and b) incredibly and embarrassingly stupid. Instead I just figured out a simple way to make the show's basic premise fit logically into the setting of professional wrestling. Now you may not really like the angle. That's fine. I actually think it's pretty good, especially considering I just made it up on the fly, but the point isn't whether or not you like the angle I created. The point is to demonstrate how I took inspiration from a simple fictional work to create a viable pro wrestling storyline.

You can do the same. Earlier in this chapter when we talked about really getting to know the characters you create, I suggested you keep a journal. Here's where that journal comes in handy again. Always keep it with you. That way, whenever you're watching a movie or reading a book and you get an idea for an angle, you can write it down so you won't forget it. As soon as you start actively asking yourself, "How can I turn this into a pro wrestling angle?" whenever you're watching TV or reading, you'll be surprised by how many good ideas start flooding your head! As ideas start to pile up, it's very easy to forget some of them, and then you're left beating your head, thinking, "Aw, darn it! I had an idea that would work perfectly for next month's show. What was it again?"

Art imitating life

In the previous section we talked about looking for inspiration for gimmicks and angles in works of fiction. But that's not the only good place to look for ideas. An even better place to look might just be real life and the real world.

That's exactly what Verne Gagne did in 1985 when he conceived the Colonel DeBeers gimmick. Believe it or not, back in 1985, segregation was alive in well in South Africa. It was called *apartheid*, and it was designed to keep whites separated from nonwhites in all parts of South African society. Apartheid was present everywhere in that country, and the one area where it really reared its ugly head for the world to see was in the realm of sports. In South Africa, nonwhites were not permitted to compete against whites in any athletic event. Nonwhites were also not allowed to be on the same teams as whites. Not surprisingly, the rest of the civilized world frowned greatly on all of this, and by the mid-1980s, pressure was mounting for South Africa to abolish apartheid once and for all. It was a very hot news topic in the United States at the time. Just about every day you'd hear something being said on the news about South Africa and its refusal to abolish apartheid.

Verne Gagne, being a pretty smart guy, saw a great angle in all of this. He conceived an arch heel from South Africa whose gimmick was that he was a racist elitist. The idea for the character was that the guy would be a pompous, anti-American bigot who absolutely refused to wrestle anyone who wasn't white. So Verne recruited a capable ring veteran by the name of Ed Wiskoski for role, which he played to the hilt. The result was Colonel DeBeers, one of the most hated pro wrestling heels of all time.

The real world is an awesome place for angle and gimmick ideas. The objective is to tap into something hot without making it obvious that's what you're doing. Here's an example. In 2009, the world was outraged when popular tennis star Serena Williams flew into a rage over a call made by a line judge. "If I could," she screamed while shaking a tennis ball in the official's face, "I'd shove this f*cking ball down your f*cking throat." Williams' unexpected unsportsmanlike conduct shocked tennis fans everywhere because Williams was so popular, had done all sorts of charitable work, and had been hailed as a role model for kids. In effect, she disappointed her fans and tarnished the reputation of the sport of tennis.

So how could we turn this into a pro wrestling angle? Well, how about using it as the basis for a surprise heel turn? Take one of your most popular wrestlers, a guy who's a big fan favorite and always plays by the rules, and put him in a big match against one of your top heels – maybe a match to determine the number one contender for the belt. Then have the guy lose the match to the heel on a controversial call, maybe a slightly fast count or maybe the ref counts the baby out even though his foot is on the ropes. So the heel wins on a bad call and quickly gets out of Dodge. Meanwhile, the baby who just lost becomes outraged and flies into a totally uncharacteristic rage over the call and attacks the ref. The guy becomes so infuriated and violent, security has to jump into the ring to protect the ref. Fans are shocked. The baby-turned-heel threatens the ref again, tells the security officers to screw off, and heads back to the locker room in a huff.

At the next show, the guy does an interview where he apologizes profusely for his actions. "I don't know what came over me," he says. "I hope the fans will forgive me." So now the fans think all is forgiven and the guy's heel turn was scrapped. Wrong. At the next show, you have the guy lash out at the same referee again! Now he's a confirmed heel, a guy who's a bit of a loose cannon, and you have an awesome feud between this guy and…a referee! Of course, as we talked about earlier, the referee is a representative of the promotion, so really, the feud is between the wrestler and the promotion. From here you have all sorts of tangents the angle can go off on.

Again, you might like this angle and you might not. The point, however, is how you can look at real world events and turn them into ideas for realistic pro wrestling storylines. Ideas for gimmicks and angles are all around you, if you keep your eyes open!

Avoid contamination

I debated back and forth on whether I should include this section, because I know it's controversial and because I know you might think I'm crazy for even suggesting it. But what the heck – I'm going to throw it out there for your consideration and as food for thought. Ready?

Here it comes.

Brace yourself…

Stop watching WWE and TNA.

There, I said it. Now please try to refrain from throwing this book against the wall.

Yes, you read it right – I'm suggesting that you not watch the big boys. Why? Because it's just so darned tempting to copy what they do. Even if you don't do it intentionally, subconsciously, it's very difficult not to incorporate a lot of things you like that you see on TV into your own storylines. As you sit down to think up ideas for your next show, whether you realize it or not, if you're regularly watching what Vince and Jeff are putting on TV, it's inevitable that the ideas that pop into your mind are going to be greatly influenced by what you saw on the tube. Now don't take this the wrong way – I'm not saying that WWE and TNA suck. I'm admittedly not a fan of what they're doing now, but that's not the point I'm trying to make. What I'm saying is, to be successful, to build a promotion that real fans will come to and come back to, you have to do things that are original. As I've already said multiple times before, you can't offer fans something that smacks of what they saw on TV. What you offer has to be unique; otherwise, why is someone going to pay to come see your show? They can just watch WWE and TNA for free and see pretty much the same things you're offering.

The only way to ensure that what you have to offer your paying customers is 100% original is to not watch what the big boys are doing. And believe it or not, this discipline is not all that uncommon. Many of the best known authors will completely shut themselves away from pop culture so that they can write a story that's all their own. They'll unplug the TV, throw away their radio, cancel their cable subscription, and disconnect their Internet service to prevent themselves from becoming "contaminated."

Now I'm not suggesting you go to this extreme. After all, as I just wrote in the preceding sections, I'm a big believer that TV, movies, and the news are all great sources of inspiration for wrestling angles. What I *am* suggesting, however, is that you not watch competing wrestling programming. This way, you prevent yourself from being contaminated as far as *wrestling* goes.

Am I crazy? Maybe. But I guarantee you, if you take this advice, the originality of your angles will improve a thousand fold.

4   The Heel

"If you only knew the power of the Dark Side."
- *Darth Vader, evil dark lord of the Sith*

The power of the Dark Side

Alfred Hitchcock, director and producer of such classic films as "Psycho," "The Birds," "North by Northwest," and "Strangers on a Train" once famously said, "The more successful the villain, the more successful the picture." The famous and prolific filmmaker knew how to make good, exciting movies. He knew that the lynchpin to a movie's success is the bad guy.

That's what this chapter is all about – pro wrestling's heels. I've already stressed the importance of villains to pro wrestling, but it can't be stressed enough. Heels make the show.

Heels make the show!

It was no accident that boxing was most popular during the title reign of Muhammad Ali. It was no accident that tennis boomed when John McEnroe was the number one player on the courts. Sure, everyone loved his archrival Jimmy Connors, but that's only because they loved to see him beat McEnroe. It was no coincidence that the world had its eyes glued to the TV when Tonya Harding – after having her rival Nancy Kerrigan brutally attacked by a thug – figure skated in the 1994 Winter Olympics.

Heels make the show! Your promotion cannot and will not succeed unless you have tremendous heels. How do you create tremendous heels? Read on.

What makes a heel a heel?

What makes a heel a heel? Well, what makes a jerk a jerk? Seriously, think about people – both famous and not – whom you don't particularly care for. What is it about them you don't like? If you look very closely at the personalities of people you don't like, you'll find a common list of qualities that applies to almost all of them. People you don't like are one or more of the following: Lazy, dishonest, disingenuous, insincere, self-centered, selfish, opportunistic, cocky, aggressive, tricky, unreliable, untrustworthy, hateful, spiteful, jealous, resentful, or self-serving. A good heel, then, is one who embodies one or more of those qualities.

But as I cautioned in the previous chapter, you don't want to create "catchall" heels. You don't want to take every one of these character flaws and roll them into every heel in your promotion. That would just make your heels unrealistic and indistinguishable.

The brass ring of every heel is to convince the fans that he's a jackass both inside the ring and out. That is, a smart heel endeavors to convince fans to believe that he's an asshole in real life. If a heel can convince fans that he really is an asshole, they'll have genuine contempt for him when he steps into the ring. If fans believe a guy is a nice guy in real life but just portrays a bad guy in wrestling, they'll have no contempt for him. They'll just kind of chuckle when he behaves badly. When he goes down to mouth off to a fan at ringside, fans will think, "Ha ha! Look at Jimmy. He's really into it. He's so funny." Thus the heel is just a joke – a clown, a laughing stock, a slapstick comedian. And make no mistake – it's impossible to get excited and into a match where the fans regard the heel as nothing but a joke. The whole match becomes a joke, like an episode of "The Three Stooges."

So to convince fans that you're an asshole, be an asshole. Look at the assholes in your life and do the things that they do, carry yourself the way they carry themselves, and say the things that they say. Focus on one or two negative qualities and really flesh them out.

The Twelve Villains

To help you flesh out your heel characters and make them truly realistic, I've put together what I call "The Twelve Villains," twelve distinct types of heels that you can use as templates to spur your creativity when developing your bad guys:

- The Hater
- The Traitor
- The Coward
- The Bully
- The Hothead
- The Whiner
- The Opportunist
- The Sadist
- The Braggart
- The Madman
- The Pretty Boy
- The Trash Talker

We'll discuss each heel type in detail in the following subsections.

The Hater

The Hater is a very jealous man. He hates another wrestler because he's jealous of him, his popularity, and his success. Look around you in your real life and you'll find haters all over the place. If you're a pro wrestler, I'm sure you can find a half dozen haters sitting next to you in the locker room. How do you find them? Easy – just say something positive about another successful worker who's not in the room or within earshot. The haters will come out of the woodwork like sharks when there's chum in the water.

"Oh, he doesn't know how to work," you'll hear them say.

"I don't know why they put the belt on him. He can't draw."

"He's just a [insert famous WWE wrestler here] wannabe."

You know what I'm talking about. A pro wrestling locker room (or an Internet message board) can be a very hateful place. So considering it's so realistic, why not tap into it when developing a heel character?

Envy is very unattractive. No one likes a jealous person, but everyone loves to hate one. That's why shows like "The Real Housewives of Orange County" are so popular – people love to watch those women envy one another and get into arguments and catfights. They love to watch the one woman who's so envious of her "friends" she goes to great lengths to sabotage them, only to see her devious plots foiled or exposed in the end. It's great – albeit a bit demented – entertainment.

To work the Hater angle properly, you need to start small and build it up. Let's illustrate this by taking two young buck wrestlers new to your promotion. Let's call them Ace and Hawk. Stupid names, yes, but just bear with me. Ace and Hawk are two young wrestlers who debut in your promotion about the same time and are billed as having loads of potential. They're pretty much on the same road – they're young, up-and-coming, talented, dashing, and so on. They're contemporaries, equals. After scoring a few wins in squash matches, they start making their way up the rankings little-by-little, match-for-match, but they never face each other. Then one day, you have Ace score a big, surprise upset victory over one of the established names in your promotion. A big to-do is made about the victory, and lots of talk starts to swirl about how Ace is the next big thing, the champion of tomorrow. This makes Hawk, our other young gun, jealous, slowly turning him into a Hater.

We first let on to this by having the ring announcer interview Hawk after a squash match. The ring announcer asks him for his thoughts on Ace's big victory and Hawk responds by saying something along the lines of, "Well, you know, Ace is a great competitor. He's got some good moves...but you know, luck had a lot to do with that victory..." Taken aback, the announcer asks, "Wait – are you saying Ace won that match by luck?" Hawks responds, "Well, you know, I'm not saying that's the only thing – again I have all the respect in the world for Ace – but he did get lucky."

And just like that the seed is planted for a great, very realistic feud. Think about it – in the real sports world, feuds are sparked by jealousy all the time, and all too often the mean-spirited things that are said out of jealousy create bitterness that lasts for years.

In 1971, for example, Muhammad Ali and Smokin' Joe Frazier were two men on a collision course. Frazier was the heavyweight boxing champion of the world; Ali was the former heavyweight boxing champion of the world. Both men were undefeated (Ali had been stripped of the title for refusing to serve in the US Army). Both men were incredible fighters. The only thing that separated them was the gold strap around Frazier's waist, and that made Ali jealous. In a spite of envy, Ali started taunting Frazier, saying terrible things about him. He called him ugly and dumb and said he looked like a gorilla. He said Frazier was too ugly to be the champion, that a champion should be beautiful, like he claimed he was. When the two men met in the ring, Frazier got even. He won the fight on a 15 round decision, making Ali even more jealous and resentful, leading him to say even more hateful and even racist things about Frazier.

Ali went on the beat Frazier in their next two epic bouts for the world title. Both men retired as legends, but the bad blood never washed away. They both continued to say bad things about each other for the next 30 years. Frazier resented Ali so much, in 1996, when Ali, who was very badly stricken with Parkinson's disease, lit the Olympic flame, Frazier told the press that he would have liked to have "pushed him in."

Now *that's* a blood feud!

Remember, what sparked this rivalry and the epic matchups that ensued was Ali's jealousy. Had Ali not said the hateful things that he did, their first fight would have been your average title fight. It would have been a great technical fight, of course, but it would not have packed the raw emotion and pure drawing power that it did, and the three fights that the two men fought may not have found their way to the history books as "the biggest fights ever fought."

Say what you will about Muhammad Ali. Maybe he was being a jerk, maybe not. But considering the fact that by his own description he developed his boxing character by watching Gorgeous George the pro wrestler, it's all quite possible that the mean-spirited things he had to say about Smokin' Joe were all just a work. A work that worked, that is. And considering the wild success he enjoyed from it all, pro wrestling promoters and bookers should do the same.

The Traitor

Everyone hates disloyalty, and disloyalty is the central characteristic of The Traitor. The Traitor betrays the trust of his friends, his allies, and of the fans. He lures you in and convinces you that he's trustworthy and that his word is true, but then when you're looking the other way or when the right opportunity presents itself, he stabs you in the back. The Traitor is not to be confused with The Opportunist, whom I'll describe in the next subsection. The Traitor is a plotter. He premeditatedly deceives a person to become his ally or friend, knowing all along that he is going to ultimately betray him. The Opportunist, on the other hand, considers a friend a friend and only betrays him when a golden opportunity presents itself and he's overcome by temptation.

More on that in just a second.

For now, understand that The Traitor is a scoundrel of the worst kind. He's a predator and a liar. He's a double agent. Probably the best example of a traitor I can give is the most notorious traitor of American history – Benedict Arnold. Benedict Arnold was a general in the American Continental Army during the American Revolution, but after getting turned down for a promotion, he decided to switch sides to the British Empire. While still a general for the Americans, he agitated for and got command of a fort at West Point, New York, and conspired to surrender the fort to the British. The plot was exposed before the fort was handed over, and upon learning that the American general George Washington was on to him, Arnold quickly ran from the fort and escaped to Britain.

In this example, Benedict Arnold turned traitor on his countrymen for his own gain. The British offered him six thousand pounds and a commission in the British military as a brigadier general. He did what he did to make some easy money and to exact a little bit of sweet revenge for getting passed over for a promotion. He was, in a word, a scumbag.

The Traitor opens up great opportunities for angles in pro wrestling. Let's take a look at one. Let's suppose you have two hot tag teams, a baby team and a heel team, and the babies are the champs. The heels are managed by a mastermind arch heel, and they've been chasing after the baby team's titles for weeks, but every time they've come up short. So the manager cooks up a scheme. He has his boys jump the babies outside of a match and "injure" one of them badly. So now one of the babies is out of commission, and they can't defend the titles. Left with no choice, the promotion gives the healthy member of the baby team an ultimatum – either defend the titles or they'll be stripped. So the baby informs the promotion that he has no choice but defend the tag titles against the heels without a partner. Then, like the cavalry riding in to save the day, another one of your top babies enters the scene and informs the partner-less baby that he'd be honored to become his new partner while his original partner heals up. The baby agrees, and a new team is set to defend the titles against the challenge of those dastardly heels.

Or so it seems.

Little does our babyface know it, but his new partner is a traitor! Behind the scenes – according to our storyline – the new partner, whom the fans think is a baby, has been offered big bucks by the evil manager to pretend to join the original baby, but then throw the match to his guys. So when it comes time for the match, the new partner turns on his partner, sucker punches him and knocks him out, steps out of the ring, and the heels make the cover. The titles change hands legally (although unjustly), and a new feud is born.

Remember, the key to making an angle like this work is the fans can't see it coming. You have to make every effort to make it appear as if the new guy offering to save the day is a 100% red blooded good guy. In fact, as a red herring, you might even consider involving the traitor babyface in another totally unrelated, unresolved feud against another heel when he makes the offer to join up with the baby whose partner becomes injured. See, if you hype up the unrelated feud, fans will immediately be under the impression that that feud must be resolved and that since our traitor is waist deep in that feud with a heel, no one will predict the heel turn!

Very sneaky, right?

Be aware that once you use The Traitor angle, there's no turning back. That is, once a babyface turns traitor, it's very, very difficult to realistically flip him back to being a babyface again. Sure, you see guys turn traitor and flip back again all the time – even in the big leagues – but as we discussed in depth earlier, doing this is cheap.

Example: WCW did it with Ed Leslie when they ran the moronic Dungeon of Doom angle that we talked about in depth in the previous chapter. They had Leslie – Hulk Hogan's best friend – turn traitor on him to join the Dungeon in their struggle to destroy Hulkamania. Then, when the Dungeon of Doom angle was finally (and mercifully) put to rest, WCW's brain trust wanted Leslie to flip back to being the Hulkster's friend again, so how did they explain away his betrayal? In the most slapdash way ever – they said Ed had joined the Dungeon of Doom as a secret agent to spy on the Doomsters' activities and report their plans back to the Hulkster in the Hulkamania Command Center.

How convenient.

Don't do this. If you're going to turn a guy traitor, that's great, but do it along the vein of Larry Zbyszko's turn on the great Bruno Sammartino, where once Larry turned on Bruno, from that day forward, Larry would forever be a heel.

The Opportunist

The Opportunist is very similar to the Traitor, but as I mentioned in the previous section, there is a very significant difference between them. Don't confuse the two. The Traitor is a conspirator. He fakes that he's someone's friend so he can deliberately turn on him. It's all planned ahead of time. The Opportunist, on the other hand, is the guy who yields to temptation. An opportunity opens up, and against his own moral code and better judgment, he goes for it.

Need an example of an Opportunist? Just tune in to "Jerry Springer" or "The Maury Povich Show." Opportunists show up there all the time. You know what I'm talking about. A guy comes on to the show to admit to his buddy that he messed around with the buddy's girlfriend. When the dismayed buddy asks, "Why did you do it?" the guy says, "I couldn't help it! She threw herself at me!" In other words, the victim's girlfriend comes on to the buddy, and instead of saying, "No way. So-and-so and I are friends," he gives in to the temptation and has a romp in the hay. This guy is an Opportunist.

The Opportunist doesn't set out or plan to betray his friends ahead of time; he just is weak when the right opportunity presents itself.

So let's put this into an angle. Let's say you're doing a battle royal to determine the number one contender to your promotion's title. Every guy on your roster – save the champion – is in this battle royal. The match is brutal. One by one, guys hit the floor. Eventually we get down to just three guys – two babyfaces and one super heel. To make it interesting, let's say that the two babyfaces are normally tag team partners – they're even wearing the same color boots and trunks for this match. They're tied to the hip, like Robert Gibson and Ricky Morton when they were the Rock and Roll Express. So it's down to these tag team partners and the super heel. One would guess right away that the super heel is outnumbered. The tag team partners take a moment, talk it over, and agree to eliminate the heel and then wrestle a clean, fair-and-square match against each other to see who's the winner. They shake hands and turn their attention to the heel. Despite his best efforts, the heel can't evade the partners. They tie him up against the ropes and work together to dump him over the top rope. The heel hangs on for dear life, but little by little his legs are getting lifted up and pushed over. At last, the combined strength of the two faces is just too much for the heel, and over he goes, but just as he goes over, he tries to prevent himself from hitting the floor by grabbing onto one of the babies' arms, almost pulling the baby out of the ring, too. The heel hits the floor and is eliminated.

But one of the tag team buddies is in a precarious position. For a split second, he's hanging over the top rope, halfway in the ring, halfway out.

His partner sees his golden opportunity and strikes. He grabs his partner by the trunks and dumps him out of the ring. *Ding! Ding! Ding!* The match is over, and The Opportunist is now the number one contender for the belt. The betrayed partner, meanwhile, is dazed and confused. In disbelief, he gets up on the apron and shouts at his longtime friend and partner, "What the hell? What's the matter with you!" But instead of staying there and facing the music, our just turned

Opportunist turns his back on his friend and retreats to the locker room without an explanation or apology. At an upcoming show you could have The Opportunist win the title and then his betrayed partner could then challenge him for it, setting up a huge grudge match for the gold with an awesome history behind it.

Unlike The Traitor, being an Opportunist isn't quite so much a one-way road. Think about it. If someone you think is a friend conspires against you and deliberately sets you up to take a fall, you'd be an idiot to take this guy back as a friend. On the other hand, if a guy let you down or betrayed you at the spur of a moment because he yielded to temptation, if the guy comes to you and says, "Man, listen. I don't know what came over me. I guess I just saw that gold and took the easy road. It was stupid. I want to make it up to you," accepting that guy back as a friend isn't such a stretch.

So if you have a babyface whom you want to temporarily flip over to being a heel because you think it would make a great feud, set up an Opportunist angle, not a Traitor angle.

The Coward

Ah, The Coward. So often are heels in pro wrestling made out to be cowards…and 99.9% of the time, it's done completely wrong.

When a person mentions The Coward, usually the first image that pops into someone's head is of a guy shaking in his boots, knocking at the knees, with his eyes big as saucers and begging for mercy – a guy reminiscent of Shaggy from "Scooby Doo."

This ain't the type of coward I'm talking about.

Sure, the shaking-in-his-boots heel has been done for ages, so much so that it's a staple. And this is one of pro wrestling's sacred cows that I'm going to go after. Ric Flair's been using this gimmick since I first saw him in the early 80s, and even then it was over-the-top.

In real life, cowardice isn't so obvious.

The type of coward I'm talking about is far more complex. He's strong and charismatic from afar, lurking in the shadows and pulling the strings of the people close to him. He talks and acts tough to his followers but has them do his dirty work, because under that tough, bad guy facade, he's nothing but a yellow coward who's way too afraid to do

146

anything bold himself. He has his followers completely fooled, and when he's around them he acts tough, cool, and confident because he knows they'll protect him, but once caught by himself, his façade melts away and his true colors are revealed.

Need an example? How about Saddam Hussein? As the strongman of Iraq, Saddam surrounded himself with thugs, hangers on, and toadies who stayed loyal to Saddam because he paid them well. When anyone dared to challenge or rise up against Saddam, he would use the most cowardly and brutal methods available to him to put them down. In the 1980s, when Saddam was losing a war he started with Iran, he decided to use weapons of mass destruction on the advancing Iranian troops. Problem was, his military "experts" had just developed the weapons and Saddam wasn't sure they would work. So he tested them – on his own people.

The Iraqi Kurds are a group of people who live in the northeastern region of Iraq who were never very thrilled about being ruled by Saddam. So Saddam decided to punish them by using poison gas on them. He sent his flunkies in military airplanes to drop canisters of mustard and tabun gas on helpless, unsuspecting Kurdish civilians while he lounged in an overstuffed leather chair in one of his many opulent palaces, smoking a cigar.

Twenty years later, President George W. Bush had had enough of Saddam and his evil, cravenly ways, so he sent in American troops to oust him from power. Like the coward Saddam was, he ran for the hills, but soon enough, he was found hiding in a hole. Like a true coward, when American troops pulled him out of his hiding place, he begged for mercy and tried to worm his way out by offering to "negotiate."

So how do you employ this type of villain in indie wrestling? There's a wealth of possibilities. One idea that comes immediately to mind again involves a tag team. One member of the team is one of these cowardly heels that I'm describing. The other is a young, impressionable heel who, if he wasn't under the yoke of the dominating coward, would probably be a babyface. The coward is domineering, demanding, and abusive of his partner. Maybe he's a veteran and his partner is a younger guy, so the coward's cover is that he's taken the younger guy "under his wing," when, in reality, he just wants someone to kick around and fight his battles for him. So in their matches, the young heel wrestles the brunt of the match and absorbs almost all the punishment. The Coward only tags in when the opponent is down and hurt, and as soon as things get a bit hairy, he tags out and lets his younger partner come in and take the beating. If the team loses, The Coward blames his partner, even though the partner effectively has to fight two men since he doesn't get much help from The Coward.

Probably the best recent example of a Coward in modern times is Randy Orton in WWE. Flanked by his two flunkies, Cody Rhodes and Ted DiBiase, Jr., Orton did an extraordinary job of portraying a classic coward who domineers and intimidates. As I've written previously, I am not much of a fan of WWE, but Randy Orton was something special in this particular role. He would send in Rhodes and DiBiase to fight most of his battles for him, and then once his opponents were hurt or weak, he coolly arrived on the scene and dished out some pain by delivering a punt to the head of whoever Rhodes and Orton had already beaten up. He then talked high and mighty, saying inflammatory things and issuing crazy challenges. If a babyface would jump to his feet and go after Orton, his flunkies cut him off and Orton would slip away to safety.

This is good stuff that fans just eat up. Tap into it.

The Bully

The Bully is very similar to the The Coward, as almost all bullies are cowards. In the context of pro wrestling, however, there are some unique characteristics between the two to be aware of. Going back to the example of Randy Orton, Orton wasn't much of a bully. He bullied his cronies, but he didn't bully his opponents much.

A bully in pro wrestling seeks out inferior opponents to dominate. He preys on the weak. He rarely challenges other contenders or any other guys of his caliber. Instead, he amasses an impressive win-loss record against a string of jobbers, and then demands a title shot against the champion. That is, he attempts to take the easy way out and leapfrog over the other contenders because he's really just a chicken. He'd much rather just beat up lesser opponents who pose no real threat to him than tangle with anyone his own size who might kick his ass. And then once he's beat his weaker opponent down, he talks trash to him as the poor guy lies injured in the ring. During the post-match interview, he flexes his muscles and talks smack about how he has no competition and how he should already be the champion.

The Hothead

The Hothead is one of my very favorite villains because if done right, he can draw tremendous heat. Notice I said, "Done right." I said that because many, many young guys wrestling as heels try to pull off The Hothead, but they go about it all wrong. They act like a hothead from start to finish. That is, from the moment they step through the curtain to the moment they step back through the curtain, they're doing the hothead act, and that just isn't realistic.

Let's talk about John McEnroe again. McEnroe was a real life hothead. He was aggressive, fiery, brash, and unpredictable. If an umpire made a call against him that he didn't like, he would explode into a raging tantrum, protesting that the umpire was blind or incompetent. Tennis fans loved to hate him. People who didn't normally watch tennis started tuning in to see what all the commotion was about. Soon they were watching to see McEnroe get his comeuppance and then, of course, watch him explode. And that's exactly what tennis did in the 80s – it exploded. It enjoyed success the likes of which it had never seen before. And much of that success was due to McEnroe's hothead behavior.

But now I challenge you to go watch some of McEnroe's classic matches. If you watch closely, you'll notice something very significant: McEnroe wasn't always a hothead. When it was time for his match, he'd come out to the court cool, calm, and collected. You could see the focus in his eyes. You could sense his readiness and his determination. Soon, the ball would be served and the match would get underway…and the time bomb started ticking. It wasn't until things got really going, until the match became very competitive and the points were being scored one-for-one, one-for-one and it became clear that this could be anyone's match, *that's* when the time bomb was most likely to detonate.

And when it did, watch out.

The pro wrestler who embodied The Hothead personality was Larry Zbyszko. He was loud, he was brash, and when a call didn't go his way, he was a crybaby. And he was the master of the stall. That is, if a baby got up on him, he'd roll out of the ring, throw a tantrum, and complain to the referee that, somehow, the baby had used an illegal tactic to get the upper hand. The referee would start the count and demand that he get back in the ring, but Zybszko would take his time, fueling fans' ire. People in the first few rows would come unglued every time Zybszko would stall, furiously demanding that he get back in the ring and receive the punishment he had coming to him. When Zybszko would finally get back in the ring, he'd use a dirty tactic to win back the advantage and then dominate for a few minutes, but invariably the babyface would recover and take Zybszko down, sending him into a blind rage all over again.

Fans ate it up.

The key here is buildup. If you're portraying a hothead character, think *steam iron*. You know how when you first turn on a steam iron to iron a shirt, it's ice cold and you have to wait a few minutes for it to warm up? Then it gets warm, but it's not steaming yet – still not good enough to get those tough wrinkles out of your shirt. Then finally after a few more minutes, steam starts emitting from the holes in the iron's metal surface, and you can start pressing out those wrinkles. Then, after a few more minutes, the iron is so hot, steam is shooting out of the iron, and if you're not careful, you'll get burned.

That's the right way to portray The Hothead. You come out cold. You're relaxed. Fans give you some lip as you make your way to the ring, but you're calm about it. You might pause for a moment and give a heckler a dirty look, but you say nothing. You're above these lowlifes. Then you make it to the ring. The ref comes over to pat you down, but you don't complain. At this point the steam iron is stone cold, but the cord has been plugged in. You get pelted by a smattering of catcalls from the fans. You cut your eyes at them but continue to say nothing. The bell rings. You tie up. You exchange a few holds and counter holds. No problem. You tie up again. The baby takes you down with a quick arm drag. *Now* you show your first signs of irritation...

You see how this works? You let the tension build. You take your time. You portray the events as they would unfold in the real world. You let the steam iron slowly heat up. You don't come out of the dressing room throwing a fit, because doing that makes it obvious it's all just a silly act. Instead, you allow the events in the ring to guide the story along. Like with everything else we've discussed so far, if you allow the real world to logically guide you, you can't go wrong.

The Whiner

Another great, real world type of villain that you can't go wrong with is The Whiner. Oh, you know this guy…and trust me, you despise him. The Whiner is that kid whose dad gives him a posh, high-up job in the family business that he didn't earn and isn't qualified for but then complains that the job is "beneath" him. The Whiner is the guy hooked on drugs who blames his drug addiction on his parents because they didn't give him every single little thing he wanted as a child. The Whiner is the guy whose parents *give* him a brand new car when he turns 16 but then he tells them it's not good enough for him and that he wants a better, more luxurious car. The Whiner is the guy at work who shows up late, does very little, and doesn't pull his fair share of the load. The other workers complain about him and tell the boss he should be fired. But the boss feels pity on the guy and decides instead to talk with him about his issues and give him a second chance. But when the boss talks with him about how he needs to improve, The Whiner calls his boss an asshole and pulls attitude.

I hate The Whiner. Every time I meet one I want to punch him in the face. Just kidding, of course, (maybe) but this illustrates how much whiners get under my skin. The Whiner is an ingrate, a complainer, a morale buster. He's self-centered and believes he's above everyone else despite the fact that he's never done anything to elevate himself above anybody else and isn't very smart, either.

Probably the very best example of a whiner in pro wrestling was Raven when he was in ECW. Played by Scott Levy, Raven was a slacker, a sociopath, an ingrate, and a "tortured soul." You know what I mean by "tortured soul" – he portrayed a character akin to those losers in the world who self-appoint themselves as "tortured" because they weren't given every little thing they wanted in life, because their moms had to work nights when they were kids, or because they're abject failures in life because, well, they never made any effort to do anything.

Here's an idea for a whiner angle, but before I describe it, keep in mind that building up a whiner character takes time and dedication. Many events have to transpire over time for the fans to get a good feel for what the character is. So start out by picking a young heel and give the guy some hype. It's best if the guy has never wrestled for you and is an up-and-comer, a new kid on the wrestling scene. Fans expect any newcomer to the sport to be grateful and eager for any opportunity to climb into the ring. It doesn't matter who it's against or what the match's stipulations are – opportunity is opportunity.

So you do some hyping of this new guy. Before he even appears before the crowd, your announcer tells the fans that this newcomer has "great potential" and is a "future champion." So the fans haven't even seen the guy, but they already have big expectations. After hyping him up for a while, you finally book him in a match against another up-and-comer. So fans are thinking, "Finally! We're going to get to see this guy they've been pushing." But then you have the guy come out for an interview and he refuses to wrestle his chosen opponent, insisting that the guy isn't at his level. He wants a bigger match against a bigger name guy – otherwise, he won't wrestle.

So the scheduled match doesn't go, because the whiner refuses to wrestle against an "inferior" opponent. So at the next show you interview him again, asking why he refused to wrestle, considering he's just a newcomer himself. The whiner then goes into a whiny rant about how he's the best, how he deserves the best, and how he's not going to waste his time on "loser" opponents.

But your promotion stands its ground. The announcer tells the whiner that he must wrestle his chosen opponent or be subject to a suspension. Outraged, the whiner refuses and storms away from the interview area. Then when it's time for the match, it becomes a question if the guy will even show up. After making the crowd wait a few minutes, he finally emerges from behind the curtain with a subtle pouty look on his face. He reluctantly climbs into the ring and the match is started. He dominates the match early, but after a few minutes of cocky behavior, his opponent turns the tables and gets the upper hand. So the whiner does the unthinkable – he quits. He rolls out of the ring and goes back to the locker room without even looking back. He's counted out.

You then repeat this pattern in several ensuing shows – the guy shows some promise but then quits. So by now, fans really hate this guy. Then, at last, you give the guy a jobber to beat up and you let him win a match after quitting all his previous matches. In the post-match interview you have the guy brag about how great he is and then you have him demand a title match! Here's a pouty, whiny brat who quits every match where the going gets a bit rough, and then he wins *one* match against a jobber and he demands a shot at the title!

Trust me, if you build this up right and coach your heel to execute The Whiner gimmick realistically and convincingly, fans will absolutely despise the guy – and then they'll buy lots and lots of tickets to see him hopefully get his ass kicked.

The Sadist

The Sadist is someone who just wants to hurt people. A sadist gets a rush on beating people up and injuring them unnecessarily. Causing someone else pain feeds The Sadist's ego and validates his own warped self-image of being a strong, bad ass tough guy.

When the Road Warriors first hit the scene in 1983, they were billed as heels, and their gimmick was that they were two sadists from the mean streets of Chicago who took pleasure in beating people up. Bookers would put them in squash matches against jobbers, and the Road Warriors would just pulverize them. This, believe it or not, is how the Road Warriors became big. Most fans remember them as a team that would pulverize top heels, but their true start came as Sadists.

If you need a real life example of a Sadist, the best place to look is baseball from the turn of the 20th Century, when legendary madman Ty Cobb terrified basemen and intimidated pitchers by just looking at them. Cobb, a man who held many of baseball's biggest records for many years and to this day widely considered one of the best players of the sport's history, was a bona fide sadist. In a past life he was probably a medieval torturer, as the man genuinely thrived on hurting people.

One time when asked about his playing style, Cobb coolly replied, "I always went into a bag full speed, feet first. I had sharp spikes on my shoes. If the baseman stood where he had no business to be and got hurt, that was his fault." Cobb tried his darnedest to hurt any man

153

who tried to stand in his way – both on the baseball diamond and off it. Sometimes he would even attack someone just for the fun of it. An unabashed racist, Cobb once attacked a Black groundskeeper allegedly over the condition of a practice field. When the groundskeeper's wife jumped in and begged Cobb to stop beating her husband, he punched and choked her, too.

Cobb's mad, aggressive style, his pleasure in hurting people, and his dominance on the baseball diamond made him the most hated man in the sport. Fans hated him. Managers hated him. Team owners hated him. Even his teammates hated him. When the man died in 1961, only four people from baseball attended his funeral. Now that's saying something. After all, the man was a legend, larger than life, and baseball's first Hall of Famer. But everything the man did outside of the "proper" confines of the sport preceded him.

This is a perfect model for a heel in pro wrestling – a guy who takes pleasure in hurting people and will punish anyone who tries to stand in his way. The best way to create this character is to ask yourself, "OK, what would Ty Cobb do in this situation?" If Ty Cobb was in a wrestling match against a jobber, what would he do? I'll tell you what he'd do – he'd beat the snot out of the jobber. He'd constantly ask the timekeeper how much time was left in the match every few minutes so that he could milk the clock and beat the jobber senseless for every possible second before being forced to make the cover before time ran out. Then when the ring announcer asks him why he was so cruel, he'd blame the jobber for getting into the ring with him.

Beating up jobbers is a heel's modus operandi, especially among Sadists and Cowards. That said, be careful not to mistake The Sadist for The Coward. Remember, a coward is brutal, but he runs from a fair fight. He's a chicken. A sadist, on the other hand, is determined to hurt anyone and will take on any challenger.

Again, think Ty Cobb. Ty Cobb wasn't afraid of anybody – even when he was outnumbered. One time he was walking the streets of Detroit and three muggers jumped him. He beat them all up and sent them running for their lives. Most men at this point would consider themselves lucky, get the hell out of there, and call the police. Not Cobb. Cobb instead relished the moment as a golden opportunity to inflict some serious pain. He chased down one of the would-be thieves, tackled him, pulled his pistol on him, and tried to shoot him. But the gun misfired, so Cobb beat the mugger's face to a bloody pulp with the butt of the gun instead, leaving the guy with a cracked skull and fractured cheek bones.

This incident – as grisly as it was – is good fodder for a sadist angle. Say your sadist is in a match against a lesser, younger heel opponent, and, as all heels do, the young heel tries to get over on the sadist by cheating. Let's say he attempts a pinfall by pulling your sadist's trunks. The Sadist kicks out at the very last instant and then goes ballistic. He sees red. In a blind rage, he grabs the guy and beats the tar out of him from pillar to post, not caring anymore about the match or about scoring a pinfall. He brutalizes the guy so badly, the referee has to call for the bell and security has to come to the ring to pull The Sadist off his opponent. When it's all said and done, The Sadist has lost the match due to disqualification, and his opponent is wheeled away on a stretcher. The Sadist then flies into another rage and threatens to attack the referee for disqualifying him. So security steps in again to protect the referee, and The Sadist jumps one of the security officers and starts pounding on him just for daring to get in his way.

When running an angle like this, remember, it's critical to make a big deal about The Sadist's actions. A guy beating up an opponent to the point he gets disqualified and then going after a referee and then beating up a security officer would be a heinous act in any real sport. Imagine if something like that happened in boxing or MMA! People would be still talking about it years afterwards.

As I've harped about before, too often in pro wrestling these days, stuff like this happens all too often and nothing ever gets said about it. It's like we have really, really bad short term memories. A guy commits some atrocious act one week and the next week it's completely forgotten and never mentioned again. This is a very *bad* way to book and ranks very high on the list of things that need to be fixed in the sport. Specifically, to run an angle like the one I just described (or any, really), you have to have a memory of it and you have to mention it from show-to-show to develop a history for the character and the angle.

The Braggart

I've written a lot about Muhammad Ali in this book, largely because he's a great source of inspiration for pro wrestlers, especially heels. If Ali had to be categorized into one of the Twelve Villains, he'd definitely be this one, the Braggart. No doubt about it. And I'm pretty darned certain he'd wholeheartedly agree with me. Mind you, Ali's braggadocio was an act, but he knew that to impress the world he had to tell everyone he could that he was the greatest.

"At home I am a nice guy," he once said. "But I don't want the world to know. Humble people, I've found, don't get very far." Now I'm not 100% sure I agree with him on that point, but it does show the method to his madness: Loudmouths who boast big about themselves and announce to the world how wonderful they are get a heck of a lot of attention, and usually it's negative – so negative, in fact, that just about everyone hates them. After all, who doesn't hate someone who brags on himself? In Muhammad Ali's case, he was able to back up his mouth with his fists, and that made people despise him even more.

Another great example of a braggart from the pro sports world is Terrell Owens, the brash wide receiver of the NFL. Owens, or "T.O." as he's more affectionately known, has no qualms about telling everyone on planet earth how great he is. A quintessential ball hog and camera hound, he is one of the most hated men on the gridiron today – unless, that is, he's on your team. If he's on your team, you love him. If he's not on your team, you love to hate him, and that's no accident.

Throughout his career, Owens has methodically worked the crowd and drawn tremendous heat regardless of what team he was on. Without question, T.O drew the most heat with his colorful end zone celebrations. Just about every time T.O. scores a touchdown, fans get treated to some creative, over-the-top celebration. Like the time he borrowed a cheerleader's pom-poms and joined the girls in a victory cheer after he scored a touchdown. Or when he grabbed a fan's popcorn and poured it into his own face. These antics delight the fans of the team he plays for but elicits rage and hate in the hearts of the opposing team...and in the hearts of anyone who doesn't have T.O. on their team.

Owens took poor sportsmanship to new heights. Not only does he excessively celebrate his own success, he openly taunts players he's just beaten for scores. Example: After just scoring his 100th career touchdown, Owens pulled a towel from his waist, folded it over his arm, and then presented the ball to the opposing team as if he were a waiter serving up a meal. Another example: In a game against his former team, the Philadelphia Eagles, Owens scored a touchdown and then flapped his arms like the wings of a bird -- an obvious mockery of the Eagles' own celebration jig. This raised a deafening chorus of boos from the fans in attendance, prompting Owens to comment later, "There's a lot of love in those boos."

His most outrageous case of excessive celebration and outright mockery of his opponents occurred a decade ago and is now known as the infamous Texas Stadium Incident. This particular event should be required study material for any aspiring heel pro wrestler. Why? Because it was classic villain behavior early in Owens' career that immediately catapulted him to larger-than-life status.

It went down like this. Owens was playing for the San Francisco 49ers at the time. Everyone knows how passionate the people of Dallas are about their Cowboys. To the good people of Dallas, the Cowboys' big blue star is almost a religious symbol. Owens knew that, too – and that's what inspired him to do the unthinkable.

After scoring his first touchdown of the game, Owens was not content with the standard end zone celebration. Instead, he decided he wanted to rile his opponents and their fans by doing a victory dance – right smack dab in the center of the Cowboys' blue star on the 50 yard line.

Fans were livid. The Cowboys' players were insulted. Owens' teammates were appalled. It was sheer poor sportsmanship and pure showmanship. It was the ultimate in self-congratulation.

But that wasn't enough. When Owens scored again, he decided to repeat the act of mockery. He ran out to the 50 yard line and placed the ball square on the Cowboys' star and prepared to outdo his previous performance. But then, unbeknownst to Owens, something else happened, something very familiar to pro wrestling fans – a babyface appeared at the last second to stop the heel from his committing his evil act.

That babyface was Cowboys safety George Teague, and he was determined not to allow Owens repeat the sacrilege of desecrating the Cowboys' star. So he ran after Owens, and right as Owens placed the ball on the Cowboys' logo and started his celebration, Teague kicked the ball away and decked Owens. Owens then did what all heels do when confronted this way: He retreated from the babyface and let his cronies do his fighting for him. Then, as both teams broke out into a fisticuffs with Teague at the center of it all, Owens abandoned his teammates and went back to finish his celebration!

In the end, Teague was ejected from the game, but he won the hearts and minds of every Cowboys fan in that stadium that day. Owens' cheeky display and Teague's heroics have made this event so unforgettable, it's now listed as one of the top ten most memorable moments in Texas Stadium history. Ironically, making history gives T.O. yet something else to brag about.

And bragging is what T.O. does best, which is where heel pro wrestlers should really pay attention. Ask just about any heel pro wrestler about how good he is (when he's in character, of course), and 99 times out of 100 you'll get a very bad Donald Trump impersonation. He'll puff out his chest, raise his nose ridiculously high in the air, and then start spouting off silly, over-the-top braggadocio: "I'm the greatest wrestler in the universe! No one can beat me! I can beat God with one arm tied behind my back!" Conversely, ask Terrell Owens, "Who's the best receiver in the game?" as Dateline NBC did in late 2006, and you get this: "I'm gonna say myself. I know there are a number of guys out there and I can name, some of the top guys in there. But, you know, that's just me having confidence in myself."

See the difference? The wrestler's boasts are nothing but a laughable case of bad acting. Owens' response, on the other hand, is sincere. This guy truly believes he is the best in the sport, and he says so. Most guys would have ducked that question or, out of humility, would have just named someone else. But not T.O. No way. He's going to tell you how good he is and he's going to tell it to you straight, so that you believe he believes what he's saying. And it doesn't matter what he's doing, either. Whatever he does, whatever project he pursues, he firmly believes he's damned good at it and is not shy about saying so.

At the end of 2009 he announced he is going to branch out and become a fashion model (!), because, well, he's so good looking: "When you've got some good looks like myself, you've got to take full advantage of it," he said.

Remember, Americans hate a braggart. To Americans, it's OK to be great. It's OK to be larger-than-life. You just have to be gracious and humble about it. It's not OK to be great and say so. And it's certainly not OK to celebrate your own success.

But of all Owens' heel-like antics, though, what stands out the most is his fierce feud with former Philadelphia Eagles quarterback Donovan McNabb. That feud is the stuff of legend, and the animosity that came from it still smolders to this day.

The year was 2005. The Philadelphia Eagles were coming off a disappointing loss in Super Bowl XXXIX, and Owens came to realize that he was slated to make "a mere" $3.5 million for the season, an amount that did not place him in the top ten highest paid receivers in the league. So he protested and demanded that he get a new contract – even though he was already under contract. The Eagles, of course, balked. So Owens became disgruntled and said to the media, "I wasn't the one who got tired in the Super Bowl."

The comment was clearly directed at McNabb, and it implied that Owens placed all the blame for the Eagles' Super Bowl loss squarely on McNabb. A few months later, Owens did the unthinkable when he proclaimed that the Eagles would be much better off if they had Brett Favre as their quarterback instead of McNabb. Soon after, McNabb and Owens were no longer speaking to each other, and the entire Eagles team imploded. To this day, the two men don't like each other, which shows us again why T.O. is such a great heel – that is, great heels spawn great feuds that endure for many years. Just think Flair v. Steamboat, Raven v. Dreamer, Debeers v. Snuka…. Enduring, heated feuds sell tickets and win TV ratings, whether your sport is pro wrestling or pro football.

Within recent times, when Dallas was in the hunt for the Super Bowl, T.O. appeared to have turned over a new leaf. He even stayed loyal to his team and Tony Romo, Dallas' star quarterback, after Dallas suffered a disappointing loss to the New York Giants in the playoffs. Romo fell victim to harsh criticism from the media for taking a vacation a week before the game, but T.O. refused to pin the blame on him: "We lost as a team. We lost as a team, man."

What's this? A face turn for T.O.?

Not so fast. Any face turn proved to be short-lived for Owens, who was back to his old tricks the following season. After a loss to the Washington Redskins, Owens whined about not getting the ball enough, even though the Cowboys threw the ball his way 18 times and handed off to him twice in end arounds. That means the Cowboys gave him the ball 20 out of 58 total offensive plays – yet to him, that wasn't enough. A couple weeks later, while basking in the glory of a 35-22 victory over the hapless San Francisco 49ers, T.O. took all the credit for the win: "They unleashed me today."

Pro wrestling heels, are you listening? This is how to be a braggart!

Heat vs. Cheap Heat

There is heat and then there's cheap heat. You need to understand the difference.

The term "heat" gets tossed around a lot nowadays. Pretty much any time someone is referring to a crowd reaction – whether it's positive or negative – that person calls it "heat." The accurate definition, however, is the negative reaction a heel gets from fans for his dastardly behavior both in and out of the ring. The distinction is important because heat by the right definition is absolutely essential to the success of a pro wrestling promotion.

A heel's job is to make the fans despise him. The more they despise him, the better. The greatest heels in pro wrestling history understood this fact intimately and were masters of manipulating crowds and generating awesome heat. Take guys like Ric Flair, Bobby Heenan, Roddy Piper, Nick Bockwinkel, Colonel DeBeers, Ted DiBiase, Raven, Triple H (as a heel), and Randy Orton and you'll find guys who, as heels, were some of the most hated men on the planet. Fans loved to hate them. Some of these guys were so despised, fans couldn't make the distinction between fantasy and reality. Fans would attack them outside of the ring, burn them with cigarettes, throw beer on them, overturn their cars in the parking lot, and challenge them to genuine fistfights. Roddy Piper once had a fan pull a long, razor sharp hunting knife and try to filet him with it. Now *that's* heat!

A good heel can draw tremendous, real heat without ever touching the microphone. Surprised that I wrote that? Well, it's 100% true. You might be scowling at that idea right now since it's so common these days for heels to grab the nearest microphone and launch into some longwinded, rambling rant where they insult everyone and everything that comes to mind. Think about it. At just about every single indie show you go to, I guarantee you at some point – and probably more often than once – some young heel will come out during his pre-match introduction, grab the mic from the ring announcer, and then start talking smack. He'll insult the fans, their families, the local sports team, the city, the looks of the local women, the weather, and the six-year-old kid sitting in the front row. Then he'll start spouting cheesy, grandiloquent boasts about how he's the king of the universe and the next coming of the Messiah. You know what I'm saying is true because you've seen it yourself way more times than you can count. In fact, if you're wrestling as a heel, you might be feeling a bit defensive right now because you do the same sort of thing and think you're great at drawing heat.

But what you're drawing is *cheap heat,* and heels that think they need to grab the microphone and launch into a bombastic diatribe to draw heat are rank amateurs, plain and simple. Again, a good heel can draw awesome heat without even touching the mic.

How? Simple – attitude and body language. Never forget that pro wrestling fans are not stupid. Not by a long shot. In fact, longtime pro wrestling fans tend to be a very attentive, savvy, street-smart bunch, and they pick up on details and nuances better than the average member of the general entertainment audience. So there's no need to spell things out for them or spoon feed them. If you're a heel, you don't have to announce to your audience in no uncertain terms that you're evil; if you act as a heel properly, the fans will figure it out on their own well enough and soon enough.

It's just like villains in good movies. The bad guys in good movies don't come out and act like an ass clown at the opening scene just to establish themselves as the bad guy.

Think of a good movie like "The Shawshank Redemption." The warden in "Shawshank" is the main villain. He's sinister, conniving, cold, and ruthless. How did Bob Gunton, the actor who played the warden, convey that to the audience? Simple – through damned good acting. He didn't have to appear in a scene and act all exaggeratedly pompous and cocky and look directly into the camera and insult the people in the audience: "Hey, you in the third row! Is that your girlfriend or a dude in drag hoping for a cheap meal?"

So if they don't have to resort to cheap heat in the movies, why are so many workers resorting to it in pro wrestling? You don't have to! In fact, it's the wrong thing to do. It's cheap, it's corny, it's bad storytelling, and it's bad for wrestling. It's like a nice Italian restaurant serving its customers Spaghetti O's out of a can and calling it pasta. That's exactly what cheap heat is – it's Olive Garden serving you Spaghetti O's out of a can and calling it Linguine al la Marinara. It's giving your girlfriend a flashy cubic zirconia engagement ring and telling her it's a four carat diamond. It's hanging a framed velvet picture of Elvis up in your living room and calling it art. It's putting dual exhaust and spoke rims on a Ford Focus and calling it a sports car. It's taking your kids to a local church carnival and telling them it's Disney World.

Cheap heat is the cheap way out. It's the easy road. It takes no special skills, little practice, and even less effort. Anybody can grab a microphone and shout that a football team sucks. It takes real talent and dedication, on the other hand, to *act*, to convince the audience – at least for a moment – that you are real life asshole.

So how do you convince the world that you're a genuine asshole when, in reality, you're a nice guy who loves his family, a good friend to many people, a hard worker, and a guy who really, really appreciates pro wrestling fans who pay good money to come see you in a show? It can be tough. So tough, in fact, that's why many guys resort to cheap heat – they just don't know how to be assholes.

So let's look at a few situations and compare and contrast the cheap heat response to the response of a truly good heel who can really work a crowd.

An autograph request

Let's say you're a heel, you're in your street clothes, and you're on your way in to the venue for the night's show. A ten-year-old kid recognizes you as you walk past the concession stand and excitedly asks you for your autograph.

Cheap Heat: You take the pen and paper from the kid and say, "Sure, you little brat! I'll give you my autograph." Then, before you sign it, you announce at the top of your lungs, "Hey, people! Look here! This kid knows talent when he sees it. At least one person in this stinking, miserable place has some class!"

Real Heat: As the kid asks you for an autograph, you keep on walking, not even slowing down. You cut your eyes at the kid and scowl just a bit. Then you mutter, "I don't do autographs, kid."

See the difference? In the first example, you're acting like Moe from The Three Stooges. It's crystal clear to the kid and everyone else looking on that you're just putting on a silly, sophomoric bad acting job and trying vainly to make people laugh. Everyone can easily tell that you're just being a goofball class clown, and who hates the class clown? He makes Mr. Baldwin's American History class a bit more fun.

On the other hand, by denying the kid the autograph and barely even acknowledging him, the kid and everyone else thinks, "Wow, what a jerk! He clearly takes this wrestling business too seriously. He must think he's a star or something." Now *that's* real heat! Those fans have a real contempt for you and will tell everyone else sitting near them in the stands how much of a jackass you are.

So are you with me so far? Yes? Good. Let's look at another situation.

A heckling fan

You're making your way to the ring when you notice a loud fan right by the crowd barrier talking smack at you.

Cheap Heat: You stop and start talking smack back. You say, "Shut your filthy mouth, you redneck trailer trash hillbilly hick! Shut your mouth or I'll shut it for you! You think you're tough? You talk so big and tough, why don't you get in that ring and I'll show you who's tough! I'll mop the floor with your sorry doublewide ass!" Then you walk a few more steps and notice a kid trying to high-five you. So you put your hand out to receive it, but as the kid is about to smack your hand, you pull it away and run your fingers through your hair, pulling the old "You're too slow" trick.

Real Heat: Your eyes are locked on the ring. You don't bother looking left or right at the fans as you walk down that aisle because you have a match to win and don't have time for fans. Then, as you're walking past the heckler, you pretend not to notice him as if he's so unimportant, he doesn't even register on your radar until the very last second. Then, as you're one step past him, you turn toward him and glower at him with a slightly confused and dismissive look on your face, the way a big movie star on the red carpet on his way into the Academy Awards ceremony would look at a heckling fan in the crowd behind the guard rail. It's a, "I don't have time for you, pal," look. Then you look the guy up and down (just with your eyes, not by moving your head) disapprovingly, as in saying with your eyes to the fan, "Are you for real? Look at you, decked out in your K-Mart clothes." Again, you *don't say this with your lips*, you say it with your disdainful *eyes*. And trust me, all you need is your eyes to communicate this message most effectively. Just furrow your brow a bit and leave the rest of your face blank. Then you turn your back to the guy and walk on, as if the guy was a complete waste of your time and is now out of your consciousness.

Again, see the difference? In the first example, you're engaging in comical smack talk, as if you're in a rap off with the heckling fan. Again, you're behaving like a hip-hop comedian who insults and lambasts someone in the crowd for a cheap laugh. The message you're communicating to the crowd is, "I'm trying to be funny. I'm trying to make you laugh. You may not think I'm funny, but at least I'm trying!" And as I wrote just moments ago, people don't hate the class clown – they love him because he's just so darn funny. Remember, your job as a heel is not to make people laugh but to make people hate you. That hate is what enables the good guy/bad guy struggle in the ring to unfold and flourish. Instead, too many matches nowadays are good guy vs. the class clown, and everybody cheers for the class clown (if they cheer at all).

Taking a bump

This example is the big daddy, because there are so many teachable moments in it. Let's say you're wrestling as a heel against a babyface who's really, really over. So you have two assignments – make the crowd really hate you and make the face look really good. So you arrange a high spot where the baby takes you over in a series of three deep arm drags, causing you to retreat to the safety of the floor.

Cheap heat: First, let's talk about the feeds for the series of arm drags. You tie up and then quickly take the baby over with a hip toss out of the collar and elbow. You strut casually away, pointing to your temple, overly obviously communicating visually to the crowd, "See how smart I am?" Then you turn to do the feed with your left arm way out absurdly out wide from your side. Then you take the next arm drag and get up, comically staggering about the ring like a drunk Barney Fife. You turn, conveniently, and take the next arm drag and the next. Finally you slip under the bottom rope and collapse ridiculously onto the floor. You then get on your knees, throw your head back, squeeze your eyes shut as if you're crying, and start furiously making the timeout sign. Then, pretending that the crowd is razzing you and the things they're saying offend your sensitive ears, you stick your fingers in your ears and shout, "Shuuuuut up!"

Real heat: You tie up and then quickly take the baby over with a hip toss out of the collar and elbow. But instead of strutting away like a peacock, you instead walk away back to your corner casually and nonchalantly.

When you get to the corner, you coolly adjust your kneepads. You pay no attention to the fans and no attention to your opponent. By doing this you're nonverbally, clearly, and realistically communicating to the crowd, "I'm so good, this is a walk in the park for me. This guy is nothing to me. I'm totally relaxed because I can beat him any time I want." You're toying with your opponent. To you, this is just a tune-up match. So you tie up with the baby again, but this time he turns the tables on you. He takes *you* over with a quick arm drag.

All right, let's hit the *pause* button for just a moment. You're a heel and you've just been surprised by an opponent you underestimated. The traditional bad acting way a heel responds to just such a situation is with mock shock. They sit up quickly from the takedown, selling their lower back ridiculously, and they make a shocked, terrified look on their face. You know exactly what I'm talking about – that look as if they just accidentally walked into the girls' locker room and saw three dozen college girls naked in the showers. They bug their eyes out of their skull and open their mouths as wide as they can, like a baby bird expecting a worm from its mama.

Stupid. Cheesy. Bad acting. This is exactly the sort of thing that makes the average non wrestling fan say, "Oh, that's so stupid. Who watches this?" and change the channel. Instead of all this slapstick nonsense, why not try some good acting, some realism? How? Simple: Ask yourself how you would respond in this situation if it were to happen in real life.

Say you're in a fight with your little brother, and for all the years your little brother has been able to walk and ball a fist, you've owned him. Any time he tries to fight you (as most brothers close in age invariably do), you take him to school. So now you're in one such tussle, and you're not the least bit threatened. But then out of nowhere, boom! He takes you down. How would you logically respond to this? I'll tell you how – first with confusion, then with anger.

Let's step through it. Boom! You're little brother just took you down out of nowhere. Your very first reaction is confusion: "What just happened? Where am I? Oh, hell…I'm on the ground! How did that happen?" Then you come to your senses and, naturally, anger and humiliation set in: "That little piece of crap! He just took me down! How dare he? He'll pay for this!" You then quickly get to your feet and go after the kid, intent on making him pay.

So let's apply this to our spot. Boom, the babyface surprisingly takes you down. You sit up, and the first thing you do is make a confused look on your face. *This look should last no more than two seconds.* Any more and the reaction looks staged and unnatural. Then, that expression should immediately give way to a look of anger. Now, if you were in a real fight and someone knocked you down, would you get back up with your back turned to your opponent? Of course not. That would be really, really stupid. The natural, instinctive response in any fight is to keep your eye on your attacker. If you get knocked down, as soon as you get your wits back about you, you start looking for him. So whenever you take a bump like an arm drag and you're going to feed a follow-up move, don't stand up with your back to your opponent and your eyes looking out to the crowd; before you even start to stand up, look over your *right* shoulder, thus silently communicating to the crowd, "Where is he?" Then when you spot him, get up and charge him, just as you would in a fight with your little brother. Make sure you have your left arm ready for the feed.

Let's go through this spot step-by-step, because it's important:

1. You tie up.
2. You take the babyface down, as expected.
3. You casually walk back to your corner, disaffected.
4. You tie up again.
5. This time, the babyface takes *you* down with an arm drag.
6. You sit up.
7. You look confused for *two seconds.*
8. You change the look on your face from confusion to anger.
9. You look over your right shoulder to spot the babyface.
10. You charge him, with your left arm ready for the feed.
11. Boom! He takes you down again.
12. You sit up.
13. Do *not* look confused! After all, there's nothing to be confused about. He just proved to you moments ago he can take you down.

14. Instead, look angry.
15. Look over your right shoulder and spot your opponent.
16. Charge again, again with that left arm ready for the feed.

Got it? Pretty simple stuff, really. I'm sure that if you play this out in your mind's eye you can plainly see how this is so much more realistic than the way boys are doing it traditionally.

Now let's get to the heat. You've just been taken down three times with three quick, deep arm drags by an opponent you had underestimated. You're surprised, confused, humiliated, and angered. This guy's gotten the better of you. He's on your tail. Time to bail out, buy some time, and regroup. So you roll out of the ring under the bottom rope. You take a couple seconds to subtly sell your lower back, then you explode.

Ever see a quarterback who's just thrown an interception because his receiver ran the wrong route just lose it when he gets to the sideline? He throws his helmet at the Gatorade table, Gatorade flies everywhere, and then he starts screaming bloody murder at the receiver. This is the same response you're looking for. You slam your hand on the mat and shout, "Damn it!" You storm over to your corner where you strategically placed an open plastic water bottle at the start of the match, grab it, and throw it against the ring steps. Water flies everywhere, hopefully on you. So now you showed your ass and are all wet. But instead of getting angrier, you try to act all nonchalant, trying to pretend that you didn't get water on yourself!

Think about it – you see this all the time! Some dude gets really, really ticked off, so he grabs the first thing nearby and flings it against the wall. The thing ricochets off the wall and it smashes the screen of his TV! Then he's all embarrassed and thinking to himself, "Oh, damn it! How stupid was that?" Meanwhile, the guy's wife is in the corner, quietly snickering at him, trying desperately to stifle it, because she knows if he sees her laughing at him, he'll get even angrier. This is exactly the same real world situation we're recreating in our spot. The heel (you) is that guy who throws the thing against the wall and ends up smashing his own TV. The fans are the wife, only they don't have to restrain their laughter.

So there you are, all wet, and the fans are laughing at you. *Resist the temptation to slip into cheap heat! Don't fly into a comical rage and start yelling, "Shut up!" and "It's not funny!" at the crowd!* Instead, put your hands on your hips, cock your head slightly to the side in resignation, roll your eyes up to the ceiling, and make a face that says, "Go ahead, you schmucks, laugh it up." But don't actually say a word. Just get back in the ring and regain the upper hand by using a dirty tactic.

So you see what's going on here in all three situations? You're interacting with the crowd without being so blatantly obvious and preposterous. Now I know you might be thinking, "Norm, you're crazy. In all three examples, you have the heel totally not interacting with the fans. Fans want the heels to interact with them. It's part of the show," but nothing could be farther from the truth. In the examples I presented, the heel *is* interacting with the fans – he's just doing it like a realistic, true jackass rather than as a bumbling, hapless class clown.

I remember way back in 1987, I was at a WWF house show in Miami. The AWA was my favorite promotion back then, but when the WWF came to town, you could bet your bottom dollar I'd be there. Anyway, I didn't realize it yet, as the Internet did not exist and kayfabe was still going strong, but Curt Hennig, the AWA's former heavyweight champion, had just made the jump to start working for Vince as "Mr. Perfect." Back then, new characters would show up at house shows long before they ever appeared on TV, so very few people – save the hardcore fans like me – had any idea who Curt Hennig was. And I was shocked that here was Hennig, the AWA's top draw, appearing under the WWF banner.

Needless to say, I wasn't very happy with Hennig for turning on the AWA and going to work for the competition. I watched as he made his way to the ring. His eyes were cast down at the floor. A contemptuous scowl was on his face. He said absolutely nothing to the fans as he walked the aisle. He pretended not to even notice them. As he approached the ring steps, he was within earshot of me, as I was sitting in the front row. So I saw my opportunity and grabbed it: "Hey, Curt!" I yelled. "Go back to the AWA!"

Let me tell you, if looks could kill, I'd be nothing more than skeletal remains right now. Holy cow, that guy either a) was a damned good actor or b) really, really did not like me saying that. His eyes bore into me like Superman's laser vision, and I knew in his mind he was saying, "Go eff yourself, punk!" For that moment – even though I was 100% smartened up by then – I was consumed by the moment. I was firmly convinced that Curt Hennig was a surly, cocky asshole, and he did not like me. And everyone around me felt the same way. "Oh, he didn't like that," a girl said behind me. "He looked like he wanted to kick your ass!" my buddy said next to me. Truth be told, Curt Hennig (rest his soul), was a nice guy who liked the fans and probably appreciated the fact that after spending so much time working for the AWA in Minneapolis, a kid all the way down in Miami recognized him. Yet he had me convinced.

That's the goal, dear reader! The goal is to convince the world that you're an asshole, a knave, a jerk, a self-absorbed ass, a cocksure son of a bitch, even though you're not. The goal is to make people hate you, make people *love* to hate you. If people prefer to laugh at you because you remind them of that kid they used to laugh at in Mrs. Crabtree's Social Studies class – that kid who in middle school would snap the bra of the girl sitting in front of him, that kid who'd stick a "kick me" sign on the back of the class geek, that kid who'd mock sneeze and toss all his papers into the air, that kid who'd moon the class when the teacher's back was turned – they'll love you, not hate you. The show becomes a silly sitcom like "Family Matters" or "Gilligan's Island," not an awards-winning, ratings-crushing drama like "Dallas," "The Sopranos," or "Lost."

Of course the difference is, "Family Matters" had Urkel and "Gilligan's Island" had Gilligan. They were funny (to some people, at least). Pro wrestlers, on the other hand, 99.9% of the time are *not* funny. Being funny takes real talent, and only about one in a million people is truly funny. That's why comedians like Jerry Seinfeld, Dave Chappelle, and Larry the Cable Guy make millions and millions of dollars. So since wrestlers try to be funny when they're not, wrestling shows become an unfunny sitcom.

And just like a sitcom that sucks, people tune out in droves. Drama we can do. Comedy we cannot. Real heat is drama. Cheap heat is comedy. Learn the difference.

A bad guy doesn't have to always be bad

One time about 20 years ago, I was booked for a show somewhere in Colorado – I think it was Castle Rock – and I was, as always, working as a babyface that night. I was to work a match with a young guy I had never worked with before, which wasn't necessarily a problem. I was used to working with people I'd never been in the ring with before. Personally, I much prefer to work with a guy in a few practices before a show, but as often is the case in indie pro wrestling, this time we just didn't have that opportunity. So anyway, I went to the guy backstage and introduced myself. He seemed nice enough, but my first impression of him was that he was a bit loud and obnoxious.

"Man," he said to me, "you're really going to get over tonight."

"Why?" I asked.

"Because people really, really hate me," he said. "I'm the biggest heel in this area."

"Oh, really?" I said, immediately suspicious. I'm always suspicious of anyone who pats himself on the back.

"Yep. You just watch and see."

So fair enough – the promoter of this show had booked me, and I was appreciative of that – so I was going to give his audience the best match I possibly could. But when the time came for my match, I came out to a crowd that was initially indifferent. They didn't cheer or boo me as my name was announced, which was logical, as I hadn't ever worked for this promotion before. The fans didn't know me. So to give them a clue that I was the baby, I smiled big, waved, high-fived, and gave thumbs up to all the kids – just the way a good cookie cutter babyface is supposed to. So I climbed up into the ring and started bouncing on my toes and stretching the ropes to warm up while I waited for my opponent to be announced. I was curious to see the fans' reaction when this guy got announced since he had bragged so big backstage about how much heat he had. So the announcer announces him, and out he comes from the back.

You could have heard a pin drop.

Fans couldn't care less about this guy.

Immediately he starts dishing out an extra-large helping of the cheap heat I described in the previous section. Acting a fool, yelling at fans to shut up, calling one guy's girlfriend fat, bending over and pretending to moon the crowd, etc., etc. Right away I think, "Ah, hell. This is going to be rough."

He climbed up into the ring and started pacing back and forth like a caged tiger. He looked like he was seriously on something by the way he was pacing and his eyes were darting around. He would scream at a fan on one side of the ring, march over to the other side of the ring and yell something stupid at someone else, then march right back to the first side and yell something else to the first fan he yelled at. It was all just completely stilted and over-the-top. Finally, the bell rings, and I hoped this guy will get into it and settle down some.

Man, was I ever wrong.

So we tie up, and, thinking I need to settle the guy down, I kind of stiff him into a side headlock with the intention of taking him to the mat with a side headlock takeover. Well, as soon as I get him in the headlock he starts screaming all sorts of nonsense and throwing a ridiculous tantrum. "Lemme go! Lemme go! Lemme go! He pulled my hair, ref! He's hurting me!" So I muscle him over with the takeover so I can talk to him a bit, but he starts screaming and kicking and flopping around spastically like a fish out of water. I said to him, "Hey, man, come on. Let's work this some first," wanting to build the match up some before he starts trying to draw heat, but he was so busy acting a fool, he couldn't hear anything I was saying.

This went on for the rest of the match. We couldn't get anything going or work a single spot because this guy was so busy trying to be a villain out of Laurel and Hardy shorts. He couldn't work a single move or hold seriously without carrying on or completely overacting. Fans started booing and yelling, "Boring!" and "This sucks!" Needless to say, it was a terrible match, one of the worst of my career, and I felt terrible about it. But the sad part about it was, after the match, this guy thought he had done great! In his delusional mind, fans yelling, "This sucks!" was heat!

This guy is one of these rank amateurs who believe that because he's booked as a heel, he has to be a "bad boy" every single second he's in front of the audience. First of all, however, he wasn't being bad, he was just being obnoxious. And second of all, if you watch the performances of the greatest actors to ever portray villains in the movies, you'll plainly see that their villains weren't always bad.

Take the movie "The Godfather" as an example. Don Vito Corleone, the title character played by Marlon Brando, is a powerful, charismatic, and ruthless mob boss. He's the head honcho bad guy, the guy who strikes fear into the hearts of his rivals. Yet in the movie, the audience often finds him endearing. He's warm, charming, and full of a love of life. He's a good father (well, as good a father a mobster can be), loves his family, and enjoys playing with his grandson. But don't let all that Mr. Nice Guy fool you – when it comes time for mob business, this guy will cut your throat in a heartbeat. This is what makes a villain *real*, folks! Remember, as I've talked about before, even the most evil villain is still human. He's going to have dreams, hopes, weaknesses, soft spots, and people he loves and cares about.

Villains aren't always bad!

So too should this play out in pro wrestling. Heels should not walk out to a match and from the word *Go!* be acting evil. This is entirely unrealistic and poor acting. It is far better for a heel to come to the ring, ready to wrestle a match and confident he's going to handily defeat his opponent. So it stands to pure reason that during much of his match, he's going to *just wrestle!* He's not going to protest or complain or resort to dirty tactics straight out of the gate.

A heel should only turn to dirty tactics when it starts becoming clear to him that he might lose the match. It's his last resort. That's what separates him from the babyface. The babyface won't stoop to using dirty tactics – he's out there to win or lose fair and square no matter what. The heel, on the other hand, is only about winning. He'd much prefer to win cleanly – as winning cleanly bolsters his image and feeds his ego – but if push comes to shove, he's perfectly willing and able to resort to a low blow or a finger to the eye to save his skin.

It's like that kid you used to play "Monopoly" with when you were little who would always try to cheat whenever you got the upper hand. That kid would much rather beat you honestly if he could, but if he started to realize that you're building up a nice string of properties with hotels on them, he'd start stealing from the bank when you weren't looking or try to put two houses on a property when he only paid for one.

Now I ask you, what are adults but grown up kids? If a person lies and cheats as a kid, oftentimes – not always – but oftentimes, that person lies and cheats as an adult. A person's character is formed at a very young age; so unfortunately, the world is just full of liars and cheaters. But the key lesson to take away is that in the real world, liars and cheaters aren't *always* liars and cheaters. Typically they only lie and cheat when their back is up against a wall.

So, too, should be the case for pro wrestling heels. Remember, pro wrestling is art that imitates life. Make it imitate life as closely as possible, and you'll put on shows that really have an impact on people.

All dirty tactics don't have to be illegal

Low blows, eye gouges, hair pulls, kicks to the crotch, chokes, foreign objects, outside interference – all par for the heel's course nowadays. And I'm here to tell you, believe it or not, that it's terribly unfortunate. Heels way, way, way overdo it with the illegal activity these days, so much so, that when it happens, fans barely even notice. Fans react to an eye gouge or a jab with a foreign object about the same as they do a punch or a clothesline. Heck, if a clothesline is done well enough, you can probably get a bigger reaction from it than a low blow or an eye gouge. Fans have become numb to it all, as if it's no big deal at all that a wrestler wins by doing something illegal. But now I ask you, how realistic is that?

Yes, competitors in other sports sometimes engage in illegal tactics – like Mike Tyson biting Evander Holyfield's ear in 1997 – but such occurrences are extremely rare, and when they happen, they're a *big* deal. Tyson biting Holyfield's ear is a perfect example. That was so outrageous, people are still talking about it today. And the rarity of such occurrences is what makes them so shocking and so dramatic. The problem with pro wrestling is, these things happen in *every…single…match!* They happen so frequently, people don't care. Fans think, "Yeah, OK, this guy's the heel…OK, he gouged the baby's eye, fair enough…ha ha, the baby is staggering around…ahh, now the heel pulled his hair…ho hum…I wonder if the concession stand sells popcorn?"

Back in the golden days of pro wrestling, if a heel like Cowboy Bill Watts, Ole Anderson, or Harley Race used an illegal tactic, the audience would get riled, enraged, and downright ugly – in some places, riots broke out! That's how well these guys could play the audience. One of the key reasons why they held that kind of sway over their audiences is that they didn't use illegal maneuvers in every…single…match like wrestlers do today. When they did something illegal, it was a big deal.

Now you might be thinking, "But Norm, how's a heel supposed to draw heat and establish himself as the bad guy if he's not allowed to use illegal tactics?" The answer is simple: Not all dirty tactics have to be illegal.

There's a host of tactics open to a heel that are perfectly legal but still downright dastardly. The key to making a legal tactic dirty is either a) using it as an easy way out or b) making it seem cowardly. Brave men go toe-to-toe against their opponents. When two brave men square off in a fist fight, one says, "Bring it!" and the other says, "All day long!" and then they start swinging away, exchanging blow for blow. The last man standing is the winner. Such a showdown is pretty easy to imagine. You see this sort of thing in the movies all the time.

But now imagine the same situation – both men have squared off and have their fists up, ready to go. The first guy says, "Bring it!" and the second guy says, "All day long!" So the first guy moves in to start slugging away, but then the second guy, instead of wailing back, kicks the guy in the shin, dropping him to his knees. Then while his opponent is vulnerable and off his feet, the second guy starts punching away upside his head. Now, was there anything "illegal" about the second guy kicking the first guy in the shin? No. But was it cowardly and dirty? You bet!

Now how do you apply this to pro wrestling? Easy. Just take any situation where the babyface has the upper hand and is on fire and then have the heel do something "cheap," like after the babyface has taken the heel down with a string of arm drags, have the heel do a quick single leg pickup and then drop into an ankle hold. See how that works? It's perfectly legal but "cowardly" in that instead of confronting the baby face-to-face in a hot spot, he instead pulls the plug on it and drops into a rest hold.

Here's another example: Let's say your two wrestlers are really going at it, exchanging stiff punches, and the baby gets the upper hand. Where they were exchanging punch for punch, now the baby is landing two for the heel's every one. So the heel gets backed into the corner, and the baby really starts laying into him. The heel covers up, and the baby is just pounding away at him. So the heel quickly bends over and launches his shoulder into the baby's midsection, doubling him over. The heel then seizes the opportunity by grabbing the waistband of the baby's trunks and catapulting him out of the ring.

It's simple, really. Just coach your heels to take some punishment and then go down low. The tactics they use don't have to be illegal; they just have to be evasive to be dirty. Now mind you, I'm not professing that heels should *never* use illegal tactics. That's not what I'm saying at all. What I'm saying is, great discretion should be exercised when using them. The use of an illegal tactic should *only* be used if it advances a well thought out and well planned angle. They should not be used at the drop of a hat. Think creatively. Think outside of the box.

The Book of Don'ts

Moses and the Stone Tablets

According to the Book of Exodus, there was a great man named Moses who led his people, the Hebrews, out of slavery in Egypt and into the desert to freedom. They wandered about the desert for a while, searching for a land promised to them by God, but wound up at the foot of a mountain named Sinai. Moses went up to the top of Mount Sinai to pray for guidance, and God gave it to him by carving out a set of stone tablets from the side of the mountain. On those tablets were ten rules the Hebrews were to obey. We know those rules today as the Ten Commandments.

God made it pretty easy on us by carving out just ten rules for us to follow. In this chapter, I present indie pro wrestling's commandments for better matches, better shows, bigger success, improved respectability, and greater profits. The only problem is, there are a heck of a lot more than ten! It's a good thing we have paper now instead of stone tablets; otherwise I'd need a wheel barrow to deliver them to you. Pay close attention to what I have to say in this chapter. Hopefully you've been paying close attention this entire time, but in this chapter, the rubber really hits the road.

Let's get this party started by discussing the first commandment: You are an athlete.

Don't forget: You are an athlete

You are not a clown. You are not a comedian. You are not a stooge. You are not a joker, fall guy, village idiot, jester, comic, cartoon character, buffoon, superhero, klutz, fool, or chucklehead.

Above all else, first and foremost, you are an athlete, and your chosen sport is a full contact combat sport. You shalt not do anything that compromises or discredits that.

What do I mean by "compromise" or "discredit"? Think about it. As you develop a gimmick or build up an angle, you start by saying, "OK, I'm an athlete. Would an athlete do *X*?" If the answer is no, then you don't do *X*! For example, suppose you're considering developing a gimmick where you're a zombie with undead supernatural powers. You plan on painting your face white and coming to the ring with fake blood oozing from your mouth. OK, would an athlete in boxing, UFC, or pro football portray himself that way? No? Then don't do it! It's stupid!

Let's take another example. Suppose you're considering a gimmick where you're a paroled (?!) death row inmate. So you plan to wear a prison jumper to the ring. For added effect, you think wearing leg chains and handcuffs like Hannibal Lecter would be cool. You'll have someone wheel you to the ring on a hand truck and even have someone unlock the chains and cuffs to allow you to wrestle the match and then lock you back up once the match is over. Think this is a good idea? Well, again, let me ask you – would a boxer, UFC fighter, or football player do this? No? Then it's an open and shut case – it's stupid. Don't do it.

Let me make this perfectly crystal clear – doing gimmicks like these causes grievous harm to the sport and business of pro wrestling.

Put even simpler, I've said it before and I'll say it again: *This drivel is killing pro wrestling.*

Stop it!

I touched on this subject in Chapter 3 when I discussed taking out the trash. I also mentioned the fact that many people disagree with me on it – and you might still be one of them. You might be saying,

"Norm, without characters, wrestling would be boring. No one would watch." And you know what? You're right! If every wrestler was some vanilla, no-personality, no-backstory guy, you're 100% right – wrestling would be boring and no one would watch. But notice I said "characters" and not "gimmicks." There's a big difference. A character is just that – a character with a history, personality, and an identity. A gimmick, on the other hand, is also just that – a gimmick. And you know what the definition of the word "gimmick" is? Well, according the Random House dictionary, it's, "To equip or embellish with unnecessary features, especially in order to increase salability, acceptance, etc." Notice the key word in that definition: *Unnecessary.*

Gimmick characters are exactly that – unnecessary. Think about it. So many gimmick characters can easily be salvaged if you think more about *character* and less about *cartoon.* For example, let's say you're developing your run-of-the-mill cowboy gimmick character, complete with the cowboy hat, riding gloves, leather vest, chaps, cowboy boots, branding iron, and bullwhip.

All right, let's apply the litmus test. Would a UFC fighter or boxer come to the ring dressed this way? No? OK, then according to this commandment, we have to throw it out, right? But we don't have to throw it all out! Why not throw out everything except the cowboy hat? Instead of portraying some silly, unoriginal character out of an old John Wayne Western, why not portray a "Don't mess with Texas" tough guy Texan? You don't need the branding iron, bullwhip, or riding gloves to portray such a character. And can you imagine a boxer or UFC fighter wearing a cowboy hat? Of course! People wear cowboy hats all the time, especially people from Texas.

You can run this exercise with almost any outrageous gimmick character and transform it from a cartoonish caricature to a realistic, dramatic real world character. Don't believe me? Let's take the death row inmate I used just a few paragraphs ago. Instead of just going completely over the top, amp it down. Instead of going with the ridiculous death row guy in the prison jumper and the leg irons, why not develop a character who made mistakes when he was younger – say he got caught stealing cars – and did some time in prison? But now he's out and ready to turn over a new leaf. He's ready to prove to the world that he's a good person and he'll do whatever it takes to reach his goals. That's a perfectly realistic character that, if done right, the audience can easily identify with and get behind.

Whatever, you do, though, remember – you are an athlete. Portray yourself as one.

Don't play hot potato with the belt

I go to a lot of indie pro wrestling shows. I mean, a lot. One thing I see way too much of (among many other things) is promotions playing hot potato with their title belts. What do I mean by hot potato? I mean, "Here, you're the champ this week. Next week, it's Jimmy's turn." Don't do this! Titles changing hands at the drop of a hat is a very bad thing for any promotion. The promotion's champion is like its president. Just as Americans wouldn't like the idea of a new president every few months, pro wrestling fans can't stand the notion of a new champion being crowned at every show.

I know why this happens so much in the indies. Part of the reason is that bookers think it's exciting to see the title change hands, but the *real* reason is locker room politics. If you've been around indie pro wrestling for any length of time, you know what I'm talking about.

Locker room politics is pro wrestling's version of office politics – workers weaseling their way around or kissing the boss' butt to get ahead. You put the belt on one guy and ten other guys start bellyaching that it's not fair and it should have been them who got to wear the strap. Never mind that the whole thing is a work. Pro wrestlers want belts, even if it's all just an act and a belt is just a prop, so if you allow them to, they'll beg and wheedle and cajole their way to a title reign. And if they get denied a title reign, they'll start talking behind your back about what a jackass you are, how your promotion sucks, and how you don't know anything about the business. So a lot of promoters try to stave this off by rotating the belt around frequently so that everyone gets a chance to hold it for a little while.

The problem with this strategy is, fans don't like it! And that's what matters most! Your primary job as a promoter is not to keep the boys in the locker room happy, it's to keep your *paying customers* happy!

You don't have to look very far to see how true this is. Just think about the golden eras of pro wrestling. You'll notice that pro wrestling enjoyed its highest ratings and highest attendance numbers when one guy held the belt for a long, long time. Hulk Hogan held the WWF title from 1984-1988. Ric Flair held the NWA title between 1984-1991. Sure, he dropped it a few times to big name contenders to keep things interesting, but in almost all cases, he won the title back within a month. Thus, defeating Hulk Hogan or Ric Flair for either title was a *major* event. It was a big deal. People got stoked about it. Those matches are unforgettable.

Conversely, when you allow your title to trade hands from show to show, fans never get used to any one guy being "The Man." Parity rules supreme, as everyone's on the same level, and who wants to watch a sport with so much parity? Just imagine if every single team in the NFL either went 7-9, 8-8, or 9-7. Boooooring! Every team would be the same. There would be no big winners or big losers. There would be no 2007 New England Patriots going 16-0 in the regular season, only to lose in the Super Bowl. There would be no 1985 Chicago Bears to go 15-1 and win it all. There would be no 2008 Detroit Lions to go 0-16 and be the laughing stock of NFL history.

The same holds true for pro wrestling. Pro wrestling fans want big winners and losers, not guys who win a title one week and then lose it the next week and then win it back the following week. Pick a guy who can carry your promotion, put your belt on him, and then push him to the moon. Remember, not everyone can be the champion. And also remember, it's a work! A pro wrestling champion is only playing a role in a show – he's not really a champion! It's not like he's actually won something in a legitimate sporting event. It's all a work.

It's like a TV show. Every TV show has a main character and supporting characters. Not everyone can be the main character. On "Seinfeld," Jerry was the main character and George, Elaine, and Kramer were all supporting characters. Had the producers of that show decided to mix it up and make Kramer the main character, well, the show wouldn't have been "Seinfeld," now would it? The same holds true with wrestling. Pick a guy, push him, and stick with him.

Don't undersell your title matches

Speaking of titles and the Super Bowl, one thing you should *always* keep in mind is that a match for your main title is *your* Super Bowl; hence, it should always be presented as such. What I mean by this is, you should present your title match as a very, very big deal. It should be the main event of main events. Again, look at any other sport and how they treat their championship events. Regardless of whether it's the Super Bowl, the World Series, or the Stanley Cup, there's all sorts of hoopla, fanfare, and buildup for the event.

When the NFL stages the Super Bowl, the teams don't just run out onto the field, play the game, hand over a trophy, and then run back to the locker room! Oh no, no, no! When the NFL stages the Super Bowl, it's a week-long event! There are interviews, investigations, analyses, in-depth looks, prognostications, and parties for the entire week leading up to the game. Then leading up to the kickoff, there's fireworks, dancers, big band performances, an Air Force flyover, and last minute player updates. Then after the big game there's the grand trophy presentation, champagne, confetti, balloons, more interviews, and formal congratulations all around. In other words, the NFL lets the whole world know, "Hey, this is the *Super Bowl*, people! This means something!"

Quite clearly we can't come anywhere close to this type of hoopla and production. However, we should still send a clear message to our fans that a title match is a big deal. How? Easy – build up and follow up. You start with the buildup. When you're getting ready for a title match, you should start planning and plugging it *months* in advance. Let's say the title event will be on May 1. Starting *at least* in December, you start building up a feud between the champ and the challenger. You have the feud build up to a boiling point. Then during your March show, you make the "big" announcement: "Fans, it's official! We've just gotten word that on May 1st, Red Myers will defend his title against the challenge of Tommy Strong! The contracts have been signed, so, fans, get your tickets *now*!"

At your next show you plug the match some more, stressing how big and important the match is going to be. Do an in-ring interview of both the champ and the challenger. Then when the day arrives for the match to go down, make a big to-do about it: "This is it, fans! Tonight's the night. Tonight's the night you will see this two men face off for the biggest prize in Acme Pro Wrestling!"

Give your fans a damned good, long match, and when it's over, follow up. Get in the ring and do the post-match interviews. If the babyface won the match, have the other faces come to the ring to congratulate him. You can even give out party favors to the fans *before* the match so that now that the baby has won, they can be tossing confetti and streamers into the ring! Make it a big deal!

Don't book impromptu title defenses

Coming right off the heels of the previous section where I stressed the importance of making a title match a big deal, I now want to make this next commandment very plain: Do not book impromptu title defenses! I repeat – do *not* book impromptu title defenses!

Damn, I hate this. I mean, I really, really hate this. Nothing cheapens a title more than having some yahoo come out from behind the curtain and lay a challenge down right on the spot, like this: "Hey, listen here, punk – if you want a shot at this belt, you got it…right now!" and then they jump in the ring and start wrestling for it. I absolutely despise this angle. Never, ever do it!

Equally as abominable is the cheap angle where at the start of the show, the heel champion is being interviewed when the promotion's "commissioner" comes out unexpectedly and says, "Listen here, Red. You've been talking a lot of smack. So guess what? You're defending your title against Tommy Strong *tonight!*" And of course, the heel champion then flies into a ridiculous temper tantrum, kicking the bottom rope and stomping his feet.

Grrrrrr! Do *not* do this!

Would Roger Goodell, the commissioner of the NFL, ever run down to the field before a regular season game between two big division rivals, grab a microphone, and say, "OK, you two teams have the best records in the NFL! You're both undefeated! So guess what? Tonight's the Super Bowl! That's right! Screw February! Screw the playoffs! We're awarding one of you two teams the Vince Lombardi trophy *tonight!*" I mean, really, how stupid would that be? It's so stupid, it's hard to even imagine it. Right now you're thinking, "Oh that's ridiculous. The NFL commissioner would never in a quadrillion years do something that stupid." And you're right! He wouldn't! It would never happen. So why does it happen at almost *every...single...pro...wrestling...show*?!

Remember, a title match is a big deal – a super big deal. It's an honor for the challenger. It's a "big payday" for the champion. Title defenses are rare. Thus, landing a shot at the title should be like getting a role in a movie, landing a book deal, or signing a record contract. It's something to celebrate. It's something to prepare and train for. It's not something that gets awarded arbitrarily here and there, at the drop of a hat.

Doing that cheapens the title!

Don't let the inmates run the asylum

Along the same vein of impromptu title defenses are pro wrestlers who decide for themselves who they'll wrestle or who they'll defend their title against. Even worse is that tired old angle where a pro wrestler somehow is named "commissioner" or "president" or whatever of the promotion. Stupid, stupid, stupid. I've seen more promotions do this than I can count. Heck, for a stretch, it seemed WCW was doing this every week. First, JJ Dillon was the commissioner. OK, fair enough – he's a distinguished guy in a suit. But then Bischoff became the boss. Then somehow Roddy Piper was boss. Then Ric Flair became "president." Then Vince Russo became the "Powers that Be." Then WCW got canceled.

OK, so this was an epic failure, and anyone with half a brain should have been able to realize that it was a very bad idea from the very get-go to have so many ridiculous leadership changes. But evidently no one working for TNA has half a brain, because they've been repeating the same idiocy! First they had Jeff Jarrett, then Larry Zbyszko, then Jim Cornette, then Kurt Angle, then Mick Foley, and now Eric Bischoff! Hey, who says a ship full of holes won't float? Just because WCW tried it and the boat sank as soon as it was launched, that doesn't mean the same thing will happen to TNA!

Folks, don't fall into this trap. Allowing a pro wrestler or manager to become "the boss" in kayfabe is a really crappy story angle to begin with. Then the damage it does to your promotion's credibility is just too much to bear. Wrestlers are athletes. They are the players. They are *not* the boss. Keep it that way. If you want to have a figurehead commissioner in kayfabe, that's fine, but don't pick a wrestler or any other active personality to fill the role. Pick an old, distinguished guy in a suit. Pick a retired wrestler, your grandfather, a stage actor, or whoever, but do not appoint a wrestler! Again, would the NFL appoint an active player like Cam Newton or Chad Ochocinco as its commissioner? For crying out loud, no. That would make the NFL a farce. Don't do the same thing to your promotion. Take control. Don't let the inmates run the asylum.

Don't let Internet trolls manipulate you

While we're at it, don't let the fans run the asylum, either! Within the past ten or fifteen years, pro wrestling has had a terrible tendency to pay too much attention to crap posted by fans on the Internet. One guy here says, "This show sucks!" and boom, the promoter's making a change. Remember, opinions are like tax burdens – everyone has one. Back in the day before the Internet, people had the same opinions they do now. The only difference is, they didn't have a forum to say it in back then. It doesn't matter what you do, someone is always going to hate it. That's true with everything in life. The key is not to allow those vapid opinions guide your way. *You* guide your way! It's your show!

It's like running a restaurant. A well run restaurant has a head chef who decides what's on the menu. Now I don't care how good the restaurant is – it could win every award there is to win – there's always going to be some jerk who walks out saying, "I didn't like it. There was too much butter in my mashed potatoes." Do you think for one minute that if that complaint got back to the head chef that he'd immediately change his recipe for the mashed potatoes? Hell no! Why? Because he knows that for every one jerk who doesn't like his mashed potatoes, there are a thousand other people who do. And if he changed his recipe to make that one guy happy, he'd end up making a thousand other patrons unhappy.

Don't get me wrong – I'm not saying that you shouldn't listen to your customers. Any business person who's so arrogant that he doesn't listen to his customers won't be in business very long. The key is to know whether or not a complaint is isolated or if many people are saying the same things. If one guy leaves your restaurant saying, "The mashed potatoes sucked," that's nothing. But if fifty people leave saying that, you have a problem.

So how do you know the difference? After all, a handful of people all saying the same things can make a heck of a lot of noise on Internet forums. You can easily be led to believe that fifty people are complaining about your mashed potatoes when it's really only two or three. Well, to find out, ask yourself the following questions: How is my attendance? Are there lots of empty seats? Is my attendance going up, staying steady, or declining? How's my bottom line? Am I making money from each show or am I taking a loss? If people are coming to your shows, you're filling the house up, and you're bringing home a profit, you must be doing *something* right. But if you're only bringing in a marginal profit or if you're not meeting your profit goals, a change is in order (which, incidentally, is the premise of this book).

Be aware that fans tend to be armchair quarterbacks. They talk big but usually have no idea what they're talking about. And that's OK – everyone is entitled to his or her opinion. They'll even jump on a message board and say, "Well, if I were running that promotion I'd make so-and-so the champ and do this-or-that…" Again, that's fair enough. Opinions are great. However, you need to understand that despite how much fans act like they want to run the show and decide what happens, they really don't.

Fans don't want to tell the story; they want the story told to them. Do you think the people who went to William Shakespeare's plays wanted to tell the story? No! They wanted Shakespeare to knock their stockings off with one of his awesome stories. Do you think Stephen King's fans want to tell him how to write his next horror novel? Oh, sure, they hop onto Internet forums left and right and babble on and on about how they could have written a better ending to the *Dark Tower* series, but would they *really* want to? Absolutely not. Fans want to be entertained. They want to be dazzled. They want a master storyteller to spellbind them and take them on a journey into another world. They don't want to do the work, because that wouldn't be entertainment, now would it?

So don't let fans run the show. Don't make sudden, ad hoc changes to your promotion just because a few blowhard smarks start talking smack on Internet forums or on Twitter. You're the boss. It's your show…and your business.

Don't be a slave to the pop

There is nothing more musical to a wrestler's ear than a good pop from the fans. It's what we all strive for. Getting a pop is equivalent to a theater actor getting a standing ovation or band hearing, "Encore! Encore!" once the curtain has dropped. In pro wrestling, there are two things that measure success – a pop and the gate. Typically good pops equate to good gates, so it stands to reason that pro wrestlers endeavor for as many big pops as possible.

But this is a mixed bag, especially today. Wrestlers have become so eager to generate a pop, they've become slaves to it. They spend their entire match trying to push the envelope, trying to one up the guys who wrestled in the match before them, trying to keep the fans making noise. It becomes a vicious cycle, like the cocaine addict who starts snorting cocaine so he can work harder and longer but then becomes a slave to the drug and eventually winds up losing his job.

Being a slave to the pop is very similar. Pro wrestlers push the envelope to get a pop, and if they get one, they push the envelope further and further and further. Soon, though, fans become bored and disaffected, because matches become nothing but dizzying, unexciting spotfests. And then once the cheers fade away, wrestlers believe they have to push the envelope further to recapture the audience, so they're jumping from balconies, breaking fluorescent light tubes over each other, power bombing each other through stacks of tables, and taking suicide dives off the tops of cages.

All of this is the result of allowing the fans to call the shots. Wrestlers wrongly believe that if fans aren't on their feet and screaming every second of the show, they're doing something wrong. But that isn't the case. Remember, as a pro wrestler, a large part of your job is to work the crowd, *not the other way around!* You pull their strings, they don't pull yours. And the key to pulling their strings is by giving them excitement in very controlled doses and at unexpected times.

There's a reason why it's called a *high* spot. It's because a high spot is one of the high moments of a match. A high spot is like a fifty yard touchdown pass, a grand slam homerun, or a game winning three point shot. You build up to it, the same way a football team builds up to that fifty yard touchdown pass with a series of four or five yard running plays. How do you build up to a high spot in wrestling? Simple – by wrestling, dummy! I'm talking side headlocks, top wristlocks, hammerlocks, standing switches, arm bars, and toeholds. A match full of high spots without traditional mat wrestling is like a football game without huddles. There's no tension, no buildup, no wonderment amongst the fans as to what's going to happen next.

I know what you're thinking – you're thinking that when you start to wrestle, fans will get bored. In fact, a lot of times when you take a guy down and put him in a reverse chinlock or an arm bar, some fans get antsy and start hollering, "Booooring!" Well, you know what I have to say about that? Who cares! So what if some bumpkin starts that nonsense? Again, it's *your show!* Just because that one troll can make a lot of noise doesn't mean that everyone else in the audience doesn't appreciate the mat action. Remember, a pro wrestling match is supposed to tell a story, and like we talked about in Chapter Three, every good story has a conflict, climax, and resolution. The mat wrestling is the conflict, the high spot is the climax, and the finish is the resolution.

More on this later.

The point is simple – the fans are there to be entertained, and you're the entertainer. It's your story to tell, your canvas to paint, your block of marble to sculpt. Just as Leonardo Da Vinci didn't allow common folk to dictate to him how he should paint the Mona Lisa, you shouldn't allow fans to dictate to you the pace or content of your matches. Again, it's *your* show, *your* match, *your* house. *You* tell fans when to cheer and when to sit down. *You're* in control.

Don't rush

You've probably figured out by now that I have lots of grievances against TNA. I openly admit it – I'm not much of a TNA fan. But if there's one thing that tops the list of things I don't like about that promotion, it would have to be how all its matches are rushed. I have never seen a promotion rush through its matches the way TNA does. I suppose it's by design, as TNA stands for "Total *Nonstop* Action." Maybe they mean that literally, that no match of theirs can ever have a slow moment. I watch a TNA match, and the first thing that comes to my mind is, "Damn, *slow down!*"

It's just move after move after move in rapid, spray and pray AK-47 machine gun style. It's dizzying, hard to follow, and entirely unrealistic. I mean, after all, a suplex is supposed to hurt, right? If yes, then how can guys so readily spring back up to their feet and be ready for the next big spot?

My point is simple – *slow down!* I mean, really, really slow down. Take your time. Allow the match to ripen naturally.

Here's an example. Suppose you're in a match against a decent opponent, and you decide to hit him with a vertical suplex. Let's also suppose the match has been going for a while…let's say fifteen minutes. Fifteen minutes into a match, you've probably broken a good sweat and are breathing fairly heavily. OK, boom, you hit the suplex. Now, a lot of young guys nowadays jump right up (almost spastically) and immediately try to hit their opponent with something else. *Wrong!* Instead, hit your suplex, and then take your time getting back up. Remember, pro wrestling is supposed to be a combat sport, so if you've been wrestling this guy for fifteen minutes, surely you've absorbed a lot of punishment up to now. So since you just hit your opponent with a suplex, the natural thing that would happen in a real fight is the guy who just gave the suplex would take a couple seconds to catch his breath. You should do the same.

Watch any of Ric Flair's classic matches (Flair vs. Bockwinkel, Flair vs. Steamboat) and you'll notice he does exactly this. Flair's best matches are considered among the most exciting matches of all time, and if you pay attention, you'll see he does exactly what I'm describing. He takes his time in between moves. He doesn't rush. He hits a move and then stands there for a moment, contemplating what to do next. It appears very realistic, because in a real match, you'd do exactly that. You wouldn't rush right into the next move – you'd take a moment to collect yourself and to be sure you weren't rushing into a trap.

Rushing from move to move looks sloppy and amateurish, especially when you're not sure of what move you're going to do next. A lot of young wrestlers allow their feet to move faster than their brains. That is, they hit a move like a suplex and then jump right up to attempt their follow-up move before they've even decided what that follow-up move is going to be! Further, when you jump right up and immediately move in for your follow-up move, oftentimes your opponent isn't ready, so you have to hesitate or back off until he is, which appears completely phony. You know what I'm talking about. Now that I've pointed it out, I'm sure the light bulb has gone on above your head – a young guy hits his opponent with a move, jumps right up and goes for the next move, but he's indecisive and his hands are jerking about, uncertain as to where they should go.

Stop, breathe, think.

OK, let's repaint the example, this time not rushing. You've been wrestling a decent opponent for fifteen minutes. You both have been exchanging various lead-up holds and a few punches and kicks here and there. So you're both a bit winded. You're not exhausted, but you are a bit winded and sweaty. You deliver a kick to the guy's gut, doubling him over. So you move in and hit him with a nice, sharp suplex. Now both of you are down on the mat. He's selling the suplex nicely. You roll over onto your side, breathing heavily. You study your opponent as he sells the suplex you just hit him with. You coolly stand up and study him some more. You do *not* move in towards him yet. Instead, you *stop, breathe,* and *think!*

"OK, what move am I going to do next? Let's see...his back is hurt since I just hit him with a suplex, so let's do a backbreaker!" So now you move in. Your opponent is ready, since you gave him a moment to get his bearings. You call the backbreaker and then hit him with it. You then immediately attempt a cover and he kicks out at two. OK...*stop, breathe,* and *think!*

What next? Well, he just kicked out of your pinfall attempt, so what's the next logical thing to do? Clearly he's not ready to be pinned, so you have to wear him down some more. So you put him in a reverse chinlock with your knee in his back to continue to sell the idea that you're working his back.

Now, don't misunderstand me here. When I say, "Slow down," I don't mean slow down the holds and moves. I mean slow down *in between* holds and moves. Nothing irks me more than wrestlers who dally right before or while performing a certain hold. Like these guys who are going to do a suplex who grab their opponent in a front facelock, throw the opponent's arm behind their head, but then before doing the move, they start dancing, acting silly, or calling out to the fans. Meanwhile, while the guy is wasting time and acting a fool, his opponent just hangs around, cooperatively, conveniently, and patiently waiting to take the bump.

Again, *silly*. If you're about to hit me with a suplex, why would I just stand there and wait for it while you shout out your catchphrase to the crowd? In a real fight I'd punch you in the stomach and say, "Let go of me!"

So the proper way to pace a realistic match is to execute your holds and moves themselves quickly and explosively, with snap and precision. *Pop! Bam!* Suplex! Then, in between holds, you slow down, pace yourself, take your time, and contemplate your next move, the way a good chess player thinks four or five moves ahead of his current one. This gives a match an extremely realistic look and feel because it doesn't look scripted or preplanned. It looks like you're actually contemplating what your next move should be.

Don't just stand there!

In the previous section I gave the example of a guy who sets up his opponent for a big move, but before he actually executes it, he wastes time by screwing around with the crowd or dancing a little jig. To a non-wrestling fan, this sort of thing is just plain ridiculous: "Oh, yeah, right," they think. "Like that guy would just stand there while the other guy's dancing."

Wrestlers just standing or lying around, waiting patiently for their opponent to perform some big, grandiose move is a serious problem that's reached epic proportions. Not sure what I'm referring to? Here are a few examples:

- A heel grabs a face after somehow knocking him silly and drapes his head over the middle rope. The heel then runs across the ring, hits the ropes, bounces off, runs back toward the baby, jumps through the top and middle rope but hangs on, causing him to boomerang back around, allowing him to kick the baby in the head. What's wrong with this? Easy – is the audience to really believe that the baby is just going to leave his head draped over the middle rope while the heel does all that acrobatic nonsense? In a real fight, if you're down and not knocked out, your survival instinct *always* forces you to get back on your feet. You don't just stay put wherever your attacker puts you so that he can continue to whip your ass.

- A babyface Irish whips the heel from one corner into the other. The heel does a Flair Flip (which, incidentally, is stupid enough on its own), but instead of flipping over the top rope and landing on the apron, the heel flips over the top rope and winds up *sitting* on the top turnbuckle! The heel then stays seated on the top turnbuckle, acting like he's asleep and waiting conveniently for the babyface to jump on to the middle rope behind him and back suplex him off. What's wrong with this? It's stupid, that's what. First of all, if you ran someone into a ring corner in real life, he would never in a million years flip upside down and then somehow wind up sitting on the top turnbuckle. And second, even if that one-in-a-billion thing did happen, the heel just wouldn't stay sitting up there, defenseless! He'd jump down. Never, ever sacrifice realism just so you can "innovate" a new move or spot. Never.

- The babyface kicks the heel in the gut, doubling him over. He conveniently stands perfectly still and perfectly doubled over while the babyface runs the ropes and then performs a scissor kick onto the back of the heel's head. This one may be the most common offender of the "Just standing there" foul. If you ever get kicked in the gut, yes, you would double over...and then quickly drop to your knees...and then quickly start writhing around in agony. You wouldn't just stand there perfectly bent over, waiting for your opponent to run the ropes and then do his signature move on you.

All of this crap stems from the desire of young wrestlers to "innovate." As I mentioned, the big problem with all this spotfest "innovation" is the fact that your opponent has to just stand there and take whatever punishment you're about to dish out, which simply does not happen in real life. The only time someone would just stay put is if he were knocked unconscious or was writhing in such terrible pain that he couldn't see the next thing coming. So this I say to you – innovation is fine so long as you keep it real.

The rule of thumb I want you to employ is actually very simple. Any time you're innovating a move or building a spot and in your head you hear your own little voice say, "Hmmm...that looks kind of fake," *don't do it!*

You know that little voice I'm talking about. It's that little voice you suppress by saying to yourself, "Yeah, but it's wrestling," or "Eh, fans won't notice that," or "Fans are willing to sacrifice some realism for pizzazz." You need to start really listening to that little voice! You know why? Because fans aren't stupid and they have little voices, too, that say, "Damn, that looked fake," and, "Wow, that was cheesy," and, "This is so phony, it's kind of embarrassing to watch."

You ever watch a movie that's really, really corny? A movie like "Anaconda," featuring an overgrown, poorly computer generated snake; "Kazaam," starring Shaq the basketball player as a genie; "Santa with Muscles," headlined by our very own Hulk Hogan as a guy who gets amnesia and then thinks he's Santa Claus; or "Indiana Jones and the Kingdom of the Crystal Skull," the 2008 stinker that brought us a 70-year-old Indiana Jones, a nuclear bomb-proof refrigerator, interdimensional aliens, and a flying saucer that emerges from under the Earth?

You know how you feel when you watch really corny movies like these? You feel embarrassed to be watching them. You ask yourself, "Why am I watching this? Who in his right mind would like this?" Then when it's all over, you say to yourself, "Damn, I just wasted two hours of my life on that." Well, I hate to say it, but I must: That's how many, many people feel when they watch pro wrestling. We're not going to grow our audiences by making potential fans feel like they're watching "Killer Klowns from Outer Space."

Missed a spot? Don't sell anyway!

Just as bad as working spots that require your opponent to sit still and just take the beating you're about to dish out is selling spots that miss. I can't count how many times I've seen a punch or a dropkick miss by a mile and yet the guy taking it sells it anyway. This really rears its head when a spot calls for a guy to go over the top rope. One guy is supposed to take a dropkick that sends him "flying" over the top rope. But the second guy mistimes the dropkick, missing by a light year. So the first guy, confused and startled by the fact that the guy missed, sells anyway by jumping over the top rope.

No!

Before I go on with the discussion of missed spots, let's first talk about the whole going-over-the-top-rope thing. What's with that? In 99% of cases, it completely defies physics, gravity, and logic. Think about it – if someone dropkicked you in real life, you wouldn't "fly." You would get knocked backwards, in which case, the ropes would catch you – which, after all, is what the ropes are for.

Same holds true for a punch. If you were in a bar fight and someone punched you, you wouldn't jump up and go flying over the bar! At worst you'd get knocked back and fall into the barstools. So the getting-knocked-over-the-top-rope thing is really, really unrealistic, and trust me, it looks that way from the audience's perspective, too. It adds nothing to the show, either, so don't do it. If you must do it, do it in a tag match where you can have one of your opponents pull the top rope down while your other opponent dropkicks you. That way you would logically *fall* (not fly) over the top rope.

OK, now back to the main point. If ever your opponent tries a move and misses, *do not sell anyway!* Do not sell at any cost! Guys who sell a move that misses typically do so because they just weren't expecting the move to miss and didn't know what else to do. So they panic. It's a lack of preparation for the worst. Remember, our military smartly runs exercises for just about every kind of disaster imaginable. They do so not because they want or even expect those to happen, but because they know they *might.* That way, if something bad does happen, our troops are ready and just react. The same holds true in this situation. Always be aware that any spot in a match can miss and be ready with an action plan for if it does.

Going back to the example of the dropkick that missed, if your opponent is supposed to hit you with a dropkick but misses badly, act like you dodged it. Then once the guy hits the mat, quickly put him in a rest hold. Talk it over, regroup, and try the spot again.

Don't beat up women!

This is the embodiment of sociopathic behavior. When did it become OK for a 250 pound, 6' 4" muscular guy to beat up on a 120 pound girl? I mean, seriously. I'll tell you where this all stemmed from, because it's a fairly recent development that I unfortunately witnessed.

Back in the middle 1990s, when Paul Heyman was trying to draw some attention to the fledgling ECW, he decided that it was anything goes. Blood, gratuitous violence, insane stunts…anything. Pro wrestling had never seen anything like it. At the time, the two big promotions, the WWF and WCW, were content to turn their shows into live action Saturday morning cartoons, so when ECW wrestlers started slicing each other open with box cutters, shooting each other with staple guns, throwing each other on thumbtacks, and setting each other on fire, a new audience took notice.

It was an audience of pimply faced, sociopathic, video game addicts. They were computer nerds who worked as telemarketers to support their gaming habit, chubby misfits who still lived with their Mom at the age of 25, comic book store losers who had never kissed a girl, much less gone out on a date. These were young Burger King and Radio Shack employees who were frustrated and angry at the world because it didn't recognize or appreciate them.

In a word, losers. And sure enough, losers like these repel girls, which, as you might guess, leads these guys to secretly resent women. So when

Sick: Seriously, now. Who in his right mind thinks stuff likes this helps our business? Who in his right mind would find this entertaining?

Paul Heyman instructed his wrestlers to start power slamming, punching, and piledriving the femme fatale Francine and Raven's evil valet Beulah McGillicutty, ECW fans were delighted and overjoyed. "Yeah! Take that, bitch!" they were secretly thinking as an attractive "mean girl" got dragged about the ring by her hair. They'd really get stoked when one of the girls – wearing a mini skirt, of course – would get grabbed and turned upside down for a piledriver. They'd get stoked not so much because the girl was about to get her head spiked into the mat, but because they got to see her skimpy underwear.

Just like everything else in the world of pro wrestling, since this got over once, it's been copycatted and repeated over and over and over again all over the country ever since ECW went under and it's unfortunately destined to continue for years to come. But, folks, this is just sick stuff, plain and simple. Call me a prude or a bleeding heart or a fuddy-duddy or Dudley Do-Right or whatever, but the fact is, it's wrong. It appeals to a very warped segment of society and drives ordinary, well-adjusted people away in droves. Really, who wants to take his kids, wife, or buddy from work who's not yet a wrestling fan to an event where women get beaten up, manhandled, and flung around like rag dolls?

In order for pro wrestling to recapture its widespread appeal, we need to exorcise it of all the sociopathic material that appeals only to those pimply faced nerds who quietly admire the Columbine shooters. If you're thinking about doing a spot or working an angle that isn't fit to be seen by your ten-year-old nephew, *don't do it!* This type of smut is a disgrace to the pro wrestling business, and it needs to stop.

Don't do hardcore

While we're on the subject of smut, I would be remiss if I didn't call for an end to hardcore – or "extreme" – wrestling. This is another abomination made popular by Paul Heyman that appealed directly to sicko teenagers that drove mainstream fans away in droves. Admittedly, when hardcore wrestling first really hit the scene in the mid-1990s, it was a phenomenon that catapulted a minor Philadelphia indie promotion named Eastern Championship Wrestling from obscurity to national prominence as *Extreme* Championship Wrestling. ECW was something no one had really seen before. It was shocking, and it tapped directly into people's natural morbid curiosity. But there's something about that lure that doomed ECW to its ultimate demise (and, incidentally, to the sad fact that it *never* turned a profit) – it wears off.

There's a great fish market in Pensacola called Joe Patti's. If you're ever in Pensacola and have a hankering for fresh seafood, I highly recommend you go check it out. But there's one thing about Joe Patti's you need to be aware of – it stinks like fresh fish. I remember one time I was there with my wife buying shrimp to grill for dinner that night and I asked the guy behind the counter, "How can you stand the smell of this place?" and he said, simply, "It wears off."

Such is the case with anything shocking, extreme, graphic, lurid, or gratuitously violent – it wears off, and that's exactly what's happened to hardcore wrestling. It's worn off. Once upon a time, fans were mesmerized by a guy getting power bombed through a table. So they bought more tickets. But then that quickly wore off, so then it became two tables. That sold some more tickets, but it, too, wore off. So then guys were jumping from the top rope through tables. That sold lots of tickets (and permanently injured lots of wrestlers), but eventually it wore off. So then guys were jumping off balconies through tables. But that, too, wore off. So then guys started smashing each other through window panes, shooting each other with staple guns, busting fluorescent light tubes over each other, setting each other on fire (briefly), lynching each other with barbed wire, and throwing each other from scaffolds.

It's amazing what some guys will do to get some attention, but you know what? Nowadays, no one really cares. I sit through indie events where guys get slammed through a table wrapped in barbed wire, and the fans sitting next to me yawn and get up to go buy a hotdog.

It's worn off! Fans don't care anymore! They've grown callous to it all. It's lost its effect.

But a bored crowd isn't the worst thing about hardcore wrestling; what's worst about it is the fact that it drives away potential new fans. Seriously, what thirty-something-year-old, reasonably successful guy with a wife and two kids and who goes to church every Sunday wants to go to an event where chubby grease monkeys bust fluorescent tubes over each other's head and cut each other's forehead open with barbed wire? It's just not something your typical God-fearing, Nautica-wearing soccer dad would want to take his ten-year-old son to see. He'd much sooner take his boy to something else – *anything* else. And considering the wide array of entertainment options available to Americans today, the very *last* thing pro wrestling wants to do is scare off potential fans. The entertainment market is just way too competitive today.

You know, while I'm on this topic, I have a few rhetorical questions to ask. Number one: Why is it that in every hardcore match there's always a baseball bat and/or a boat oar wrapped in barbed wire, but instead of the wrestlers using it to hit an opponent over the head and bust open his skull, they instead use it to scratch the barbed wire across their opponent's forehead? Number two: How come baseball bats, stop signs, boat oars, two-by-fours, glass panes, railroad spikes, and staple guns are legal, but hunting knives, machetes, and Samurai swords are not? And number three: How come if you hit someone in the head with a bat in a hardcore match he gets back up in, oh, five seconds, but if you slam him through a flimsy banquet table, he's finished and ready to be pinned?

All three questions have the same answer: Because hardcore wrestling is stupid. Enough already!

Don't oversell

Overselling is bad acting. And most guys don't even realize they're doing it. They think they're putting on a good show, when in reality, fans are rolling their eyes in disgust.

To best illustrate this point, let's do a little exercise. Right now, right after reading this paragraph, I want you to put this book down and do your best acting job of being sneaky. Yes, I'm serious – do it right now. If you're worried about your family members thinking you're crazy, go to another room and close the door. But then I really want you to do your very best acting job of being sneaky. Sneak your way from one side of your bedroom to the other. Put the book down, do it, and then come back. I'll wait.

Done? OK, great.

Now, let me ask you this – I bet you felt like you were auditioning to be the new Hamburglar, didn't you? I bet you were way up on your tiptoes, hands out to the side like you were walking a tightrope, head stooped, and looking side-to-side like you were doing Barry Darsow's old Repo Man gimmick.

OK, now I want you to do the exercise again. Only this time I don't want you to be sneaky, I want you to try to walk from one side of the room to the other without making a sound. Go ahead…seriously…I'll wait.

You see the point I'm trying to make here? In the first case where I told you to act "sneaky," you did just that – you gave it your best interpretation of what "sneaky" was to you. Maybe you didn't act like the Hamburglar, but I'm sure you understand where I'm going with this. In the first case I asked you to *act* a certain way; in the second case I asked you to *do something*. When you act like you're doing something, you're pretending. And when you pretend, it becomes very clear to your audience that you're faking. Academy Award-winning actress Helen Mirren once said that the best actors are dogs. Why? Because they don't act. They just do.

Remember, pro wrestling is acting, and to give the very best, most believable performance possible, you have to be a damned good actor, and the way to be a good actor is to *do,* not *act.* That's the lesson that B-grade actors haven't learned. It's also why those crappy movies on the SyFy Channel suck – the actors in them try to *act out* a scene rather than just *do* the scene. When a good actor is in a scene that calls for him to have a conversation over lunch, he does just that – he eats lunch and makes conversation with the actor across the table from him. He listens intently to what the other actor has to say, enjoys the food he's eating, and then responds naturally to the conversation. *That's* how you make a scene convincing! It looks real because it is.

An excellent recent example of this in action is the movie "Paranormal Activity." If you haven't seen that movie yet, make a run to the Redbox tonight and rent it – just don't watch it alone! It has a very simple premise – a young couple living in a California tract house become haunted by an evil spirit. If you were to just read the description of the movie on the back of the DVD cover, you'd probably just think, "Ahhh, been there, done that," but if you watch it, I guarantee you, you'll think differently.

The movie is terrifying because it's a) very simple and b) extremely realistic and well-acted. And why was it so well acted and realistic? Because the director didn't give the actors a formal script. Instead he just gave them a rough idea of what to expect and then just let them act out their reactions on their own. He unleashed the actors and let them do their thing naturally.

Now let's apply this directly to pro wrestling. In the world of acting, acting poorly or unrealistically is typically described as *overacting;* in the world of pro wrestling, acting poorly or unrealistically is *overselling.* Overselling is a pervasive problem in pro wrestling, and it stems largely from well-intentioned pro wrestlers trying to give the audience a good show. But the fact is, they're trying too hard. If you've been watching pro wrestling for any amount of time, I am positive you've seen hundreds of examples of what I'm talking about – a guy gets body slammed and as soon as he hits the mat, he bounces himself up off of it like he's on a trampoline, or a guy gets suplexed and then he flops around spastically like a fish out of water.

I always like the guys who take bumps that make them "sleepwalk," like the guys who take a bump from, say, a clothesline, and then immediately sit up, pretending like they're asleep or drunk, they shudder a couple times like they have the hiccups, and then they comically flop back down to the mat and spasm a couple more times. You've seen this. You know you have.

Fake! Phony! Cheesy!

This is a classic example of guys *acting* rather than *doing*. They probably have never gotten clobbered by a clothesline in real life before, so they don't know how to react to it. And to make the move look really "devastating," they really ham it up, but their overselling has just the opposite effect – instead of making the clothesline look devastating, they end up making it look like a joke. Again, folks, think logically when you sell a move. Think *realism*. If you were running full tilt, returning a punt on a football field, and out of nowhere a defender stuck out his arm and clotheslined you, would it knock you into a drunk, state of sleepiness where you spasmed comically or flopped about like a fish? No! If some guy clotheslined you for real on a football field, it would rip your feet out from under you and you'd lie on the turf, writhing slowly in pain.

The key to proper selling is to ask yourself the question, "If someone did this to me in real life, how would I react?" If someone punched you in a bar, would you turn your head with the punch, open your eyes up wide with a shocked look on your face, and then turn your face back towards your attacker so he can hit you again? Of course not! If you were in a bar and someone was just punching away at your head, your natural reaction would be to *close* your eyes (not open them wide), turn your ahead *away* from your attacker, and put your hands up to try to block the punches from hitting you!

So let's talk about properly selling both these attacks – the clothesline and the punch. If you're taking a clothesline, the proper thing to do is *bump*. And I mean *bump!* When your attacker sends you into the ropes, charge them, hit them hard, and ricochet off like a bullet. Then run full tilt back towards your opponent, and when you feel that clothesline hit your chest, *bump!* Throw your feet as high up into the air as possible and land square on your shoulders. Then *stay on the mat!* Writhe about slowly, side to side, with your arms crossed across your upper chest. Squeeze your eyes shut tight and grit your teeth like you're in agony. Maybe cough once or twice (but no more than that!). Pretend like you're a quarterback and you just got drilled by a linebacker. The key here is to stay on the mat and move very little. Remember, when someone gets hurt bad on the football field, you don't see them move very much. They writhe about a bit in pain a bit, but it's very limited. If you do this the way I describe, the fans in attendance will be thinking, "Is he really hurt? Maybe he really got hit!"

Getting the fans to think that you are really getting hit is even more important when taking a punch. Unfortunately the punch is probably the most oversold thing in the bump bag. For some reason, guys nowadays just don't seem to know how to take a punch. Again, ask yourself, "If this were real life, how would I react?" So if you were in a fight and somebody punched you in the face, how would you react? If you're not sure, watch some UFC or boxing bouts on YouTube. When a guy gets punched for real, he *closes* his eyes. This is an involuntary reaction to prevent the eyes from getting injured. He also puts his hands up over his face to try to prevent any more punches from landing.

With this in mind, let's say you're backed into a corner and your opponent is just wailing away at your head. Put your hands up in a mock attempt to "block" his punches. Don't just have your arms dangling uselessly by your sides. When you put your hands up to act like you're trying to block the punches, just be careful not to put them too high where your opponent inadvertently hits your hands and forearms. Next, when a punch "lands," don't turn your face away, drop your mouth open in mock shock, and then conveniently turn your face back to the starting position to receive the next blow. Instead, when a punch lands, *close* your eyes like you're wincing in pain and turn your head *away* from the punch. Keep blindly trying to "block" the punches with your hands as your opponent continues to just lay them in, bam, bam, bam!

Can't you just imagine this in your mind's eye? Doesn't it look realistic? You bet it does! I can just see a guy backed into a corner, trying desperately but vainly to block a mad flurry of punches. His head is turned away to the punches, but they keep on coming. It's just like how a hurt boxer gets pinned up against the ropes and tries futilely to block his opponent's assault. Then, boom! The dominant fighter lands a big right cross and the guy on the ropes is dropped to his hands and knees.

That's the way you sell! Remember, the goal is to make a move look devastating and realistic, not comical or burlesque. The goal is to sell without overselling.

Don't skimp on punches

Pro wrestling is a combat sport. As such, you should make it combative, and the best way to do that is with lots and lots of punches. Think about it – any time a fight breaks out, whether it's in a bar or in a prison, the fighters invariably resort to their fists to settle it. A fist is a man's most basic weapon. It's the weapon God armed him with to defend himself. So it only stands to reason that when a pro wrestling match becomes heated, fists should start to fly. I'm a big proponent of lots of punching in pro wrestling matches, and the biggest matches of history back that up. Look at any match that really packed the house and blew the roof off – Steamboat vs. Savage, Hogan vs. Andre, Steamboat vs. Flair, Austin vs. The Rock – and you'll see fists flying like popcorn in a Jiffy Pop kettle.

The key is to not go with the fists too early in the match. Let the heat develop slowly, gradually, and logically through tit-for-tat wrestling before having it break down to a fisticuffs. If the tension is built up right, really letting the fists fly will let the crowd's anticipation explode like the cork popping out of shaken champagne bottle.

Hulk Hogan, as I'm sure you know, was the master of this. Hogan was criticized for constantly using the same formula over and over again in every single one of his matches, but as they say, it's hard to argue with success. While Hogan's matches were arguably repetitive and predictable, fans would always go absolutely nuts every time he would "hulk up" and dish out a beat down to whatever heel he was feuding with at the time. So don't be shy with the punches. Dish them out back-and-forth. Let your babyfaces get the best of your heels in toe-to-toe slugfests and watch your fans gobble it up.

Don't employ drug addicts

Drug addiction is a terrible thing, and it's especially terrible for business. That said, it only stands to reason that if you're in the pro wrestling business, employing drug addicts or drunks is a bad, bad idea. People with drug habits, unfortunately, are undependable, unpredictable, and oftentimes desperate. Many hardcore addicts will do just about anything to get a fix, and this includes lying, stealing, and cheating.

And let me not forget to mention that addicts are ordinarily pretty easy to spot, and having addicts in your show makes a very bad impression on fans. It gives the show a seedy, sleazy feel and conveys the message that the only people you can get to fill out your card are dope fiends and meth heads. If your average, family-oriented fan decides to give your show a shot but then sees meth heads climb into the ring, you can rest assured he won't be back. To me it's just common sense, but considering how often I see guys who clearly have a problem in shows, this touchy subject is worthy of mentioning.

If you're a promoter or a booker and you know a guy has a problem, have a talk with him about his problem, but don't book him until he cleans up. And if you're a worker with a habit, do yourself a favor and kick it.

Don't let wrestlers touch the mic

All right – I know this may upset a lot of workers, but I haven't pulled any punches this far, and I'm not about to now. So as the title of this section reads, do *not* let wrestlers touch the microphone! If you're saying, "Whaaaaaat?!" right now, allow me to explain.

Clearly pro wrestlers need to do promos and interviews; there's no way they could develop their characters otherwise. However, during those promos and interviews, the announcer should be holding the mic! Again, think real sports. When the on-field correspondent goes over to interview the Indianapolis Colts star quarterback Peyton Manning after a big game, do you ever see Manning grab the microphone out of the interviewer's hand and just start talking about whatever he wants to talk about? No, of course not. The interviewer holds the mic and asks all the questions. The player's job is to answer them. The big networks do this deliberately to steer the player's comments to help tell the story of the game. Otherwise the player might just start babbling and ranting and talking smack about things that the audience has no idea about.

Sound familiar? It should, because that's exactly what pro wrestling promotions do at every single show. They hand the wrestler a mic, the wrestler haughtily steps through the curtain, climbs up into the ring, and starts ranting incoherently and boringly about nothing in particular. It's all, "Blah, blah, blah, I'm great, blah, blah, blah, I'm going to win the belt, blah, blah, blah, I'm going to kick his ass, blah, blah, blah, you need to respect me, blah, blah, blah..." And this continues until predictably, conveniently, and mercifully, another wrestler pops out from behind the curtain and interrupts him with his own brand of smack talk.

No, no, *no*: Don't let workers pick up the nearest microphone and start ranting. The microphone is the property of your ring announcer. Ranting wrestlers are boring.

Doing this is counterproductive in so many ways, but the two main reasons are that it's a) 100% silly and b) not a good way to advance your storylines. In the golden era of pro wrestling, master interviewers like Gordon Solie, Gene Okerlund, and Larry Nelson would shape and guide their promotions' angles by asking intelligent, leading questions. Instead of just handing a wrestler a microphone and letting him rant disjointedly, the interviewer would ask things that tied the story together neatly, like, "Last week you lost the title due to a questionable call by the ref. Do you think the league should hold the title up?" or, "The league has heavily fined your opponent for injuring your neck. Do you think that's enough or do you want to dish out some payback of your own?" or, "By winning last month's tag team tournament, you've earned a shot at the titles. Do you think you're ready to face the champions?"

You see how important this is and how it works? The interviewer is afforded the opportunity to recap the events of the last show to remind fans of what happened and to stress the fact that what happened in the past has a bearing on what happens in the future. The past is important; the entire angle from show-to-show has continuity. Moreover, the wrestler is not permitted to just rant randomly – he has to answer the question! And if his answer sucks or he starts to ramble, the interviewer can cut him off by just asking another question.

The difference is, by the interviewer holding the microphone and asking the questions, he controls the exchange. Give a wrestler a microphone and rest assured he's going to talk way, way, way longer than you want him to. On the other hand, when the interviewer holds the microphone and competently conducts the interview, your promotion has a realistic "sport" feel and angles are much easier for the audience to follow. Plus the whole rant-in-the-ring-that-gets-interrupted thing has been so terribly overused, it's become as dull as it is stupid.

Don't book gimmick matches

Three man dance. Four corners of hell. Item on a pole. Falls count anywhere. Empty arena. Mixed tag. Handicap. One arm tied behind the back. Indian death strap. Reverse battle royal. Lumberjack. Bra and panties. Tuxedo. Parking lot brawl. Taped fist. Boxer vs. wrestler. Beat the clock. Fans bring the weapons…

What do these all have in common?

They're all stupid gimmick matches.

Probably the most overused and entirely dull match is the three way dance (or triple threat or whatever other stupid name it's given). Think about it. What inevitably happens in a three way dance? One guy gets dumped out of the ring for a few minutes while two guys wrestle a singles match. Then the guy on the floor jumps in, dumps one of the two guys out of the ring, and then he and the other guy wrestle for a few minutes…until the guy outside the ring jumps in and dumps one of those two guys out…and so on and so on. This happens every…single…*time!* It's stupid and predictable. Just book a singles match, for crying out loud!

Then you have the plodding, uneventful, hard-too-watch falls count anywhere match. What ends up happening in this match? Two guys kind of just amble about the arena committing random improbable acts of violence on each other. And invariably, since they're not in the ring and they're wandering down an aisle or through a row of seats, at least half the audience in attendance can't see what's going on.

Then we have the ridiculous item on a pole or ladder match where there's some object high above the ring and the wrestlers have to fight to get it. First one to get it, wins. What ends up happening? The heel gets really close to getting high enough to grab the item, but because the babyface is out of position, the heel has to just stall and inexplicably not grab the item – even though he could easily do so at any time.

Gimmick matches are invariably boring and disappointing. Because the gimmick obviates the need for actual wrestling, a proper wrestling match can't be developed in a gimmick match. For example, in falls count anywhere match, the wrestlers can't do full bumps since they're not in the ring. So what do you get instead? Two guys lazily brawling where wrestler A casually leads wrestler B by the back of the neck, slams B's head against something, B sells it for a couple seconds but then grabs A by the back of the head and runs him face first into something else. Same thing holds true with those stupid strap matches – the strap gets in the way, so the two guys can't actually wrestle. So they just work a boring you-punch-me-a-couple-time-I-punch-you-a-couple times deal that always ends anticlimactically.

If you look at the greatest matches of all time, you'll see that none of them was a gimmick match. That's because gimmick matches suck. Now you may be scoffing at me again, thinking, "Come on, Norm, you need some variety!" but to that I ask you, when was the last time you watched a gimmick match that was great? I'll tell you when – never. Gimmick matches are just that, gimmicks. They're overhyped crap that sound deadly, innovative, exciting, brutal, or whatever, but when the match actually goes down, it sucks. So here's my guidance to you: Singles, tag, or battle royal.

Pick one.

Don't play offensive ring intro music

Let me let you in on a little secret: Not everyone likes the things you like. This holds especially true with music. Some people love country but hate pop. Some people love classic rock but can't stand grunge. So rest assured, whatever kind of music you like – whether it's big band, salsa, or modern jazz – there are plenty of people who despise it. This is even more true with niche music. For example, many people don't care much for rock; an even greater number of people hate punk rock. So it's safe to say, the more specialized a certain genre or subgenre of music is, the fewer people like it.

So it's no wonder that many, many, many people absolutely loathe music like hip hop and death metal. Not all of it, but a lot of hip hop is just downright vulgar. As a consequence, a lot of "regular folks" have been turned off by it and see it as the music of thugs and punks. Death metal, on the other hand, is that abrasive metal music where the lead singer screams into the microphone in a scratchy voice where it sounds like the guy is trying to sound like Satan. Granted, you might be a big fan of these types of music. You might think they're edgy, innovative, in-your-face, and on the cutting edge – and that's fine – but many "average Joes and Janes" just can't stand it. To them it's offensive and juvenile.

Now let me ask you this – you know when you go into a fun family steakhouse and they have music playing? Listen to what they're playing. They're either playing classic rock, southern rock, or country. Now, I ask you, would a family restaurant ever play death metal or hip hop? Absolutely, unequivocally, 100% no. Why? Because the owners of those restaurants aren't stupid. They know the patrons of their restaurants are the average Joe and Jane, and they don't want to offend their paying customers. So instead they play it safe by playing music that almost everyone can tolerate.

I'm shocked, however, by just how many indie pro wrestling promotions haven't learned this lesson. They blast vulgar, abrasive, and inappropriate music during each wrestler's introduction not because the fans like it but because the wrestlers think it's cool. But let's never forget that a promotion isn't about what the wrestlers like – it's about what the fans like.

Remember, a pro wrestling promotion is a *business*. Don't scare your paying customers away by assaulting their ears with gansta rap or deathgrind. I mean, *duh*!

Don't be vulgar

Many workers today look back on the WWF's "Attitude Era" and ECW's heyday of the middle and late 1990s with great fondness. They wax nostalgic whenever they lovingly recall the images of Stone Cold Steve Austin up on the middle rope, flipping off the fans, the Sandman guzzling beer out of a can, and Degeneration X doing the "crotch chop" and yelling, "Suck it!" into any available microphone. Without any doubt, these were heady days for pro wrestling; some people even consider this period as one of pro wrestling's Golden Eras. And you know, they might be right. But while this time was very good for the nationally televised promotions, it was one of the worst things to ever happen to indie pro wrestling.

Once again, you might be thinking I'm crazy. You might believe in the "trickle down" theory of pro wrestling – that is, when the big leagues are doing well, that prosperity trickles down to the little guys in the indies. Well, there may be some truth in that line of thinking, but in the case of the Attitude Era, it didn't pan out that way. It actually had the opposite effect – it was very good for the big leagues but was devastating to the indies.

Why? Let's talk about that.

As all true pro wrestling fans know, the 1990s gave rise to the infamous Monday Night Wars, where WCW and the WWF went head-to-head in an all-out blitz to outdo the other in television ratings and pay-per-view buys. ECW was in the mix, too, as a fringe element that was "reinventing" the sport. Meanwhile, "trash TV" was becoming hugely popular. Jerry Springer, Howard Stern, and Morton Downey, Jr. were scoring big in the TV and radio markets by airing shows that focused on foul language, dysfunctional guests, in-studio fistfights, and extremely lurid sexual relationships, particularly among family members. It was "shock entertainment," and it was winning big. Why? Because teenagers and young men all across America could tune in in the privacy of their bedrooms and get their jollies. If mom should pop her head into his room, a kid could quickly change the channel. The pro wrestling bigwigs at the time saw the popularity of trash TV and decided they could score big, too, by emulating it. So pro wrestling abandoned its mandate to be family-friendly and went straight for the young male demographic. That way they could score big on advertising from companies with products that appealed to young males with money to burn – video games, acne treatments, electronics, sporting goods, bodybuilding supplements, etc.

It worked. Young males tuned in in droves, and the WWF and WCW made money hand over fist. The indies, meanwhile, as they always do, mindlessly and robotically followed suit – they started doing the trashy, vulgar, shock value crap, too. They didn't really know why other than because it's what the big leagues were doing. What they failed to realize, however, is that big league wrestling and indie wrestling have completely different business models and thus, different target audiences. Consequently, very often, what's done in the big leagues will *never* work in the indies.

Think about it. Let's say you're Vince McMahon and you decide you want to go after the coveted young male audience. The young male audience is coveted because young males are dumb and impulsive and because they have parents with fat wallets. So you, Vince McMahon, decide to hire some really skanky girls from the local strip club to become "stars" on your show by performing all sorts of sexually provocative stunts. Sure enough, that draws the horny young men to watch your TV show. And remember, if mom or girlfriend pops her head in, they can easily change the channel real quick. So now you, Vince McMahon, have a huge audience of horny young men watching your trashy product week-to-week, and you're selling millions in advertising to companies that hawk video games, Axe body spray, and "Girls Gone Wild" videos. A young male sees that crap and either runs out and buys it with what little he earns from his Taco Bell job or just pesters his parents to buy it for him. So it's a very successful model – Vince dishes up some smut, young males tune in, and advertisers rake in the cash, prompting them to buy more advertising.

Now let's say you're not Vince McMahon anymore. You're Jimmy Podunk, the local indie pro wrestling promoter. Will the trash TV model work for you? Absolutely not. Why? Well, think about it. The two main profit avenues for indie promoters are admissions and concessions. *That's* where you make your money. So if you do like Vince did with the Attitude Era by injecting a bunch of whores, vulgarity, shock music, gratuitous violence, and sexual innuendo into your shows, do you think the pimply faced teenagers are going to show up? Heck no! Half of them aren't even old enough to drive, so they'd need their parents to drive them to the show. And as the parents get wind of what kind of show you're running, they're going to say, "No way you're going to that!" Plus, even if a few pimply faced dudes of driving age do show up, how much money is in their wallets? Not much, I assure you. Thus they have very little money to spend on hotdogs and boiled peanuts at your concessions stand.

A much better target audience for indie pro wrestling is the audience drawn to the NFL and Major League Baseball. Who are they? They're thirty-something men *and women* who enjoy going to clean, safe, and respectable sporting events so they can get into it the game and have fun rooting for their favorite team or athlete. These are people with good *jobs* who have *money* in their wallets and purses. These are people with *kids* who get *hungry* for hotdogs and cotton candy and *thirsty* for Coca Cola! These same kids tend to be under the age of ten who tend to beg their parents for t-shirts, caps, and action figures. So now, if your show is an "Attitude Era" show, do think for one minute that that couple with kids is going to stick around? Heck no! They'll take their kids to the high school football game or the movies instead.

This is how the Attitude Era grievously damaged indie pro wrestling. I saw a recent indie show where a young wrestler decided it would be funny to "hide" a plastic water bottle in his trunks right where his "family jewels" were, thus making an obscene fool of himself. When the referee challenged him about it, he said, "What? No, that's not a foreign object – that's all me!" Now, seriously, do you think people with families find this sort of sophomoric behavior entertaining? No! But too many indie promoters and workers have been too dumb and too naïve about business to stop and think, "OK, who do we really want to appeal to? Who do we want buying tickets?" Instead they've largely just been marks themselves who liked the crap they saw on ECW and the WWF and just decided, "Hey! That's so awesome! I'm going to do that, too!"

Too many indie pro wrestling promoters have been marks first, businessmen second. And I'm here to tell you, if we truly want to make indie pro wrestling mainstream and make it profitable, we need to switch that around. Again, like I said in the previous section, it's what the ideal fan wants, not what you want.

I'm going to talk a lot more about this in the upcoming chapter on marketing, but for now, remember, your target audience is adults with kids, not pimply faced teenagers. Get rid of the skanks. Get rid of the sophomoric frat boy humor. Get rid of the lurid angles and the foul language. Take out the trash!

6 | Back to the Basics

"Learn the fundamentals of the game and stick
to them. Band-Aid remedies never last."
- Jack Nicklaus, champion pro golfer

The essentials

I've been to lots and lots of indie shows over the years, and one thing has struck me too often – many guys clearly never learned the essentials of the sport and art of professional wrestling. This probably has a lot to do with what I wrote about in Chapter One of this book – that nowadays there are just too many chintzy pro wrestling schools and too many unqualified trainers. Or worse, many guys are just self-taught. They watched wrestling growing up as kids and then just "learned" how to do the moves on their trampoline in their parents' backyard. And the unmistakable end result is crappy wrestling.

I can spot a poorly trained worker a mile away and in about three seconds of watching him work. Further, many young workers not only don't know how to only perform the essentials, they don't know how to sell them, either. Thus, a lot of essential moves that can be used so effectively to build a match get glossed over or forgotten about all together.

A perfect example is the collar and elbow. I am shocked by how many guys can't execute or sell this most basic maneuver. Lots of young wrestlers rush through it as if it's just a necessity to bridge to a high spot, when, in actuality, you can tell an entire story with just a collar and elbow alone!

So that's what this chapter is all about – the basic essentials of pro wrestling matches, from pacing to performing to selling. I'm approaching this chapter under the assumption that you already know how to perform the basic mechanics of the various moves and holds. So I'm not going to teach you every in and out of each move from scratch. That's not the objective. I'm operating under the assumption that you have already learned the fundamentals of pro wrestling, so my objective is to teach you how to execute and sell the moves *correctly* and *convincingly*. So let's get at it, starting with a concept very near and dear to me – ultra realism.

The guiding principle: Ultra Realism

This is a subject I've talked and written about ad nauseam. I've talked with hundreds of workers about this concept, as it's what I believe should be pro wrestling's guiding principle. Put simply, make it look real! Make everything you do, every move, every reversal, every bump, and every sell look real. And when I say, "real," I mean *ultra*-real – so real that fans are left marveling, "I thought wrestling was fake!"

Ultra realism is the underpinning of everything I'm going to talk about in this chapter. Everything we'll go over, every bit of guidance, is aimed at making pro wrestling more realistic. We'll go over making moves more vicious, more hard hitting, more devastating, more convincing, more pronounced, and more leveraged all in the name of ultra-realism. If you endeavor to make *everything* ultra-realistic (and I do mean *every*thing), your matches and your shows will improve exponentially. Realism allows fans to lose themselves in the show, to invest themselves in the characters and in your stories, and remember – *that's* what sells tickets.

Think schoolyard when feeding

We talked quite a bit about feeding in the chapter on heels, but I want to touch on the topic again because feeding is one of those things that lots of guys are doing wrong, and when done wrong, feeding looks 100% phony baloney.

Here's how most guys feed. Let's say the babyface takes the heel down and the spot calls for the heel to feed the baby another quick arm drag. Most guys today feed the arm drag by getting back up to their feet with their back turned to the baby. They take a few over-the-top, stumbling steps like a bad actor playing a drunkard and blink a few times at the crowd, as if silently saying, "Duhhhh...what happened?" Then they abruptly turn to their right to face their opponent with a ridiculous, confounded look on their face. Then the baby locks in the arm drag and takes him over. There are three things wrong with this:

1. It looks absurd. As we discussed before, in a real fight, who gets back up to his feet without first turning to face his opponent?

2. It slows down what should be a lightning-fast spot. Think about it – you take the heel down with one arm drag. Then you get up and have to wait on him to get up, stumble around a bit, gawk stupidly at the crowd, and then *finally* feed the next arm drag. A spot like this is so much more exciting when it's, *bam!* takedown, immediately on your feet, and *bam!* another takedown.

3. The guy feeding the move has to take a forward roll from a standing, stopped position, flat on his feet. It's much better to be charging at your opponent and then feed the arm drag, as you can forward roll with a running start, which looks much more natural.

So how should you feed? Let's talk about it.

Remember, realism is our guiding light. You want the feed to be as realistic as possible. Imagine for a minute that you're in a fight on the schoolyard and the kid you're up against grabs you and throws you down to the dirt. The natural thing to do is immediately get back up so he can't pounce on you or kick you while you're down. OK, so you get back up. Now at this point, do you get back up with your back turned to the kid? Do you take a few seconds to say something stupid like, "Awww, that didn't hurt!" to the other kids watching on and then turn blindly back toward your opponent so he can catch you with a surprise punch in the face?

No!

If some kid throws you down into the dirt, 100% of the time, the first thing you do is whip your head around to get the kid back in your sight. *Then* you get back up to your feet and charge at him to make him pay for getting your new North Face fleece dirty.

The same rules should always hold true when you're feeding a move in a spot. Every time you get taken down, the first thing you do is look for your opponent. Do *not* stand back up blindly with your back turned to him! Spot your opponent, face him, get back up, and charge him with your left arm ready to feed the next takedown. Think *schoolyard!*

The back bump

The very first time I stepped through the ropes of a wrestling ring, it was to learn how to bump. Being nothing but a starry-eyed mark who dreamt of one day seeing his name (or stage name) up in lights, I was eager to learn how to bodyslam and suplex, not fall down. But I learned very quickly that the entire appeal of pro wrestling hinges on guys taking awesome back bumps. If you can't bump, you can't work, and the better you bump, the better your bookings.

The awesome *ka-boom!* of a properly executed back bump is music to my ears. It's the sound of victory. *Ka-boom* equals *ka-ching.* As such, it's critical that you learn and master the *proper* way to do it. Learning it is not difficult, but mastering it can be.

There are three keys to remember when performing the back bump – *high, square,* and *loud.* When I say, "high," I mean hit the mat high on your upper back and shoulders, not your lower back or backside. Hitting high makes the bump look and sound devastating; hitting low makes it look weak.

By "square" I mean land square on your upper back and shoulders, not to one side. Again, landing square makes the greatest, most awe-inspiring sound and is the least painful way to land. So, logically we can conclude that if you're landing high and square, you're sure to be *loud.* Remember, a bump should sound like a cannon going off, not like a shoe kicked off after a long day at work.

The art of the collar and elbow

Imagine a pristine, candy apple red, 1968 Camaro stacked with a 375 horsepower V8 engine…driven by your grandmother…to church. That's exactly what today's young pro wrestlers have done to pro wrestling's most foundational and visceral move, the classic collar and elbow tieup.

Too many wrestlers nowadays tend to give the collar and elbow "lip service." That is, they either approach it with a very soft, limp wristed touch or they perform it rotely as an irrelevant but mandatory transition into an opening spot. Oftentimes guys barely even tie up at all, and when they do, the collar and elbow lasts little more than two or three seconds.

In talking with countless young pro wrestlers, I've discovered that many guys don't know the origins of the collar and elbow or its significance. As such, they often don't know how to properly sell it. The hold predates both modern professional wrestling and has its origins in a bloody form of grappling known as – believe it or not – Collar and Elbow (C&E).

C&E originated in Ireland and was brought to the northeastern United States by Irish immigrants. C&E had very well defined rules that barred punching, biting, scratching, kicking, etc. It was often called "scuffling," as both men would shove and pull to jockey for the advantage. This is exactly what the collar and elbow in pro wrestling should look like – a physical struggle for leverage and the upper hand. A collar and elbow should look fierce and vicious. If you take your time, the collar and elbow can be a story all by itself.

But you have to execute and sell it correctly. Do it right, and you can generate serious heat in just the first few moments of your match. So here's how to do it right, step-by-step:

1. Start by assuming a south paw's fighting position – left foot back, right foot forward, hands up and open. This may feel a bit unnatural if you're right handed, so you might want to practice to get used to this. I also realize this may be a bit different from what some trainers teach, but bear with me.

2. While standing in the south paw's fighting position, the next step is a prolonged stare down. Think about this. Imagine two rams staring each other down in preparation to lock horns. Each one studies the other, waiting for a slight flinch or blink of the eye to make his move. Now, take that imagery and incorporate it into your collar and elbow. The stare down should last at least a solid 10 seconds.

3. Step forward toward your opponent with your left foot. As you're stepping forward, simultaneously "expand" your chest. Do this by pulling your shoulders back and squeezing your shoulder blades together.

4. Lean your head slightly to your right to avoid knocking heads.

5. Tie up. The tie up should appear sudden, violent, brutal, dramatic – and stiff.

6. Try to shove your opponent toward the ropes. Your opponent should do the same to you. When I say "shove" I mean *shove*. Don't pretend you're shoving – really shove him. Remember how I said the best acting occurs when you *do* rather than *act*? Well, this is the perfect example. And since your opponent will be doing the same back to you, clearly the stronger man will win. If you happen to be the man who loses and gets backed into the ropes, that's OK. Break clean, tie up again, and repeat this process.

7. As you're muscling your opponent toward the ropes, you should dip up and down for dramatic effect.

8. After you've repeated a few tieups like this, tie up one final time and *then* transition into your first spot.

So what I'm advocating here is what's commonly referred to as "going stiff." That is, you're injecting a spot of legitimate competition into your matches in the name of realism. Keep in mind, of course, that to do this, your opponent needs to be aware of it! Don't jump in the ring with a completely unsuspecting opponent and start trying to go stiff. The guy will be confused and threatened and will probably attempt to kick your ass for real. However, if you practice this method and use it effectively, it makes for one hell of a very good looking and realistic opening to any match, which sets the stage perfectly for everything that follows. The collar and elbow is the concrete slab that the rest of your match's skyscraper will stand upon. Do it right!

The top wristlock

Ahhh, the top wristlock – one of wrestling's oldest and most fundamental holds is also one of my favorites. It's such a logical and realistic hold and it transitions beautifully from the collar and elbow. To describe this lucidly, let's refer to the wrestlers as the attacker and the defender. The attacker is the guy executing the hold; the defender is the guy trying to block it and get out of it.

The hold typically comes out of the collar and elbow but doesn't have to. For simplicity's sake, let's discuss it out of the collar and elbow. The hold begins in the collar and elbow tieup with the attacker forcibly knocking the defender's hand off his left elbow. In a fluid, sudden motion, the attacker floats his left arm over the defender's left

while simultaneously sliding his hand forward from the defender's left elbow to his left wrist. The attacker then bends the defender's arm at the elbow, using his own left forearm as the pivot point. He then grasps his own right forearm with his left hand, thus completing the wristlock. The attacker should then forcibly position the defender's wrist slightly behind the defender's head. To make this hold look vicious and convincing, practice these finer points:

1. The attacker should always be either comparable in size or larger than the defender. This hold looks absolutely ridiculous when it's executed by a guy on a much taller opponent. Remember, the top wristlock is supposed to be all about leverage. A short attacker has no leverage in this position over a tall opponent.

2. The attacker should assume a very wide stance to maintain his balance. If you put this hold on someone for real and didn't spread your feet wide, it would be easy for the defender to just shove you a little and knock you off balance and thus free himself.

3. The defender should drop to one knee and grab his left hand with his right, giving the impression that he is desperately resisting the hold. Remember, in kayfabe the defender's wrist is being forcibly bent against itself, and that would cause anyone some serious discomfort. Just imagine if you had your forearm pinned to a table with your wrist off the edge and someone has pushing as hard as he could on your wrist. That's how to sell this hold.

4. Take your time! Work this hold for a while to make it convincing. If you're the attacker, never immediately transition into the takeover. Putting a guy into a top wristlock and then almost immediately taking him over is unrealistic and illogical. That is, you've got the guy in a painful hold, so why take him down immediately? Again, work the hold. Struggle back and forth. And right when it appears as if the defender is about to escape the hold, boom! Then you take him over. Remember, *every* move should tell its own story. Don't cut it short or undersell it.

Running the ropes

I hope by now you've gathered that I'm big on realism. Realism, realism, realism! I've preached this long and hard in this book up to this point, and I hope I've delivered the message loudly and clearly. In my conversations with many young pro wrestlers, I often try to impress upon them the importance of realism and why they shouldn't attempt corny, improbably moves that clearly require the cooperation of both men to pull off. Interestingly, the response I often get is, "Yeah, but what about [insert classic wrestling move here]?" Their assertion is, since some moves and holds in pro wrestling require fans to somewhat suspend their ability to disbelieve, *any* move or hold is fair game. If, for example, fans will accept, say, a standing German suplex, then they should be OK with a quadruple German suplex off the top rope!

Let me make something very clear: It is OK to stretch the imagination; it is *not* OK to insult the intelligence. There is a huge difference.

How does all that relate to running the ropes? I'll tell you how – running the ropes as a move walks a very fine line between stretching the imagination and insulting the intelligence. After all, how many times do you see guys get Irish whipped in a bar fight? How often do UFC fighters whip their opponents into the corner of the Octagon?

Never.

That's because whipping someone across any space – especially when there are no ropes involved – is impossible. No one would a) allow themselves to be whipped to begin with and b) even if you were able to somehow whip me, I'd just stop after two steps and turn around and punch you in the face.

Yet pro wrestlers have been Irish whipping each other for 100 years and fans have accepted it. Furthermore, so much of pro wrestling's most exciting action absolutely depends on the Irish whip. You can't have awesome, devastating clotheslines, back elbows, or running dropkicks without an Irish whip. It's absolutely indispensible. So the key with an Irish whip and running the ropes is to make it as realistic as possible so that it lands on the side of stretching the imagination instead of on the side of insulting the intelligence.

How? Well it all begins with backing the opponent into the ropes. When backing a guy into the ropes, the guy being backed should not just go along for the ride. I see this all the time, and it's just plain ridiculous. One should be *forced* into the ropes, not go willingly. As such, this sloppy crap where the attacker lightly puts his hand on the defender's chest and politely escorts the defender back to the ropes has to stop. The right way to back a guy into the ropes is from a deep front waist lock.

When done properly, this resembles a football player hitting a tackling sled. When football players are taught how to tackle, they're taught to hit the sled low, wrap their arms around the pad, and then drive the sled with short, choppy steps. They're taught to do this because this is what gains them the most power and leverage. It's how to tackle an opponent who doesn't want to be tackled. Same holds true in backing a guy into the ropes. The defender doesn't want to go, so the attacker has to *force* him.

So when sending a guy into the ropes, start with the waist lock. Forcibly back your opponent into the ropes with your shoulder. Your opponent, meanwhile, should actively resist you by trying to push back and by throwing some desperate forearm shots to your back and shoulders. Then when your opponent is against the ropes, release the waist lock, but then grab the middle rope and really press your shoulder into your opponent. This creates the illusion that you're really bending the ropes and storing up potential energy.

For this illusion to work, you have to give the impression that bending the ropes takes lots of strength. You want the fans to believe that the ropes are very tight and elastic, like a stretched rubber band. Then as you prepare to Irish whip your opponent, you should step waaaaaay back, lean waaaaaay forward, and then really heave your opponent off the ropes, like you're mountain climbing and you're pulling a buddy up from a lower rock. Then, as your opponent runs past, shove the guy with all your might, giving the appearance of adding momentum. He should then run *full tilt* towards the opposite side. He should then turn his back and fully lay into the ropes, bending them as far as possible. He should hit the ropes with his back, not his ribs. Then on the return, he should again run full tilt back towards you.

And that's the most important thing about running the ropes – do *not* pull up! No sissy short steps, no tiptoeing your way in, and no slowing down before you hit the ropes to soften the impact! If you hit the ropes with your back and not your ribs, it does not hurt! On the return, no slowing down to soften the impact of the clothesline or back elbow you're about to receive! Run full tilt toward your opponent and then bump big and square on your upper back and shoulders.

The arm drag

There are two ways to give an arm drag: Basic and out of a bridge. A basic arm drag – as its name suggests – is very easy to execute and, in my book, should never be used. To execute the basic arm drag, you lock arms with your opponent, elbow nook to elbow nook, drop down on your right knee, pivot, drop your left knee, and place your right hand square on the mat. Now you're on your hand and knees, forming what I call a "table" for your opponent to post from and forward roll over.

Why do I say not to do this? Because the arm drag out of a bridge is so much more impressive.

To execute an arm drag out of bridge, you start just as you would a basic arm drag – by locking arms with your opponent, elbow nook to elbow nook. But that's where the similarity stops. From here, you lean back toward the mat and arch your back as if you're doing a gymnastics bridge (hence the name). You allow yourself to free-fall toward the mat up until the very moment you feel as if you're about to hit it. Then you quickly and sharply roll away from your opponent, as if you're trying to do an alligator roll. Then land on your stomach. The sudden roll is your opponent's trigger to execute his forward roll. If done correctly, this is a thing of beauty. It looks like you ripped the guy out of his boots in taking him down.

That said, it is essential that when you *take* an arm drag, you take it right. The proper way to take an arm drag is by performing a shoulder-tucked forward roll straight over your opponent. If performed correctly, when you're halfway through the bump, *both* your legs should be pointing straight up toward the ceiling. This is another mistake I see a lot of guys making these days – they're not taking the arm drag correctly.

Instead of executing a proper forward roll, they flop to the side and perform a sloppy back bump.

Wrong!

It's the forward roll that makes an arm drag look devastating. Again, the illusion we're shooting for is that the move is so leveraged and sudden, you're getting ripped out of your boots. This illusion only happens if you do a forward roll.

So to sum up, when giving an arm drag, do it out of a bridge. When taking an arm drag, execute a proper forward roll. If you do it right and time it perfectly, nothing is more exciting.

The clothesline

While nothing is more exciting than a properly executed arm drag, nothing looks more devastating than a textbook clothesline. I love the clothesline. I love anything off the ropes, and the clothesline is king of moves off the ropes. When done properly, it looks as if a guy's head has been ripped off his shoulders and his feet are running out from underneath him. It's awesome.

There are two keys to a properly executed clothesline: Running full tilt and the point of impact. Let's discuss running full tilt first.

I mentioned running full tilt in the previously when we discussed running the ropes, but I want to foot stomp it again here because it's especially important when taking a clothesline. Too often today I see guys get sent into the ropes, run toward the clothesline, and right before they take it, they pull up, take a wimpy shot, and then do a back bump almost from a standing position.

This looks awful. It's so obviously fake, it causes the entire audience to roll their eyes in unison. It's for soft candy asses who really don't take any pride in their work. I've said it before and I'll say it again and again – pro wrestling *hurts*. If you can't take the beating, stay out of the ring. It's not for you. But if you do choose to step through those ropes, go full tilt. Take the shots. Bump impressively. Make it your goal to convince the audience – *every* audience – that whatever shot you just took hurt like hell.

Now let's discuss the point of impact. A common mistake made by workers giving clotheslines these days is whipping the opponent into the ropes and then stepping into the *center* of the ring, stand there and wait for the opponent. This really looks silly from the audience's perspective, because why would the opponent keep running into the clothesline? Why not pull up or duck?

When you stand in the center of the ring and wait for the opponent to come to you, it's plainly obvious you're telegraphing the move. As such, if pro wrestling were a real sport, the opponent would just duck the clothesline. It's just common sense. The simple solution to this problem is to chase your opponent into the ropes rather than just standing in the middle of the ring waiting on him. To do this, right after you whip your opponent into the ropes, count "One…two," in your head and then run right behind him. Your opponent will hit the ropes and boom! As soon as he rebounds off the ropes, you nail him with the clothesline.

If done correctly, this looks just devastating. It's moves like the clothesline that, if done properly, can revive the sport of pro wrestling and restore realism and excitement to it. Instead of attempting riskier and riskier and sillier and sillier gymnastic quadruple tumbleweed summersaults off the top rope, focus on making the simple, logical moves more realistic and more devastating.

Go back to the basics!

The punch

Ah, yes, the punch. The thing that sells tickets. The thing that makes matches. The thing the makes a show a show. Pro wrestling wouldn't be pro wrestling without the punch. Terry Bollea wouldn't have become Hulk Hogan without the punch.

It's a bit of an oxymoron. We're supposed to be *wrestling*, not boxing, but when it comes time for the comeback and finish, the punch rules supreme. It's all but impossible to mount a thrilling comeback without dishing out some wild and furious punching. It's what makes a comeback a comeback.

The problem is, too few indie wrestlers know how to punch correctly and convincingly these days. Even worse, too few indie wrestlers know how to *sell* a punch these days. So let's talk about both – how to properly throw a punch and to properly sell one.

There are three parts of throwing a punch: The windup, the contact, and the follow through. All three parts need to be in place to make a punch effective. If you study the best punchers in the history of pro wrestling – Terry Funk, Jerry Lawler, or Terry Gordy – you'll very clearly see all three parts of the punch expertly demonstrated.

First, there's the windup. The windup for a punch is very much like the windup for a pitch in baseball. In baseball, the pitcher starts with his throwing hand holding the ball in his glove. He moves his hands above his head and then deliberately cocks his throwing arm way back, like a catapult being armed to throw a huge boulder at a castle wall. OK, boom, hit *Pause*. Imagine the pitcher frozen in that moment and in that position. This is the *windup*. This deliberate buildup – the deliberate cocking of one's arm – is exactly how you should start every punch. You have to cock your arm waaaaay back to communicate to the crowd that a big hit is coming. Too often today I see young wrestlers throw these wimpy little pokes with no windup at all. These don't even qualify as punches in my book. It's clear to me that a) these guys never learned how to punch from a qualified wrestling trainer and b) never got into a fistfight on the recess yard as kids. Anybody who's ever gotten into a real fight and lived to tell about it knows that any real punch that's thrown with the intent of hurting one's opponent needs windup. And the more you wind up and the bigger the wind up looks, the more dramatic the whole punch will appear.

Next is the contact. Many young wrestlers believe that they shouldn't make any contact at all when throwing a punch. Wrong! That may be true in Hollywood where directors use clever camera tricks to protect the pretty boy faces of guys like Brad Pitt and Tom Cruise, but in pro wrestling, we don't have those luxuries. Plus, we're not that delicate – we're tough guys! So to those guys who believe they shouldn't make contact when they punch somebody, I say baloney. The key is not to avoid contact but to make contact and avoid hurting your opponent.

The key to proper contact is what I call *the sweet zone.* The sweet zone is that area along your neck right below your ear and just above your shoulder. It's a soft, fleshy area close to your jaw but well enough away from it such that you won't actually pop the guy in the chops. This is the area where you want your loose fist to land when you throw a punch. If you throw your punches quickly and in rapid succession, it's almost impossible for the audience to see that you're not actually punching your opponent in the face. It's very, very convincing.

Always keep in mind that when you throw a punch, your fist should be loose and soft. If you hit a guy with a closed fist *anywhere,* it's going to hurt! But if you hit a guy on the sweet spot with an open fist, it'll sting a bit but not really injure him.

After you've made contact, the next and final part of the punch is the follow through. If you ever played Little League baseball, you know this lesson well. Your coach would tell you over and over again, every time you went up to bat, "Follow through! Follow through!" A tendency of inexperienced batters is to stop swinging the bat once they've made contact with the ball. But to make the ball really fly, you have to follow through. Follow through adds tons of energy to the hit. The same holds true with punches in wrestling. If you don't follow through, you look like you're obviously pulling your punches.

Think about Batman comic books. Whenever artists draw Batman punching out a bad guy, they always draw his arm having traveled in a wide arc, with the word "Pow!" right in the middle of the arc. This type of artistry suggests a big, powerful hit that just crushed the bad guy's chin.

You want to create this same effect. So when you throw a punch, start with a deep, way back windup, throw the punch and make contact in the sweet spot with a loose fist, and then move your fist along the same arc in a long, sweeping motion that suggests that you threw all your might into the punch with every intention of really hurting your opponent.

So now that we've talked about throwing a punch, let's talk about selling one. Selling a punch is just as important as throwing one – maybe even more important. If you've never been in a real fistfight, let me tell you right now, getting punched in the face hurts. Bad. It both hurts you and stuns you at the same time. Yet watch any modern pro wrestling – like TNA, for example – and you'll very infrequently see a guy sell a punch any longer than two seconds. Typically one guy will punch the other guy, and the other guy will turn his head ever so slightly to give the punch lip service, but then that's it. He's perfectly fine, no worse for the wear, and ready to get hit with a super triple tumbling side salto inverted atomic seton bomb with a bridge off the top rope.

You know, it's really sad when a guy will sell a missed leg drop more than a punch to the face. Think about it – if a guy misses a leg drop, what does he do? He jumps up, makes a ridiculous grimace, and then hops around the ring, holding his butt. If the same guy gets punched in the face, however, he sells that less than a second.

Let me assure you this: Getting hit in the face with a bare knuckled fist hurts much worse than landing on your butt on a cushioned, spring-loaded mat. The moral of the story?

Sell those punches!

The vertical suplex

Pro wrestling just wouldn't be pro wrestling without the vertical suplex. It remains one of the most impressive moves in the entire sport, especially when it's combined with a very fluid float-over into a pinfall attempt. It's just plain awesome.

Like just about everything else, though, the vertical suplex has been badly bastardized and watered down over the years. Like running the ropes, the vertical suplex walks that fine line between realistic and implausible; it requires the viewer to suspend his disbelief in order for it to go over, because, let's face it, you don't see many guys get stood straight upside down in barroom brawls.

To make a standing vertical suplex believable, you have to take the standing out of it. In other words, this nonsense where you elevate your opponent and then stand there for 10 or 20 seconds so "all the blood can flow to his head" is straight up silly. It would never happen in any real contest. It so obviously requires the cooperation of both men to execute. Further, holding a guy up like that is dangerous. The longer you hold a guy up, the greater the tendency for the guy to start arching his back and bending over backward. When you finally drop him – if he's in that bent-in-half position – chances are good his feet will hit first instead of his back. If his feet hit first, his knees can hyperflex and rupture a ligament.

Don't do that. The proper execution of a vertical suplex is to do it in one fluid motion from start to finish. Start by cinching in the front face lock. Toss your opponent's arm over your head and immediately grab his trunks. Without hesitating, lift and elevate your opponent, but don't stop along the way to hold him up "for effect." Instead move him all the way through the suplex and drop him square on his back on the mat. This somewhat resembles a snap suplex in that it's a very quick and sudden movement, but unlike a snap suplex, a vertical suplex actually involves lifting your opponent.

The move should come across as unexpected, like it came out of nowhere. And once you've properly and successfully executed the suplex, don't forget to float over into an immediate pin attempt.

"Don't be stiff" isn't "Don't try"

You can learn a lot by just looking at pictures – especially when it comes to pro wrestling. Take a look at the one on the following page. There sure is a heck of a lot going on there. It's a target-rich environment. I could probably write a chapter just based on this picture alone. But let's ignore the enormous beer gut poking out from under the guy's shirt and the fact that the referee is wearing jeans. Focus instead on the guy administering the hold, which, I guess, is supposed to be a sleeper. Look very closely at his spindly arms. Notice that what little muscle is in those arms is totally flaccid – there's no contraction whatsoever. His arms are just totally loose and limp. He doesn't even look like he's trying. Am I seriously supposed to believe that some pencil-necked dude is going to be able cut off the blood flow to an opponent's head by just loosely and gingerly placing his arms around it?

Any pressure hold requires, well, *pressure*. If you're supposed to be squeezing off the blood to a guy's brain, you have to pretend to be squeezing. If you've got a guy in an arm bar and you're supposed to be apply heavy pressure to said arm, your muscles have to contract to supply that pressure. It's basic common sense. Remember, you're *acting*. So in order to properly sell a rest hold, you have to really flex your muscles and let the crowd see them

contract and bulge. Your muscles have to actually work to convince the crowd that you're doing something.

Now when I say your muscles have to work, I don't mean you should actually be wrenching down on your opponent; what I mean is you should be contracting your muscles against each other statically, like the way you do when you flex in the mirror to show off your pecs or your 20-inch-python arms.

But now you might be thinking, "Wait a minute! That would make me *stiff*. Workers aren't supposed to be stiff." I understand lots of guys think this way, but let's clear up some misconceptions. The idea behind not being stiff is two-fold: One, when throwing a punch or kick you don't want to be stiff because stiff shots hurt. And two, you don't want to be stiff because being stiff prevents chain wrestling. The point we want to discuss is the second one.

Think about it. Let's say you have an opponent in a standing side headlock, and the spot calls for your opponent to grab your wrist, do a duck under, and reverse your headlock into a hammerlock. Fair enough, right? That's basic wrestling. But if you're holding that hammerlock tightly and refuse to loosen up when your opponent grabs your wrist, you're being genuinely stiff. Behaving this way prevents your opponent from doing the planned duck behind and reversal. That's bad.

A lot of young wrestlers respond to that by barely holding the headlock at all. They're as loose as soggy egg noodles. Being loose like that enables the planned chain wrestling to occur, but it looks just completely fake.

What you *should* be doing is not be stiff, but to tense up at the right times. So let's say you've got that headlock on your opponent. You know what's coming – you know at some point he's going to grab your wrist and initiate the reversal. While you're waiting, however, you should be selling that headlock by really flexing your muscles, like Arnold Schwarzenegger doing a side chest pose. You should be giving the impression that you're really squeezing down on the guy's head, trying to render him unconscious. In reality you're not squeezing anything except your own muscles against themselves. Your opponent feels nothing.

Then as soon as you sense your opponent's hand on your wrist, you know he's about to initiate the reversal, so completely relax your muscles and get loose to let him perform the escape and the ensuing hammerlock. The key, as I've said over and over again, is to slow down the pacing of the match and take whatever time needed to sell the side headlock (or whatever move you're doing) for a few moments. Once it's been sold convincingly and the fans have had an opportunity to see your muscles flexing and working, then you can transition to the next move.

Conclusion

Today's pro wrestling is very much like an action movie – the audience knows it's not real but they want it to look real anyway. Think about it, had the dinosaurs in "Jurassic Park" looked fake and rubbery – but everything else about the movie remained exactly the same – do you think for one minute that it would have made as much money as it did? No, of course not! Why? Because even though the movie would have had the same story and the same actors, the people would come away saying, "That movie sucked. Those dinosaurs looked so fake."

Whether you realize it or not, that's *exactly* what so many people say while sitting through pro wrestling shows: "Oh, man, that was so fake," and, "That was really stupid." And guess what? A lot of those folks never come back.

Pro wrestling is not real. The results are predetermined. The participants are not truly trying to harm or pin one another. Kayfabe is dead. No one other than hillbillies who've never even seen a computer much less been on the Internet is still under the impression that pro wrestling is real. Yet to make the show enjoyable and marketable, it still has to *look* real. Fans want to be fooled. They want to be entertained. And the process of entertainment is all about creating an illusion. That's our job. We're illusionists.

7

Marketing: The Key to Bigger Gates

"Late to bed, early to rise, work like hell and advertise."
- Wernher von Braun, Apollo rocket scientist

Light your lamp

A man much, much wiser than me once said, "No one lights a lamp and then puts it under a basket." Instead, you put your lamp up on a lamp stand, where everyone can see its light. After all, how stupid would it be to light a lamp and then cover it so that the light doesn't get out? Yet many, many people do this sort of thing in their day-to-day endeavors.

As an example, I knew a guy once who opened up a new barbecue restaurant but didn't advertise it. And guess what? The guy was out of business in less than three months.

He had lit a lamp and put it under a basket.

Unfortunately a lot of promoters do this in indie pro wrestling. Too many guys do it, in fact. They either don't promote their shows at all or they don't promote them enough. The result? People don't show up.

If you want people to show up to your show – and everyone does – you have to light your lamp, burn the light brightly, and put it up on a really tall lamppost so that people from all over will see it and come check it out. How do you do that? Well, that's called marketing, and that's what this chapter is all about

I said it at the very beginning of this book and I'll say it again now – pro wrestling is all about sales. Whether you're a promoter, booker, worker, or referee, you're selling an entertainment product. And you're selling that entertainment product to make *money*. Marketing is the indispensible key to making all that possible. So in this chapter we're going to explore lots of crucial marketing concepts and then I'm going to give you a full host of low cost (or free!) marketing ideas to get more people to come to your shows.

Sneaker power and elbow grease

You're not Bill Gates or Richard Branson…not yet, at least. So obviously you don't have the deep pockets of a multimillionaire to fund a full blown traditional marketing campaign. Instead you have to substitute money and glitzy advertising firms with sneaker power and elbow grease. You can get very good results with a low budget marketing campaign if you're willing to put in the time and work very, very hard at it. You have to treat your marketing efforts as a second job. You have to throw your heart and all your dedication into it to get the results you want and make your promotion a success, but if done correctly, it'll pay off in spades.

It won't come easy. You have to work hard and you have to work diligently. The marketing techniques I outline in this chapter could be best described as grassroots. You don't need to spend a lot of money, but you will need a lot of sweat, time, and perseverance.

Repeat, repeat, repeat!

Let's say you have $10,000 to spend on advertising. OK, don't fret – I realize you probably don't have $10,000 to spend on an advertising campaign, but just go with the example anyway. So you have $10,000 in the bank set aside for an advertising blitz. Let's also say that you have two options: You can run a commercial for your show on TV twenty times or you can run a radio ad 100 times for the same amount. Which is the better option?

Many people would say TV because TV allows the viewer to actually *see* what you're selling, but the truth is, if the size of the audience is comparable, the radio ads would be more effective. Why? Because you repeat your message over and over and over again.

I talked a lot about this concept in the very first chapter of this book: Repeating a message is critical in advertising. The first few times an ad runs, it doesn't even register in the viewer's (or listener's) consciousness. It just looks and sounds like every other ad bombarding us every second of the day. People have learned to just tune the noise out. But when you repeat a message over and over and over again, people lower their defenses and start paying attention – whether they want to or not.

Remember that horribly annoying commercial for the product "HeadOn"? It went like this: "Head on, apply directly to the forehead. HeadOn, apply directly to the forehead. HeadOn, apply directly to the forehead." And that's it! That's all they said! They didn't make any claims, provide any testimonials, or even ask you to buy the stupid thing. They just repeated the same six stupid words over and over in the most annoying way possible. It drove people crazy!

But guess what?

Sales of HeadOn boomed!

And guess what else?

HeadOn didn't even do anything! Most people concluded that it was a headache medicine, but it wasn't. It wasn't a medicine at all – it was wax! Yes, like the stuff they make candles out of. But it sold! It made people rich!

All because those people understood the power of creating a very simple message and repeating it over and over and over again – literally!

You need to do the same thing when promoting your shows. You need to pick a message, keep that message extremely simple, and then repeat it over and over and over again until people get sick of hearing it. And then once they've become completely sick of it, you repeat it some more.

A good logo says it all

The next time there's a pro football game on, pull up a chair and pay attention. Then play a little game – count how many times you see the

NFL logo appear somewhere on your TV screen. You'll see it everywhere – on the field, on the screen, on the scoreboard, on players jerseys, on helmets, on the play-by-play guy's microphone...it's everywhere! Why? Because the National Football League, of all business ventures, understands the importance and value of branding. They want you to know without a doubt what you're watching. They want their logo burned into your subconscious mind.

It's an essential ingredient to a good marketing plan. Your customers need an easy way to immediately and distinctly identify your company and your product. When your customers see your logo, right away it should say something to them. Think about it. If I gave you a DVD with nothing on the cover other than the WWE logo, you'd right away get a very clear idea of what you were about to see and what level of quality you should expect.

That's the power of branding. It makes your business instantly and subconsciously identifiable. And if you take care that your product is of top quality and good value, that logo will immediately scream to your customers, "But this!" or "Come to this show!" If your product is exceptional, when your customers see a flyer in a window, they'll see your logo and that's all they'll need. They won't need to see who's on the card or what the main event is; all they need to see is your logo and you have them.

This type of marketing is very powerful. It appeals psychologically, but it takes great care and a lot of work for it to happen. You need two things: First, a quality product. Hopefully if you've read this book to this point you have an idea of what a quality pro wrestling show should be. Second, you need a professional, topnotch logo. Don't underestimate this second requirement. A professional, clean, high quality logo speaks volumes about your business. If your logo looks like crap, people are automatically going to assume your product is crap.

Now let me say this right away and let me say it straight – if you are not a qualified, trained graphic designer, do not attempt to design your own logo! Way too many promoters do this and in almost every single case, the logo looks homemade. Homemade screams low rent. Remember that. Homemade equals low rent.

How many pro wrestling promotion logos have you seen that incorporate flames, barbed wire, or blood? You know what I'm talking about – you go to a promotion's website and their logo is made out of letters that are "on fire." How many big, successful businesses have you seen where their logo is made out of flames?

I'll tell you how many: None!

Another huge mistake promotions use is *aliased* imagery for their logos. What is an aliased image, you ask? An aliased image is one that is jagged or blocky, not smooth. Like this:

The letters on the left are *aliased*. Notice how jagged and blocky they look. The letters on the right are *anti-aliased*. That means the graphics editing software that I used to create them worked some magic to smoothen them out and make them appear cleaner, like lettering out of newspapers.

Another big mistake I see a lot that just screams low rent is stretching images to make them bigger. Ugh! Don't do this! For example, the picture to the left is a simple, original image. Not too bad, right? We have our old friend Val Venis with his fists up, looking like he's ready for a fight. The image is clear, sharp, and in the correct dimensions. It looks very professional, probably good enough to appear in *Pro Wrestling Illustrated*. I've inserted this image here in its exact dimensions and in its original resolution. I like it.

The mistakes a lot of promoters and amateur web designers make is stretching images with software to make them fill up a bigger space. The image to the right is the same very picture as the previous one, only stretched wider to fill up the page horizontally. See how terrible it looks? Val now looks like a standard aspect movie stretched wider to fit into a widescreen TV. It looks stretched, unnatural, and cheap. And making pictures appear cheap is the biggest downside of stretching photos from their original dimensions to appear larger. They go from being clear and professional to blurry and blocky.

Don't do this, especially with your promotion's logo! A lot of guys slap together a logo using Microsoft Paint or Gimp or whatever and then when they go to put it up on their website, they decide it should be bigger, so they stretch it. This is one of the biggest and dumbest amateur mistakes a graphic or web designer can make. If you want your logo to appear in different sizes in different places on your website or your flyers and ads, resize them with your graphics design software, not your word processor or webpage making software. How do you resize images using graphic design software, you ask? Well, that's why I suggested hiring a graphic designer. If you don't know how, hire a professional.

Trust me, it will pay off. Do not underestimate the power of a professionally designed, clean and simple logo.

Remember, keep it simple!

As you ponder what you want your promotion's logo to look like, remember, keep it simple. If you look at the logos of the biggest, most successful companies in the world, companies like IBM, AT&T, McDonald's, and Major League Baseball, you'll notice that they all keep their logos simple. They don't use lots of colors or flashy design effects like shadows, glare, or beveling. Pretty much they pick two or three basic colors and they use very simple designs. For wrestling promotions, I recommend using the initials of your promotion and simply using heavy block letters.

Again, I highly recommend hiring a graphic designer, but at minimum, remember to avoid frilly font types and effects that are flashy or garish.

It's OK to trick out your ride, but you do *not* want to trick out your logo!

Slogan time

Ever notice how all the biggest companies have a slogan? It's a quick little catchphrase that's easy to remember and typically only five words or less. McDonald's has "I'm lovin' it," Burger King has, "Have it your way," Walmart has, "Save money. Live better," and even WCW had, "Where the big boys play."

A slogan is like a logo in that it's catchy and it gives your promotion an identity. Developing a unique brand, an identity of your own that's clearly distinct is absolutely critical in the vast sea of indie pro wrestling. Think about how many hundreds or even thousands of indie wrestling promotions there are today, with a new one forming about as often as it rains in Seattle. You need to distinguish yourself from the pack. You need to stand out. You want people to notice you and immediately recognize what you're doing.

A good slogan will help you do that. What makes a good slogan? Well, for starters, it must be five words or less. It has to be concise, clear, and easy to remember. Need an example? No problem. Let's say your promotion is called Power Pro Wrestling. A great slogan for your promotion would be, "Power it up!"

Here's another one. Let's say your promotion is called All Pro Wrestling. A great slogan would be, "Where the pros tie up."

Simple, right?

Now here's a word of caution. I've noticed a lot of indie promotions attempt to employ the good practice of developing a slogan, but their slogan doesn't reflect well on their promotion! For example, I've seen the slogan, "Tomorrow's champions today," or something to that effect used a lot. Bad idea! Why? Because you're just blatantly admitting that your wrestlers aren't ready for the big time yet! Another bad one is, "Where champions are made, not born." Why not just make your slogan, "Our sport is fake and we choose who wins!"?

In both the previous examples, you're underselling your promotion, which defeats the purpose of a slogan. A slogan is supposed to say good things about your promotion and your business. It's your way of putting your best foot forward. But that said, you don't want to go the other extreme, either, where you *over*sell yourself. I've seen promotions with cheesy slogans like, "The best pro wrestling in the *galaxy!*" and, "The best in the world!" Come on, now. Seriously? While you want fans to believe you have great talent working for you, your guys aren't better than the guys who work for Vince. Everyone knows that. So making grandiose statements like these just leads fans to roll their eyes and laugh at you.

Keep it real.

Once you've developed a good slogan, plaster it everywhere. Put it on your flyers, your website, your banners, and your ring apron. Repeat it over and over again. Using my example from earlier, if your promotion is called Power Pro Wrestling, when your ring announcer grabs the mic to welcome the fans to your show, he should say, "Welcome to Power Pro Wrestling! Let's get ready to *Power It Up!*" When your top babyface cuts a promo, his very last words should always be, "Power It Up!"

Much more to come on this topic in just a bit.

A web presence

Welcome to the 21st century! In today's ultra-digital age, businesses can't afford to not have a web presence anymore. It's just out of the question.

Starting a new wrestling promotion without a well-developed website is like a new casino opening up without a big neon sign out front – it's just plain dumb. There is an enormous potential customer base out there in cyberspace, just waiting for you to reach out to them. Give them a reason to come to your show and they will. Tell them about your promotion and they'll listen.

There is a gamut of opportunities on the web to market your promotion, but the first one we need to talk about is your website. You need one, and it needs to look good. It needs to be kept current. It needs to be fresh and alive. You *never* want a fan to hit your site and see a flyer still posted for *last* month's show! As soon as a show is history, all the promotional stuff for it on your site must immediately come down.

Not only should your site's content be fresh and current, it needs to be well presented. Spelling mistakes, grammatical errors, improper punctuation, and sloppy language all scream crude and chintzy. Your written communications speak volumes about your professionalism. If you write well, people will trust you and buy from you. If you write poorly, people will be suspicious of you or think you're a joke.

The colors, pictures, and graphics of your site are also critical. Remember our discussion of color schemes in chapter two of this book? Well those lessons apply to your website (and flyers), too. Your website's colors should match *exactly* the colors of your logo. If your logo's colors are navy blue and blood red, then your website's colors should be navy blue and blood red. Also remember that any graphics used on your site should be developed by a professional and any pictures you post should be taken by a qualified photographer. Your layout and navigation should be simple and logical.

Sound like a tall order? Well, it is! That's why I always recommend hiring a professional to do it for you. Unless you really know what you're doing, find someone who understands these concepts through and through. I can't emphasize this enough. An attractive, professional website will sell tickets; a crappy website will generate empty seats.

Get a domain name

Once you've found someone to develop a professional website for you, get your own domain name. What's a domain name? It's your website's address. Do not, repeat, do *not* use a domain name from a free web hosting service like Blogspot, Angelfire, or Weebly. Your domain name should be dedicated for your promotion. For example, if your promotion's name is Ultimate Pro Wrestling, you want a domain name like *www.UPWrestling.com*, not *www.UPWrestling.blogspot.com*. Using a free domain name looks cheap, especially considering domain names are very inexpensive nowadays.

Where do you get a domain name? Almost every reputable web hosting company offers them along with their hosting service. I have used both Host Papa (www.hostpapa.com) and 1&1 (www.1and1.com) and have received excellent service with very affordable rates.

A picture is worth a thousand words

Pictures! You need them! Lots of them! And good ones! You may not realize it, but posting good photos on your site is a great marketing move.

People love to look at pictures, especially if they're sharp, interesting, and full of color. You should have tons and tons of pictures on your website. There's a reason why both TNA and WWE both dedicate entire sections of their websites to high resolution photos from all their shows: People love 'em. Pictures are a great draw to your website. If you post high quality, fresh pictures regularly on your website, people from all over will visit your site just to view them. And while they're there, guess what else they'll see? That's right – your ads for your next show!

The key, though, is your pictures have to be *good*. Unfortunately, though, most pictures taken at indie wrestling shows suck. They're taken by amateur photographers who do little more than point their cameras in the general direction of the action and take snapshots. The results are muddy, grainy, blurry, washed out shots that look unprofessional and blah. A good photographer, on the other hand, can take a picture of the same event and the same subject and his photo will come out looking vibrant, sharp, and alive.

Nerds rule

So I've been talking a lot about web design, photography, videos for YouTube and other high tech must-haves for any pro wrestling promotion, and I've stressed that you need someone who really knows what he's doing to do these things for you. I've suggested hiring professionals. Professionals are great, but, well, they're *professionals,* which means they cost money.

Lots of money.

So what do you do if you need a good photographer, web designer, or desktop publisher but can't afford one? Simple – look for a nerd.

If you haven't realized it yet, here's a great pro wrestling promoter's inside secret – nerds love pro wrestling. Not all of them, but many, many do. And guess what? Nerds typically are great photographers, web designers, and computer people! That's what makes them nerds. All you need to do is find a qualified nerd to help you with the production of the promotional materials you need, whether it be a website or a layout for next month's flyer. You'd be surprised by how many nerds would jump at the chance to help out a wrestling promotion…and all for *free!* They just want to be part of the action, part of the team. So let them.

Just be sure that if you go this route you find nerds qualified to do the jobs you need done. For example, let's say you need a photographer for your shows. Let's also suppose you have a hunch that you know a nerd who may be up to the task. All you have to do is ask him, "Do you know anything about photography?" If he says yes, tell him you're looking for a photographer for your promotion. The nerd will probably tell you he'd love to help out. So then you just ask him if he has any sample pictures for you to look at. If he doesn't have anything for you to look at, he's probably not a good photographer (or web designer or desktop publisher or whatever). People who do things professionally or as a serious hobby will always have a sample of their stuff to show you. If your nerd doesn't have any samples, move on. Find somebody else. But if he does have sample pictures to show you, take a good look at them. Do any of the pictures he provides look like they might be good enough to print in the newspaper or in a magazine? If yes, you've found your man!

You'd be surprised at how many people would be willing to help you just for the experience or the fun of it. These people can be great assets; however, remember that they need to be *qualified*. Don't agree to have someone do something for you that doesn't look professional just because the guy will do it for nothing. That defeats the purpose of getting it done in the first place. Remember, in most cases – especially with things like web design – it's typically better to hire a professional, but if you can't afford one or if you know someone who's especially good, enlisting the help of an enthusiastic volunteer is smart business.

Nerds rule!

Give back

It's time to pick a charity. Why? Because charities will help you big time in promoting your shows. How do charities help you? Simple – if people know that part of the proceeds of your show are going to a good cause, they will be more inclined to buy tickets. Further, regularly donating money to charity improves the image of your business in the eyes of the community. It helps your reputation and makes you appear more legitimate. Further, it opens a few doors that otherwise would be closed to you, which I'll talk about in a moment.

What you want to do is pick a good, reputable charity that benefits one of two things – the troops overseas or kids. Not only are they very worthy causes, but nothing pulls people's heartstrings more than the troops or children. You want people to identify with and feel for your charity. For example, if your cause is saving the Gulf Coast beach mouse, well, that might truly be a worthwhile cause, but it's not really going to move the general public into action. But helping kids get treatment at St. Jude's Hospital will. And so will sending care packages to the troops on the front lines of Afghanistan.

All right, pick a favorite charity. Here's a few ideas if you're coming up blank: St. Jude's Hospital, The Fisher House, Boys Town, The Children's Hospital, The Wounded Warrior Project, and The Boys and Girls Club. Just pick one. This is your adopted charity. Then once you've adopted a charity, go to the charity's website and read about its mission. Learn what it does, why, and how it does it. Once you've learned about the charity, prepare a ten second elevator pitch for it. The elevator pitch should be simple and to the point and be committed to your memory. That way, if someone asks you what your adopted charity does or is all about, you can quickly and professionally tell them.

For example, suppose your adopted charity is The Fisher House. Let's also suppose that you're running a show in the summer and half the show's proceeds are going to The Fisher House. So you're talking to a couple fans about your show and one of them asks you, "Fisher House? Never heard of them. What do they do?" If you haven't done your homework and prepared your elevator pitch, your answer might sound something like this: "They, um, well, they, uh, do go stuff for the vets." If your answer sounds like that, right away those fans are going to question your integrity and sincerity. However, if your answer is something like this: "The Fisher House is a charity that builds comfort homes near VA hospitals so that veterans' loved ones can be near them while the vets undergo treatment," people will realize you know what you're talking about and that you're sincere about it.

Once you've developed an elevator pitch for your charity, write it down neatly on a notecard and keep it handy. You'll need it for marketing efforts we'll discuss in upcoming sections.

Charity Show

OK, so you've chosen a charity, educated yourself on it, developed an elevator pitch for it, and written the elevator pitch on a notecard. The next step is to organize and promote a charity show.

A charity show will really help you build a good reputation in the community. Here's what you do – you organize a special show and announce that 100% of the proceeds will go to your adopted charity. Yes, you read that right, 100%. You can promote one or two of these shows per year. Now don't get me wrong – you should be donating a percentage of *every* show's proceeds to your adopted charity, but one or two of your shows per year should be 100% for charity. This is an excellent way to get word out about you. Just think about it – you can announce: "Fans every single dime we make on this show goes to [insert your charity here]!" This sacrifice will pay big dividends in the future. Sure, you'll lose money on that show, but you'll make it up and then much, much more on future shows.

Flyers and Handbills

Flyers and handbills are the mainstays of affordable, highly effective guerrilla marketing. You can really increase attendance at your shows through an effective flyer campaign. But before you go hit the streets and canvas your entire city, let's first talk about flyers and handbills, what they are, and how they should be made.

A well-made flyer or handbill can very affordably get the message out about your promotion, but a poorly made one can do just the opposite – drive people away. If your flyer looks amateurish, cheap, homemade, or full of gore, barbed wire, and thumbtacks, *most* ordinary people will stay far away from your show. Sure, you might attract a few shady underworld undesirables with that kind of flyer, but, as we've discussed before, that's not the type of fan you want in your audience. You want normal people – people with good jobs, nice homes, kids, and lots of money to spend. And the best way to attract those people is with a very up-and-up, professional, and safe show. If your flyer is professional, people will conclude your show is professional; if it's cheap, people will conclude your show is cheap…and seedy and unsafe.

So what makes a flyer professional? We'll get to that in just a moment, but first, let's talk about the difference between a flyer and a handbill. A flyer is a full page ad on eight by eleven or larger paper. Flyers work best when they are printed in full color and posted in storefront windows and bulletin boards. A handbill, on the other hand, is a much smaller flyer, typically one fourth the size of a piece of paper (that's two inches by three inches), intended to be handed out to passersby. In a nutshell, then, flyers are full color paper ads to be posted in windows; handbills are smaller ads to be handed out. Many promotions hand out full size flyers as handbills, but you can save a lot of money and get just as good results by using quarter page handbills.

Below is an example of an excellent flyer or handbill. I want you to study it very closely. Take a few moments and then I'll catch up with you on the other side…

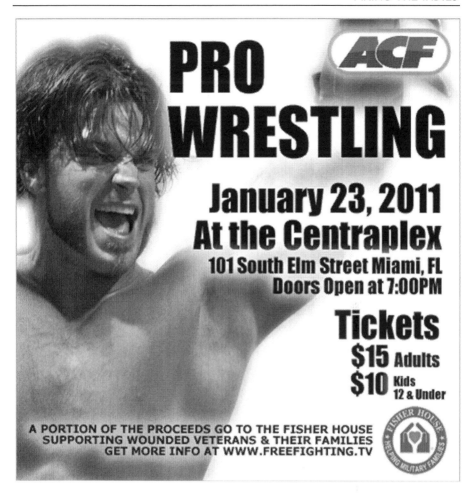

All right...now that you've studied the flyer, let's take a look at its finer points.

First, notice its simplicity. It has one picture of a wrestler that bleeds all the way to the edge. The design is clean, simple, and perfectly clear. There's no need to clutter up your flyers with pictures of every single guy on your card. All you need is a picture of your top draw. In fact, you don't even need to list the names of the other guys on the card – this is the indies we're talking about, not WWE! It's not like those guys have well-established names.

Next, notice the text. The text you use on a flyer should always be a wide, basic, sans serif font like Impact, Franklin, or Futura. Such fonts make your flyers really stand out and easy to read. Also notice there's not a lot of text going on here, either. Pretty much we're saying, "Pro wrestling show...come!" That's all you need to say. You don't need to harp about the matches, what the main event is, who has bad blood with whom, etc. All that does is muddy your message. You want people to know, without having to read much, is that you're putting on a pro wrestling show. Tell them clearly where it is, when, and how much the tickets cost. Put a link at bottom of the flyer that directs the reader to your website for more information about the show. That way if you have reached someone who cares about who's on your card, he can check your website and find out.

Next, your promotion's logo should be prominently displayed on the flyer. It doesn't need to dominate the space; it just has to be clear and obvious. Realize that many people who get a copy of your flyer won't be familiar with your promotion. All they care about is that there's a wrestling show, and by the looks of your flyer, it appears like it will be a professionally run show.

Finally, at the very bottom of the page, notice I've written a blurb about the charity I'm sponsoring and I've printed the charity's logo next to it. Remember, a reputable, well-known charity helps your credibility.

Once you've designed your flyers and handbills, take them to your printer to have them professionally printed. Your flyers should be printed in full color; your handbills, on the other hand, can be black-and-white to save money.

You can also order flyers online. You send them a copy of your flyer design by email and then they print your flyers and mail them to you. A great online printer I've used before that offers very affordable prices is *NoBSPrinting.net*. At the time of this book's printing, you can order 10,000 quarter page black-and-white handbills for just $150.

I recommend you order as many handbills that your budget permits. You should also print at least 100 full color flyers. Remember, the handbills are to be handed out on the streets, while your color flyers are to be posted in storefront windows. Once you get your flyers and handbills back from the printer, it's time to hit the streets.

Getting flyers in windows

The first thing you want to do once you get the flyers and handbills back from the printer is get those full color flyers up in storefront windows. This should be done *at least* 30 days before the show. Assemble a team of volunteers to help you do this. Get up very early and spend an entire day getting every one of those 100 flyers up in storefront windows.

Here's what you do to get a business owner to agree to allow you to post your flyer. First, make sure you're dressed professionally. Then approach the business owner by saying, "Hi, we're organizing a pro wrestling show. We're donating a portion of the proceeds to [insert your charity here]. Would you mind if I taped up a flyer in your window?" Nine times out of ten, if the business is local, the owner will tell you to go right ahead.

Notice I said the business should be local. What I mean by that is the business you target to post a flyer in should be a locally owned business rather than a chain. Chain businesses like McDonald's or Walmart typically have to get corporate approval before they'll let anyone post a flyer in their window, and they're not going to bother attempting to do that for your pro wrestling show. Local businesses, on the other hand, don't have to ask a bunch of corporate suits before they do something – they make their own decisions right there on the spot. So look for businesses that aren't chains. You'll have the most success. In particular, look for these local businesses in this order:

- Comic book stores
- Video game stores
- Sporting goods stores
- Arcades
- Hardware stores
- Restaurants
- Auto part stores
- Convenience stores
- Bars, particularly sports bars
- Fitness centers

These stores are both high traffic locations *and* have patrons who are often pro wrestling fans. Look in your local phonebook and on the Internet for these businesses local to you. Make a list of them, and then go hit the bricks. Focus on businesses closest to your show's location at first. Make it a goal to get at least 100 flyers up in store windows all over town. If you live in a big city like Atlanta or Houston, you might want to set a goal of 500 or more. Get started early in the morning – leave the house at 7AM – and dedicate the next ten hours to getting flyers up in windows.

Hand out those handbills!

Now that you have those flyers up in windows all over town, the next step is to start canvassing the place with your handbills. Your goal is to hand out 10,000 handbills.

Of course, handing out 10,000 handbills won't be easy. You need help. That's when "street teams" come in very handy. A street team is a team of volunteers – typically fans of your promotion – who agree to hand out handbills for you on the streets. Lots of fans like the idea of being "in." They like the thought that they're part of the show. You can assemble street teams by advertising for volunteers on your website and at your shows. Get everyone you can – get your workers, your friends, your brother…even your Mom to hand out handbills for you.

Once you've assembled a team of volunteers, pick your target locations to hand them out. Here are the best places to hand out wrestling handbills, in order of preference:

- Outside live WWE or TNA shows, if they come to your town
- At other indie wrestling shows
- At other fighting events like boxing, MMA, or UFC shows
- At other sports events like rodeo, auto racing, and football
- Outside big box stores like Walmart
- Outside theaters, especially if a big action movie is playing

You can also place stacks of handbills at the registers of the businesses I mentioned in the previous section. As someone is checking out at the store, they might notice your handbill and take one. Another good idea is to place a copy of your handbill in each of the stalls of men's rooms in those locations, too. And in some men's rooms there are corkboards right above the urinals. Tack up a copy of your handbill there, too.

Another great and fast way to hand out handbills is by putting them on cars. Go to a big parking lot like the one at Walmart or at the local mall and put a handbill on every car you see. The best way to do this is to roll the handbill into a loose tube and stick it in the door handle of the target car. That way you don't have to touch the person's car to put the handbill on it. Some people are sensitive about their cars being touched, and putting handbills on the windshield often requires you to lift the windshield wiper. Well guess what – lifting someone's windshield wiper is touching someone else's car! The last thing you need is some thug coming at you, shouting, "Hey yo! What the eff are you doing to my car?" If some guy does do that, you want to be able to say, "Hey, man, I didn't touch your car. We're just handing out flyers for a charity show."

A lesson in advertising conversions

You want your handbill campaign to be a success (duh!). You want as many people as possible to buy a ticket to your show as a result of receiving one of your handbills. That's called your *return on investment* (ROI). You spend money to have the handbills printed, expecting to make more money than it cost to print them. The more money you make compared to the money you spent (invested), the higher your *return on investment.* That's one of the fundamental building blocks of good business.

In the world of advertising, a successful advertisement is one that *converts.* If you see an ad on a website for a DVD, and you click on the ad and buy the DVD, the ad has just *converted.* That is, the ad led to a direct sale. It made money. Ads that don't convert are worthless…they're just a waste of money. You don't want to waste money on ads that don't convert. You want to get the most bang for your buck. After all, your advertising budget is limited. It's not like you're Donald Trump with hundreds of millions of dollars at your disposal.

So, that said, you want your handbills to *convert*. Let's look at an example. Say you spend $150 to print 10,000 handbills. Let's suppose you hand out all 10,000 flyers and, as a result, 100 people buy tickets to your show. That's a 1% conversion rate. If you sell your tickets for $15 apiece, multiply $15 by 100 and you get $1,500. Subtract the $150 you spent to print the handbills and you rake in a net profit of $1,350! Not bad, right?

So the key to take from this is, the better your conversion rate, the more money you make. You want the highest conversion rate possible. So how do maximize your conversion rate? Let's take a look at some ideas.

Know your audience

OK, so you have 10,000 handbills to hand out. That's a lot of handbills! It can be a very daunting task to hand them all out. As you get to work on passing those things out, you might find yourself getting tired and wanting to just get rid of them all. This might lead you to handing out flyers to people who clearly don't want them.

Resist this temptation. Handing out a handbill to someone who clearly won't come to your show is just a waste of money, time, and effort. Think about it – would it be a good idea to hand out handbills for a pro wrestling show to people going in to see a ballet performance? How about to people coming out of a modern art studio? Rest assured your conversion rate for those handbills would be right around 0%. You'd just be wasting your time and money and annoying the people you hand the handbill to. That's why I gave you the list of the best places to distribute handbills and post up flyers – because that's where you'll get the best conversion rates.

When you get your handbills back from the printer, remember, you want to hand out as many of those handbills to people who are already pro wrestling fans. This is your golden target demographic. Where do you find pro wrestling fans? Why, at pro wrestling shows, of course! So go to the other indie shows in your area and give every single person there – from the fans in the seats to the ref to the guy taking money at the door – a handbill to your show. If you're lucky and WWE,

TNA, or ROH runs shows in your town, *be there!* Again, give every single person who comes out of that arena a copy of your handbill.

Once you've done that, you'll have lots of handbills still left to hand out. That's when you go to other places where potential pro wrestling fans are. Think *working man.* That's who's most likely to buy a ticket to your show. Go where working men go – bars, hardware stores, sports events, sporting goods stores, auto part stores.

Maximize your conversion rate!

Girls, girls, girls!

Wherever you decide to go to handout your handbills, it's always a good idea to bring some attractive, well-endowed young ladies along with you. Get some t-shirts made up with your logo printed huge on the front and the back. Give a shirt to each girl. Your logo should be right there, you know, where guys' eyes tend to be drawn. Then have the girls smile, say hello, and hand out a handbill. I guarantee you – no straight guy on the planet would refuse the handbill. He's going to take it, smile back, and be very receptive to whatever you're selling. Trust me. Even if the dude is old, married, and dorky, when that girl smiles at him, he's going to be on Cloud 9. He'll then walk in a happy stupor to his car with that handbill in his hand. Once in his car, his brain will finally regain control of his senses and he'll say to himself, "Wow, that girl was hot! She smiled at me! Now what is this thing she gave me? Oh! A pro wrestling show. I wonder if she'll be there?"

Ka-ching!

Attractive girls are so powerful in increasing your conversion rates in a handbill campaign, you might even consider hiring some if you don't know any pretty girls who will do it for you for free. They're very effective advertising.

Smile and let them know who you are

Everyone handing out your handbills – whether they're attractive young ladies or not – should always remember to do one thing: Smile. When you approach someone with a handbill, smile big, say hello, hold out the handbill, and enthusiastically say, "Here's some info on a charity showing we're promoting!"

Never underestimate the power of a smile. People are automatically disarmed when you approach them with a warm, genuine smile. If you approach someone with a scowl or a disinterested, unenthusiastic look on your face, well, you can expect to get a disinterested, unenthusiastic response.

Not only should you approach with warmth and a friendly smile, but you need to let the people who see you know who you are. Every member of your street team should wear matching shirts with your logo largely emblazoned on them. Just think about it – imagine walking out of Walmart and suddenly you see ten people (some of whom are very attractive young ladies) all wearing bright blue t-shirts with a logo on them. Immediately these people have your attention, right? Of course! So do the same. Remember, light your lamp!

Be warned – Don't break the law!

With all this discussion of flyers and handbills, you need to be aware that there are certain legal pitfalls associated with them. Don't fall into one of these pitfalls; you might wind up getting fined.

First up, realize that some townships and cities require you to buy a handbill license before you can pass them out. Check with your local town hall. They typically cost only about $20 - $30 and can actually be a bit of blessing. If a security guard or police officer gives you a hard time about handing out your handbills, you can just say, "Sir, I have a license to do this," and they will typically leave you alone.

Another common pitfall you want to avoid is posting flyers up on city property. This is illegal in most cities. For example, posting flyers on telephone poles and light posts is illegal in many places. In some places there's a fine for every flyer posted on public property. You can wind up with hundreds or even thousands of dollars in fines! So be careful about this.

Double sided handbills

I really love this tactic – form a symbiotic partnership with another business by handing out double sided handbills. Your ad for your upcoming show is on one side, an ad for your partner business is on other. Here's how it works. Pick a local pizza joint, one that does lots of deliveries. Tell the owner you'll make a deal with him – you're handing out flyers on the street and at stores to promote your charity wrestling event. Tell him you'll agree to hand out handbills with an ad for his pizza joint on the back of it *if* he agrees to give out a copy of the handbill to everyone who buys a pizza! You both benefit. You advertise his pizzas, he advertises your show. Of course it doesn't have to be pizza; it could be any business with lots of traffic – a buffalo wings joint, a bar, a movie rental place, etc. You might even be able to get your advertising partner to split the cost of printing the handbills with you.

Call-in talk radio

Most cities have radio stations with call-in talk shows. Typically these shows discuss a gamut of topics – news, politics, local community events, sports, etc. These radio shows are an excellent free venue for you to promote your shows and reach thousands upon thousands of new potential fans. All you have to do is call in and tell the host or the call screener that you're promoting a charity show and that you would like to tell the show's listeners about it. Trust me, most call-in shows are more than willing to put you on the air if your charity is legitimate and reputable.

Remember the elevator pitch I encouraged you to develop and write down on a notecard? Now's when you need it. When the call screener or show host puts you on the air, you want to be ready to talk freely and confidently about your show and chosen charity. Here's what you want to tell the audience once you get on the air:

- Who you are
- The name of your promotion
- That you're putting on a charity pro wrestling show
- That proceeds will go to your chosen charity
- The name of your charity and what your charity does
- When and where the show is going to be
- Your website's address for more information

Once you've communicated all these points, spend some time extolling the good works of your chosen charity. Do *not* harp about your wrestling promotion! Keep the focus on your charity so that people will understand that you're sincere about your charity and not just trying to promote your business.

It's a very good idea to talk big about the recent works and successes of your chosen charity. For example, suppose your charity is St. Jude's Research Hospital. Let's also suppose the call-in show's name is Ted. You could say, "You know, Ted, as we speak, right now, researchers at St. Jude's are studying the genomes of the deadliest childhood cancers to figure out how they tick and how to cure them. This is groundbreaking research, but they need our help..." If you're professional and well prepared, the radio host will likely endorse your efforts right there on the air! This is a great win-win situation for your promotion and your chosen charity.

Radio ads

While we're on the topic of radio, don't rule out the idea of paid radio advertising. In many, many markets across the country, radio advertising is extremely affordable – probably more affordable than you might think. One ad on some stations can cost you only $10 - $20! And some stations offer 15 second spots for half that amount. For just about $150, you can run an ad on ten consecutive days leading up to your show. Tens of thousands of listeners will hear your ads and hear about your charity of choice.

I always recommend running spots on either news talk radio, country, or classic rock stations, as they typically have the highest conversion rates for pro wrestling advertising. In your area things might be a bit different, but in my experience those three tend to work best.

Curbside campaigning

You know it's election season whenever you start seeing politicians standing on the curbs of busy streets, waving and smiling big while their supporters stand by their side, holding big signs with the politician's name on it. Why do politicians do this so much? Two reasons: One, because it's cheap…almost free. And two, because *it works.*

Why not borrow a page out of the playbooks of our shyster politician friends? Go to your local sign shop and have two signs made up – one that says in huge bold letters, "PRO WRESTLING" and another that says when and where. Get two pretty girls, one to hold each sign and wave to passing cars. Then get at least two (preferably more) of your best wrestlers and have them actually mock wrestle right there on the curb! The guys you choose should be your top draws, guys with awesome physiques. They should be in their wrestling trunks, pads, and boots, just as if they were doing a show.

Imagine the reaction of the drivers of the cars passing by as they see – just out of nowhere – a ripped pro wrestler gorilla pressing another pro wrestler over his head right there on the street! And right when they're wondering aloud, "What the hell are those guys doing?" your hot divas holding the signs start waving and cheering at them. If that scene doesn't leave an impression, nothing will! During rush hour, you can easily reach thousands of people this way, and it won't cost you a dime.

If you employ this tactic, and I encourage you to, keep these points in mind:

- The girls holding the signs should be very attractive
- The girls should be wearing your t-shirt and skimpy shorts
- The workers you choose should be in excellent shape
- Smile and wave a lot
- Be a showman! Get people's attention

Be sure to select a location along a very busy road or intersection. Be sure the location is safe and well away from traffic. And be sure that the place you're standing is public property, not private. A sidewalk next to the road is perfect. If you do this on private property, the property owner might get annoyed and call the police. Also, do not wander into traffic to hand out flyers or talk to people while they're stopped at a stoplight. The police may come out and write you a ticket for blocking traffic or jaywalking.

If you're on public property and the police show up to chase you off, respectfully inform the officers that you're exercising your Constitutional right to assemble publicly. Also inform the officers that the proceeds from your show will benefit your chosen charity. Typically that quickly softens a reasonable police officer's attitude.

Just don't get hostile or disrespectful, or you might get hauled off to jail on a disorderly conduct charge!

Put your ad on wheels

Own a pickup truck? If yes, you have an awesome mobile advertising platform. In fact, you can build your own mini billboard, strap it securely in the bed of your truck, and then ride all over town with it and effectively reach tens of thousands of potential customers. All you have to do is go to your local sign shop and have two identical, large signs professionally printed up that advertise your show and when and where it will be. Again, make sure the lettering is bold and dark against a white background. Construct a frame for the signs out of 2x4 lumber and then, using a good staple gun, staple the signs to the wooden frame. Then strap the whole deal to the bed of your truck and take a few joyrides all over town. Just make sure you build the frame tall enough so that the signs show above the sides of the pickup bed.

Oh, and also be sure to wash, wax, and detail the truck before you go for the joyride. A dirty truck will convey a low rent message to any onlookers.

Internet forums

In most regions there are Internet forums dedicated to local indie wrestling. If you haven't already, join the forums close to you and post electronic copies of your flyers there. Also be sure to plug your card, talk up why your promotion is different, and rain some praise on your chosen charity.

Be sure to post a message early about your upcoming show – at least 30 days in advance – and then add updates to the message at least twice a week leading up to the show. That way you'll keep the message about your show fresh and active, meaning fans won't forget about it or miss your original message. You want to hype your show online as much as possible. Don't be shy. Really sell up your main event and any other big match on your card. Remember, oftentimes if you just tell someone something is going to big, they end up believing it. Don't sell yourself or your promotion short.

The thank you note

In addition to your flyers and handbills, print up some thank you notes. Print up at least one for every fan you expect to come through the gate. These should be a quarter page in size and should have a big "Thank You!" printed across the top in a bold font. Directly underneath the big "Thank You!" should be a blurb that expresses your appreciation, something like this: "We're happy to have you as a fan! As a token of our appreciation, we have two special offers for you!" You then hand these out to the fans at the end of the show. Here are the two special offers that you extend: A buddy pass and a free gift. Let's discuss both.

A buddy pass is just that – a coupon that allows the fan to bring a friend for *free* to your next show. Effectively this is a buy one ticket, get one free deal. The concept is very simple: Grow you audience. If you put on a show and 200 people come, if you give out a buy one, get one free coupon, at your next show you might just get 250 people! Hand out the coupons again, and at the next show you might get 300. See how this works? You don't just want your established fans to keep coming back, you want them to come back and bring a friend along with them next time. Pack the house!

Also on the thank you note should be a free gift to thank your fans for their patronage. Here's how it works: Offer something for free – say a free soda from your concessions stand. All the fan has to do is go to your website and sign up for your newsletter. When you generate your newsletter, just include a coupon for the free drink. This kills two birds with one stone – it encourages fans to sign up for your newsletter *and* the free soda coupon encourages the fan to come back for your next show. Just make sure you have plenty of sodas to give away!

Ticket affiliates

A great way to increase your ticket sales without even having to work very hard is to sign up ticket affiliates. What's a ticket affiliate, you ask? A ticket affiliate is someone who sells tickets to your shows for you and keeps a cut of the profit for himself.

Typically the way this works is you approach local business owners and propose an offer whereby they agree to sell your show tickets on consignment. They make a cut off every ticket they sell. For example, suppose you charge $15 for a general admission ticket. You offer the business owner a deal – for every ticket he sells, he keeps $5. If he doesn't sell any of the tickets, that's OK – he makes nothing, he loses nothing. But if he *does* sell some tickets, he makes a nice little profit. Thus he has nothing to lose and everything to gain.

Let's take a look at an example of how this could work. You simply approach local business owners in your area and offer them to sell tickets for your show. Emphasize that the business owner has absolutely nothing to lose. If he agrees, you give the business owner a professional-looking standup sign to place on his checkout counter, right by his cash register. The sign says, "Buy [insert your promotion's name here] wrestling tickets here!"

You then give the business owner a stack of tickets to sell. For the sake of the example, let's say you give him 20 tickets one month before your upcoming show. Every time a customer checks out from his store, that customer will see your sign and potentially ask to buy a ticket. In fact, if the business owner you enter this deal with is smart, he'll even actively sell the tickets to every one of his customers by saying something like, "Sir, there's a great pro wrestling show coming up next week. You can get your tickets right here!"

After all, why wouldn't he do this? He has nothing to lose. If you agree to give him $10 for every ticket he sells, if he sells just 20 tickets, that's $200 in his pocket, and he barely has to do any work at all to make it. It's another item for him to sell at his store…only your tickets cost him nothing to add to his inventory!

OK, so let's discuss the details of making this work.

First you print up a very professional, full color sign that says something to the effect of, "Buy pro wrestling tickets here!" It goes without saying, but be sure to follow all the same design rules we covered when we talked about designing flyers. The sign should be professional, simple, and to the point. The ticket price should be clearly marked on the sign, too. Then you get some plastic standup sign holders from Office Depot. They cost only about $3 apiece. Slide the sign into the holder, and voila! You have a perfectly professional looking sign. Make several signs like this, one for each ticket affiliate you reach an agreement with.

Next you print up your admission tickets the way you normally would. Go to each of your affiliates and give him a set amount – say 20. The affiliate should know exactly how much to charge for the tickets and keep them safe somewhere behind the counter. For this example, let's suppose the agreement you hammer out is that he's to sell each ticket for $15. He keeps $10 and gives the remaining $5 to you.

After the show goes down, go to each affiliate and collect your earnings. Let's say one of your ticket affiliates is the local hardware store owner. If he sold 12 out of the stack of 20 tickets you gave him, he gives you $60 ($5 x 12) and the eight unsold tickets.

It's critical that you collect the unsold tickets! That's the only way to keep your affiliates honest. If you don't collect the unsold tickets, your affiliate may sell all 20 tickets, pocket all the cash, and then tell you, "Oh, yeah, sorry. I couldn't sell any of those tickets you left me." By collecting the unsold tickets after the show, there's no way this can happen.

This is a great way to dramatically increase your ticket sales. It's a divide-and-conquer approach. Remember, when looking for potential ticket affiliates, go to local businesses pro wrestling fans tend to go to – hardware stores, auto part stores, sports bars, comic book stores, pizzerias, etc.

Use your workers as affiliates

This is, by far, the most controversial tactic I have in my arsenal – that's why I saved it for last. Controversial as it may sound, who has more incentive to sell tickets than the workers on your card? Now, don't confuse this tactic with a common tactic used by shady promoters where they require their workers to sell X number of tickets if they want to appear in a show. Effectively those promoters require their workers to *buy* a spot on the card.

That's not at all what I'm suggesting. Workers should *never*, ever be required to sell tickets to get on a card, move up a card, or go over. Never. Instead, use the approach I just outlined in the previous section – print up tickets in advance and give them out to the wrestlers. Let's say the tickets are priced at $20. Tell the wrestlers, "Here are some tickets to next month's show. I really want you to help pack the house. So here's the deal – for every ticket you sell, you keep $10."

How's that for incentive? You see what we're doing here? We're fostering that win-win relationship between the worker and the promoter that I talked about at the very beginning of this book. The wrestlers don't *have* to sell the tickets, but it's definitely in their best interest to do so. It's money in their pockets! Tell them to sell the tickets to their friends, family, co-workers, enemies…whoever. Your workers should be sure to say to potential buyers that a portion of the ticket sales is going to your chosen charity. That way they don't feel quite as cheesy about approaching their friends and family about buying tickets. Instead of saying, "Hey, Tom, will you buy a ticket and come watch me wrestle?" they can say, "Hey, Tom, can I interest you in a ticket for a charity wrestling show we're putting on? We're donating a portion of the proceeds to the Boys and Girls Club!"

If you really want to push the envelope and you've got the guts, you could offer your workers *all* of the money from the tickets they sell. That is, if each ticket costs $20, your worker pockets the whole $20. That gives them even more incentive to sell! But then you might be thinking, "All right, Norm…if I let the workers keep all the money from the tickets they sell, how will I make any money?" That's a fair question. Here's your answer: Concessions. Pack the house and offer an awesome concessions stand. You'll make up the difference by selling more hotdogs, nachos, sodas, and candy.

If you're still skeptical, let me put it to you like this: What's worse, an empty seat where you make nothing at all or a guy sitting in that previously empty seat that you effectively gave away for free who might just go buy a hotdog and soda from your concessions stand and a t-shirt from your gimmick table? To me, some money is always better than no money, and a full seat is better than an empty one. Further, think about the potential here – if your workers start selling tickets, they can make serious money and be very happy doing it. You, meanwhile, now have a much fuller house with more opportunities to sell concessions.

Think about it. I really love this marketing tactic. It fosters a sense of collective teamwork throughout your promotion. Everybody is working in unison toward a shared goal, and everyone is rewarded fairly and, potentially, handsomely. Resist the temptation to lord over your ticket sales. In almost every single case, promoters who lord over the tickets may make more money in the very short run, but they fail over the long term.

Sharing ticket sales with your workers – and even your staff – delivers the potential to really pack the house and build up a raving fan base for your promotion. It could be the revolution indie pro wrestling needs to reinvent itself and become mainstream.

Concessions & Gimmicks

"For every sale you miss because you're too enthusiastic, you will miss a hundred because you're not enthusiastic enough."
- *Zig Ziglar, legendary salesman*

The lifeblood of indie wrestling

Is money.

Period. End of story. No more discussion necessary. Thou shalt make money. Imagine a big stack of cash piled up on one of those tables wrestlers love to throw themselves through. Wait. Scratch that. Those tables aren't strong enough to hold up that big stack of money. Instead, imagine a huge pile of money in the center of your ring.

Visualize it. Burn it into your memory.

Hear me when I say this to you: Your pro wrestling promotion or career is not a hobby. It is not "just for fun." It is not volunteer work or charity.

It's a money making machine.

You must make money. It's not your dream, it's your duty. As a promoter or worker it is your charge to preserve the sport of independent pro wrestling. Indie wrestling cannot survive without *you*. You are its keeper. You are its steward. You are its ambassador. You are its caretaker. You must keep it alive and make it thrive.

To do that you must make money. If no one makes money at this business, sooner or later it will dry up and wither away. As I write these words, there are immensely talented young workers contemplating hanging up their boots for good because they've decided there's nothing in it for them. As I type this sentence, there are promoters who have given up and are locking their rings away in storage lockers, hoping they'll be able to sell it to someone.

What a tragedy.

Why?

Because very, very few people in the "business" of indie pro wrestling understand that pro wrestling is just that – a business. And to stay in business, you must make money.

That's what this chapter is about. Making money through concessions and your gimmick table. This is a huge potential for raking in the dough, if you know how to maximize it. And I'm going to tell you how.

Not by bread alone

Man does not live by bread alone; nor can indie wrestling live on just ticket sales. Ticket sales are great, but they alone won't keep you in business. To stay in business you must make money through other channels...and a lot of it.

I have been to thousands of indie wrestling shows over the past 25 years, and I can say with confidence I have never been to a single one with a properly run concessions stand.

Not one.

Sure, at just about every one there was what they *called* a concessions stand, but by my profit-focused expectations, they all fell woefully short.

The experience almost always goes something like this. I walk up to the table and have to figure out for myself what's being sold. Then there's some standoffish or shy kid taking orders. He's wearing sagged pants and a death metal t-shirt. He just stares at me as I walk up to him.

"Uh, hi," I say. "Can I get a hotdog and a Coke Zero, please?"

The kid looks blankly back at me with no emotion, no expression on his face at all. Then he turns to a girl cooking food behind him and asks, "Do we have Coke Zero?" to which the girl says no.

"We don't have Coke Zero," he says.

"Uh, OK, how about Diet Coke?"

"Do we have Diet Coke?" he asks the girl, to which she answers, "No. We have Diet Pepsi."

"We have Diet Pepsi," he informs me.

"OK," I say, "I'll take a Diet Pepsi."

"Two fifty," he mumbles.

I give him three dollars. He hands me fifty cents with that blank, zombie-like expression still on his face. Then he just stands there, frowning, with his long, skinny arms dangling. He stares out into space, completely ignoring me.

The girl delivers the hotdog. "Here you go," she says.

I pick up the dog and can tell right away it's one of those nasty, cheap *boiled* hotdogs...you know, where all the flavor is boiled out of it.

I ask the zombie, "Do you guys have anything else to go with it?"

He snaps out of his stupor, points lazily to the mustard and ketchup and says, "Yeah. The toppings are over there."

That's not what I meant, of course, but since this guy isn't interested in selling anything and since he's behaving as if he's doing *me* a favor, I don't bother asking for a bag of chips or boiled peanuts. Forget it. I'll just eat my nasty boiled dog and watch the show.

But then I remember my Diet Pepsi.

"You got my Diet Pepsi?" I ask the kid.

"Huh? Oh, yeah, did you order one?"

Fail. This is an epic fail in so many ways. This is so fail I can't even believe that it happens. Yet it does. Almost always.

I remember at a recent show I attended, the air conditioning was out, so I decided to go buy a bottle of water. "One bottle of water, please," I said to the concessions girl.

She replied, "Oh, we only have bottled water for the wrestlers."

Fail! Here I am with money in hand, willing to fork it over, but instead you're going to give said water bottle to a worker for *free*?!

So I said, "OK, how about a Diet Coke?"

"We only have Pepsi and Mountain Dew."

I sigh. "OK, fine. I'll take a Pepsi."

She delivers the Pepsi without saying a word. And guess what? It's warm.

Fail!

This is not any way to run a business. If you're running a concessions stand like this (and you may not even realize it's happening), you are losing gobs of money. You're bleeding cash. You're missing opportunity after opportunity after opportunity. That's money you could be banking to improve your promotion, pay the boys with, increase your advertising, improve your ring, etc.

Instead you let it *literally* walk out the door.

We're going to fix this problem…right now, in this chapter.

Do not be ashamed of making money

Making money is a good thing. Don't let anyone tell you otherwise. In any business, the only thing better than making money is making *more* money. Remember, it's your duty as a wrestling professional to *make money*. So don't let anyone get down on you for that.

We are not doing this for our health. We are not doing this as a charity. We are not doing this as an expensive hobby. We are not doing this just to get ourselves and our buddies booked and over.

We are doing this to make a profit.

We are doing this to grow the business of indie wrestling, and the best way to do that is to get our customers to fork over all the cash in their wallets to us.

Think of it this way. Each person who walks through your gate has a certain amount of cash in his wallet. Typically a fan brings enough money for tickets *and* other stuff. Your mission is to sell that fan enough *other stuff* so that fan leaves your building broke.

I don't mean this in a crooked carny way; I mean this in a legitimate *business* way. If a fan leaves your promotion with $20 in his pocket, he's going to spend it. He's going to go buy a six pack of beer, a bunch of lottery tickets, or an extra-large pizza. So if the guy's going to spend that money anyway, why not deliver something he wants so that he gives that $20 to you instead of that convenience store or pizzeria?

If you run a concessions stand, you are in competition with far more than the other indie promotions – you're in competition with anyone else who sells food. And in the world of business, he who competes best survives; he who competes worst perishes.

Do not perish.

Also, don't be afraid to charge the going market value for what you're selling. If you're selling bottled Cokes, you can buy them in bulk at Sam's Club for about 50¢ apiece. When you turn around and sell them at your show, don't sell them for $1.50 if you can get $2 for them! Don't try to "be nice" by offering prices below what you

Making money: Remember, each fan that walks through your doors has a set amount of money in his wallet. Your mission is to get it.

SCOTT WALDRON

could get for them. Again, you're not running a charity. You need to make money to stay in business and keep indie wrestling alive. You need to make money to be able to pay those boys behind the curtain for risking life and limb for you.

That said, don't attempt to fleece your fans, either. If you feel you can get push the envelope and get $2 for a Coke, don't jack the price up to $3. If you do that, fans will feel ripped off. As a rule, don't charge any more for a Coke or bag of popcorn than you would pay at a minor league baseball game.

Now, if you do raise your price from $1 to $2 for a Coke, if someone says to you, "Oh, you're just trying to make money," say, "You're damned right!"

Operating a successful concession

In this chapter we're going to talk about operating both a concession stand and a gimmick table, but I want to talk about concessions first. This is a lengthy topic, so I'm going to divide the discussion into several subtopics, starting with what you should be selling.

What to sell

There are three considerations when deciding what to sell at a concessions stand: How much fans want it, how difficult it is to prepare, and, most importantly, the profit margin on said item.

Obviously you don't want to sell something wrestling fans don't want. For example, offering spinach salad at your concession stand is probably not a good idea. I have always abided by a simple rule: Sweet, salty, or hot. All the items you offer should be one of those three. That's because people find these foods irresistible. Popcorn and peanuts are salty. Candy and soda are sweet. Hotdogs and pizza are hot.

With this method in mind, is a spinach salad sweet? No. Is it salty? No. Is it hot? No. Then it's off the list. What about pasta salad? Is it sweet? No. Is it salty? No. Is it hot? No. Off the list. Got it? Good. Don't forget it.

The next consideration is the difficulty of preparation of a given food item. For example, to cook hamburgers you need a big grill. Plus there's a great danger in cooking hamburger – if you don't cook it enough, people can get sick. This makes preparation difficult, so scratch hamburgers off the list. You want items that are very easy to prepare and very easy to store.

Finally, there's profit margin. How much does the item cost versus how much you can sell it for? That's the key consideration, assuming you can sell it.

So some excellent things to offer at your stand would be hotdogs, nachos, pizza, potato chips, popcorn, peanuts, candy, chocolate chip cookies, and sodas. You can probably think of many other good items to add to this list, but the ones I listed should be your mainstays, especially popcorn and cookies. We'll discuss why popcorn and cookies are extremely important in just a bit, but first, let's discuss the art of sales.

Introducing Ms. Rainmaker

Remember our zombie-like friend wearing the death metal t-shirt who took my order in the story I related earlier in this chapter? Yes? OK, great.

Don't hire him. Don't hire him even if he agrees to work for free. Don't even hire him if he agrees to pay *you*. Don't hire him unless you

270

have something totally behind the scenes for him to do, liking slinging the ring or picking up trash after the show.

Death metal zombie kid working your concessions stand will cost you serious money, even if he's a volunteer. Do not let a dud like him fill such a vital position in your promotion.

In fact, let me make something crystal clear: After the promoter, the person taking orders at your concessions stand is quite possibly *the* most vital person in your promotion. This person, if he or she is the right person, is the key to you making lots and lots of money. This person is critical. And you must have the right person for this job.

Who's right for the job? Here are the qualifications: A young, well-endowed attractive girl who's very outgoing, friendly, and not shy. She should be able to smile easily, have a sunny disposition, and be extremely motivated.

This girl is going to make you serious money. She's Ms. Rainmaker. She's going to make it rain cash.

To demonstrate how, let's rerun the scenario I painted earlier, but this time we're going to replace the death metal zombie kid with Ms. Rainmaker.

There she is, Ms. Rainmaker: Chain restaurants are excellent places to find intelligent, outgoing, and attractive candidates for the role of Ms. Rainmaker.

So here we go. I walk up to the concessions stand. Ms. Rainmaker is standing ready and eager to serve me. She's attractive, her hair is tied up professionally, and she's wearing a bright t-shirt with the promotion's logo on it. Before I even get to the table, Ms. Rainmaker smiles big at me and says, "Hello, sir! You look *hungry*! How about one of our kraut dogs?"

Right away I feel good. I feel comforted, welcomed. This girl is nice. She wants to help me. She's not going to spit in my food for fun.

"Kraut dog? OK, that sounds good," I say. "Sure. I'll have that."

"One kraut dog coming up! And you want chips with that, too, right?" she says as she grabs a bag of chips and places them on the counter. Then she smiles at me.

"Uh, sure," I say.

"And what would like to drink? Coke?" she says as she reaches into a cooler and retrieves a Coke from the ice.

"Actually I'd prefer Coke Zero," I say.

She puts the Coke Zero on the table and then turns to assist the girl cooking in preparing my kraut dog, which is ready in a snap. She places the *grilled* (not boiled) dog on a fresh bun and smothers it in sauerkraut. She sets it on the table along with the Coke Zero and chips.

Then she motions toward a stack of giant chocolate chip cookies and says, "Oh, yeah! You *really* need to try one of those chocolate chip cookies. The promoter's grandmother makes them from scratch from a secret family recipe. I *love* them."

"Really? All right, I'll try one."

Then she picks up a box of Hot Tamales and says, "And how about a box of Hot Tamales to snack on later during the show?"

Since I like Hot Tamales, I say, "Oh, OK, sure…"

You see what's happened here? Compare the experience above to the one I had with the zombie kid. When the zombie kid was "running" the concessions, I bought a hotdog and a soda. And he didn't sell it to me, he just handled the transaction (and poorly, at that). On the other hand, with Ms. Rainmaker at the helm, I bought a kraut dog (which is logically more expensive than a plain dog), a bag of chips, a soda, a cookie, and box of candy. Ms. Rainmaker *made* the promotion money!

She made money that will enable the promotion to continue to run shows, thereby contributing greatly to the survival of indie pro wrestling! If you believe indie pro wrestling is a good thing – I certainly do – Ms. Rainmaker is doing us an invaluable service. She's not only keeping us on the map, she's helping us expand and grow.

You *need* a rainmaker. If you don't have one, no problem. You can train one. I show you how in the next few sections.

Why a girl?

Because the majority of people in a pro wrestling audience are men.

272

And men like girls.

A 2009 study published in the *Archives of Sexual Behavior* found that, surprise surprise, waitresses who were flirty, had big breasts, and wore nice makeup made much bigger tips. It's simple, really – heterosexual men have a very hard time saying no to an attractive, friendly young woman. Knowing this, it only makes sense to capitalize on it. If an attractive young woman can increase your profits, by all means, find an attractive young woman to run your concessions!

The two things a salesperson should never say

There are two things that salespeople – regardless of what they're selling – should never, ever say: "May I help you?" and, "Anything else?" These are two of the very worst things you can say if you want to maximize your profits.

Of course you might be thinking, "Wait a minute, Norm…I hear workers in stores say those things all the time! I thought that was good customer service!"

Wrong.

Those workers who say these two things – while they mean well – are committing the most flagrant foul in the world of selling. Why? Because we have become conditioned (like Pavlov's dogs) to say *no*.

Think about it. If you walk into a store and an employee walks up to you and says, "May I help you?" nine times out of ten, you're going to respond with, "Uh, no thank you. I'm just looking."

Same holds true with, "Anything else?" Our conditioned, automatic, unconscious answer to that question is almost always, "Uh, nope. That's all."

The "Anything else?" question is particularly stupid. If I wanted something else, wouldn't I just ask for it? Plus, it's not like I'm going to stop the clerk from completing the transaction to stand there and ponder if there's anything else I want. No, I'm just going to say, "That's it," and expect the guy to ring me up.

So what should salespeople do instead of saying, "May I help you?" and, "Anything else?" Simple: Suggest something.

Anything. Suggest something! Show the customer something!

Twenty years ago, when I was just a buck private (airman) in the Air Force, I wasn't making much money. As they say, you won't get rich by digging a ditch.

So to make some extra cash, I moonlighted at the local Radio Shack. It was actually an excellent learning experience for me. One of the best things I learned was the art of selling. When I first started that job, I knew nothing about selling anything. But we got paid on a commission, so I knew that if I would put my nose to the grindstone, I could make lots of money. And sure enough, within just a few months I was the number one Radio Shack salesman in the entire Denver area.

How did I do it? Easy – by taking the bull by the horns. I realized that Radio Shack had tons of cool things for sale, things that most customers knew nothing about. Most customers didn't even know that they even existed.

There was one item in particular that I found very cool. It was a pocket computer. Now mind you, this is the early nineties. Digital cell phones, iPhones, and iPads hadn't been invented yet. Personal computers were available then, but most of them were hulking behemoths that took up an entire desk. Radio Shack, however, sold one that was the size of a pocket calculator.

It had one feature in particular that made me a mint – an appointment calendar. You could type your appointments into the calendar and the thing would remind you of them by beeping at you at the designated time. I knew that was very cool at that time, so I decided I would show it to my customers.

Every single one of them.

If a guy came in to buy batteries for a flashlight, I'd say, "Hey, you got a minute? Check this out. It's so cool," and I'd proceed to show the guy the appointment calendar feature of the pocket computer. Sure enough that guy who came in only wanting batteries was raising an eyebrow when the little beeping alarm went off.

"You'll never miss another appointment," I said. "Never be late for meetings."

To my amazement, people bought them hand-over-fist. And what was really great was I made $12 for every one I sold. Before I started showing the little computer to people, no one ever even bothered to look at them in the glass case. No one knew what they were. We had boxes of them in the stockroom, collecting dust. But then when I started showing them to people, we couldn't keep them on the shelves!

And the best part was, I didn't have to be pushy, didn't have to be annoying, and didn't have to be a huckster. All I had to do was show the thing to people.

That's why you don't say, "May I help you?" or "Anything else?" Imagine had I said to the guy who came in to buy batteries for his flashlight, "Anything else?" Do you think he would have bought one of those pocket computers? Heck no! He'd pay for his $2 batteries and walk out and I'd bank a whopping ten cent commission.

You can see this in action in the example I painted featuring Ms. Rainmaker. When I walked up to the concessions table, she didn't say, "May I help you?" she said, "How about a kraut dog?" She planted the beautiful image of a scrumptious hotdog in my head, which I yielded to. Had she not done this, I might have just bought a Snickers bar.

Also notice that Ms. Rainmaker never said, "Anything else?" Instead she *suggested* other things for me to buy, like the chocolate chip cookies and the box of Hot Tamales. You see what I'm getting at?

She's using the power of suggestion!

Do not underestimate the awesome persuasiveness of the power of suggestion. I sold hundreds of pocket computers at Radio Shack simply by suggesting it.

Good salespeople know that big sales don't just happen; you have to work for them. A good salesperson also realizes that merchandise will sell – if customers know about them and are encouraged to buy them. Again, think the kraut dog, the cookies, and the Hot Tamales. When I walked up to that concessions stand, I had no idea they were even selling Hot Tamales, not until she suggested them.

And since she suggested them, I bought them, thus depositing more operating capital into the promotion's coffers.

Assuming the sale

This is an extremely potent sales tactic used by all expert salespeople. It takes some practice, and you may need to overcome some initial shyness about it, but once you've mastered this tactic, your sales will skyrocket.

As mentioned previously, this is a tactic you want to teach to your own Ms. Rainmaker. But before you can teach it, you must master it.

Here's how it works. When you assume the sale, you do just that: You assume that the customer has already agreed to the sale before he ever does. Remember in the scenario I painted earlier where Ms. Rainmaker sold me the kraut dog? Remember when she said, "You want chips with that, right?" A moment later she said, "What would you like to drink? Coke?"

Go back and reread the scenario if you need to. Notice that I never asked for chips or a soda – she just assumed I wanted them! In fact, when I walked up to her table, I may not have wanted them at all, but by her assuming that I did, I agreed to buy them.

Here's another example of assuming the sale. Let's say you walk into a furniture store with your spouse. You're interested in a new sofa for the living room. As you enter, the salesman greets you by saying, "Hi, folks! How are you? Thanks for coming in. Take a look around! We have some really great specials this week."

He then leaves you alone.

Or so you think.

Notice he did *not* say, "May I help you?" Instead he just invited you in and encouraged you to look around. Now as you and your wife browse around, that salesman is secretly watching you. He's taking note of what you like and what you don't. He's watching your body language and your expressions. He watches for nods and smiles. Then when he thinks the moment is right, he moves in.

"That sofa is on sale this week," he says with a smile. "It's a Broyhill, one of the best brands of furniture on the market today. I haven't seen a Broyhill sofa marked down this low in a long, long time."

You ask him how much it is, and he tells you. He then proceeds to extol the quality of the fabric, the seams, and the springs. He encourages you to sit on it and appreciate its plush coziness. So you do. You and your spouse nod in agreement to each other but don't make a decision to buy it yet.

The salesman excuses himself for a moment to get something. A moment later he returns with a clipboard and a pen.

"Where do you folks live?"

"In Longwood Estates," you say.

"Great!" he says. "That's in our delivery area. We deliver free in our delivery area."

And now here it comes…

He's going to assume the sale…

"So," he says, "when would you like your new sofa delivered?"

Bingo! There it is.

You see how it works? Neither you nor your spouse said that you wanted to buy the sofa, yet he just assumed you did. In effect, he made the decision for you. He could tell by your expressions and your nodding in agreement that you liked the sofa, so he just made the buying decision easy by making it for you. He knew you wanted it but sensed your hesitation.

Everyone hesitates when they're about to buy something. A good salesman always assumes the sale to gently nudge you past that moment of hesitation. Remember this: People love to buy. Buying stuff is fun. People like to own new things. It's part of the human experience. Yet when they approach the moment of exchanging cash for the item, indecision strikes. A good salesperson reassures the buyer by effectively saying, "Hey, it's OK. It's already yours."

As I mentioned at the very beginning of this section, you may feel a bit uncomfortable using this tactic at first. You might feel shy or worry that you're being presumptuous. Relax. It's OK. If you use this method correctly, there's nothing wrong with it. It's like your customer is on a fence, teetering back and forth between buying and passing. He wants you to push him. By assuming the sale, you do just that. You nudge him over the fence to the side of buying.

And there's nothing wrong with a gentle nudge.

So the next time you're working your concessions stand, don't say, "Would you like chips with your hot dog?" say, "Would you prefer Lays or Doritos?" Don't say, "Would you like something to drink?" say, "What do you want to drink? Coke, Diet Coke, or Sprite?"

The key is to try not to give the customer the opportunity to say no, because nine times out of ten, if you give a customer a chance to say no, instinctively he's going to say it.

Remember, assume. Assume the sale is made. Assume the customer has already said yes.

Assume, assume, assume!

Building trust

Let's talk some more about death metal zombie kid from the bad indie wrestling concessions experience. I've been picking on that kid a lot in this chapter, but he's just so darned easy. He scored an *F* in every possible category.

The category he really failed in was building trust. Whenever you attempt to buy something from someone – especially food – whether you realize it or not, you want someone you can trust. You are far more apt to buy something from someone you trust than someone you don't.

That, of course, is just common sense.

Or is it? If it is, why in the heck was zombie kid permitted to work that concessions stand? Right when I walked up, I got a bad vibe from him. He was standoffish, his appearance was poor, he showed no human emotion, and he seemed as if he couldn't possibly care less about working there. Did I trust this guy? Heck no! In fact, as soon as I ordered my hotdog from him, I started having second thoughts. I began worrying that the people preparing it hadn't washed their hands first. Or maybe zombie kid spat in the water as they were boiling. Or maybe zombie kid is a meth addict with a contagious disease. Who knows?

Any way you look at it, my appetite was killed and I wanted out of there.

What about buying a new car? Let's say you go to the car dealership to buy a new car. You're looking at a new pickup when you get approached by a really cheesy salesman. He's got an orange fake tan, his hair is greasy and slicked into place, he has a pencil thin mustache, and he's trying to cover up his cigarette smell with lots and lots of cheap cologne. He comes up to you and says, "Hey, how 'bout it, chief? Let's put that baby in your garage *tonight!*"

Would you feel comfortable buying a car from a guy like this? Would you trust this guy? Would you feel confident this guy isn't going to try to rip you off any way he can or try to pull a fast one on you, like charge you $500 to spray a $5 bottle of Stainmaster on the truck's seats?

Of course not. In fact, not only would you not feel confident, you'd probably also feel uncomfortable and creeped out by the guy. You'd want to get the heck out of there.

So let's say you do. You somehow shake this guy off you and drive to the next dealership over. You start looking at another pickup when, again, a salesman approaches you. But this time the guy is dressed very professionally. He's wearing a crisp dress shirt and a perfectly knotted tie. He's clean cut and clean shaven. He extends his hand for a shake, smiles genuinely, and says, "Hello, sir! My name's Tom. Thanks for coming in. Hey, why don't you take a look at the interior of that truck? Hold on, I'll go grab the key. Be right back."

He eagerly jogs off to the dealership building and then returns with the key. He unlocks the truck, turns it on and turns on the air conditioner for you. "Come on, sit inside," he says, allowing you to sit in the driver's seat. He stays out of the truck and leaves you alone, allowing you look around and take it all in – the plush interior, the wood instrument panel, the new car smell…

So now compare the two experiences? Who are you most likely to buy from? It goes without saying it would be the second guy, Tom. Why? Because he worked at establishing trust. You didn't feel pressured by him, uneasy, or cornered. He came across as confident and knowledgeable. He appeared down-to-earth. Put simply, you felt you could trust the guy.

This lesson must be applied to our concessions stands and gimmick tables, too. When a fan (customer!) walks up, the person working that table should immediately try to establish some trust. Smile. Make eye contact. Say hello. Tell him how good tonight's show is going to be. This will immediately and subconsciously disarm him. He'll lower his guard and will immediately begin to trust you. And once he trusts you, he'll even begin to *like* you, making him much more apt to buy something from you.

Know your stuff. Know what you're talking about. Whether you're selling hotdogs or DVDs, sodas or action figures, know what you're selling. If the customer asks you, "What brand of hotdog are you selling?" don't say, "Uh…I'm not sure…" say, "We have Nathan's Famous Franks, the same ones they sell at Yankee Stadium!" By knowing your stuff, not only do you come across as confident and enthusiastic, you have an opportunity to expound on how great what you're selling is.

So building confidence is essential. Remember, smile, be warm and genuine, welcome the customer, know your stuff, and most importantly, be a real human being.

Let's go to the movies

Movie theaters are the masters of the concessions stand. They have to be, you know why? Because, believe it or not, movie theaters don't make any money off the movies they show. So how do they make money? You guessed it – from the concessions stand. Almost all the money made from ticket sales goes back to the movie studio.

Don't believe me? Take it straight from Howard Edleman, owner of Movieland Cinemas: "Theater owners joke about being in the candy business. If you didn't have concessions at a movie theater, there would be no movie theater. We have movies just to get people in to buy popcorn and candy, where we make our money."

Make no mistake – this holds true for indie pro wrestling, too. Follow the same model used by the movie theaters. The movie isn't the product, it's the bait. It's the draw. Likewise, a well-run wrestling promotion should understand that the wrestling is the bait, too. It's the draw to get people all packed in to one place where you can then sell them popcorn, candy, Coney dogs, and ice cold soda pop...oh, and DVDs, t-shirts, action figures, and toy belts. You shouldn't be running your promotion such that your wrestling is the main focus and concessions are just there to make you a little side cash. It's just the opposite – concessions and the gimmick table should receive equal attention to the show you put on in the ring.

Since movie theaters are obviously very successful at running concession stands, let's take a look at them. The very first thing you will always notice about a movie theater concessions stand isn't what you see, it's what you *smell* – fresh, buttery popcorn. Right when that wonderful aroma hits your nose, you think, "Mmmm...popcorn..."

Then you walk up to the counter and are awestruck by light and color. The glass case under the counter is jam-packed with M&Ms, Hot Tamales, Junior Mints, Sour Patch Kids, Snickers bars, and Sno-Caps.

On the wall behind the counter are pictures of tubs of popcorn, hotdogs smothered in mustard, and nachos covered in cheese. They make it perfectly clear what they're selling. It's the land of plenty.

This is the look you want to strive for when you set up your concessions stand. Remember the central lesson from Chapter Two – appearances are everything! This holds especially true for your concessions stand and your gimmick table. You want to project a polished, clean, professional appearance to your customers. Further, you want your operation to appear topnotch, alive, well stocked, and ready for business.

We'll talk about that in just a bit, but first, let's talk about quality.

Make it good

An indie pro wrestling show shouldn't just be a show, it should be an *experience*. And everything about that experience should be excellent. The matches should be good, the workers should be good, the booking should be good…and the food should be good.

I mean, really good. Think about it. One of the main reasons fans love to go to Wrigley Park is the food. Grilled Chicago hotdogs, juicy Polish sausages, thick hamburgers…fans say all the time, "I can't wait to get to the ballpark and have one of those huge foot-long Chicago dogs!" The food is all part of the *experience.*

Thus it's a complete no-brainer that if you're going to sell food at your wrestling shows (and you better), that it be absolutely delicious. Don't skimp! Don't cut corners! Don't try to save a few nickels and dimes by buying cheap no-name hotdogs or grocery store generic cola. Get the good stuff! Make the stuff taste good! Sure, you have to charge more for it, but trust me, almost everyone in the world would rather pay $3 for something delicious than $1 for something that tastes awful.

All your food should be super fresh. Sodas should be ice cold. Hot food should be served steaming hot. Packaged food like candy and potato chips should be new, not expired.

You want your fans to finish eating what you serve them and say to each other, "Wow, that was really, really good!" This will encourage two things: a) They'll go back and buy more food and b) they'll be much more inclined to come to your next show. The next time they see your flyer up in a window, they'll think, "Oh yeah! That show was awesome. And I could really go for another one of those awesome Coney dogs they sell there."

Quality! Quality in everything! Give your fans the highest quality experience and they'll come back. Give them quality food and they'll buy lots of it. Give them food that tastes good and they'll gladly pay a higher price for it.

The operation

At last, without further ado, we discuss how to operate the concessions table. First, start with the table. You actually need two banquet tables, set up end-to-end in an *L*-shape. This will give you plenty of working space. Both tables should be covered with dark banquet table cloths. Designate a central, highly visible spot on the tables for your Ms. Rainmaker to do her work.

You should have a big, professional, colorful sign or banner hanging on the wall behind the tables. The sign should say in big, bold letters, "Food & Drinks!" Also have the logos of the products you're selling (Nathan's Famous Franks, Coca-Cola, Pepsi, etc.) printed on the sign underneath the big bold letters. Don't worry about a copyright infringement. No one is going to sue you for using their logo to sell their stuff at an independent wrestling show. Just be sure you're selling those companies' products.

Next, create a basket display to showcase the packaged items you're selling at your stand. Fill the basket with boxes of Hot Tamales, bags of M&Ms, bottles of Coke and Sprite, bags of chips, and lots of king size candy bars. This will attractively advertise what you have for sale. It's a substitute for that jam-packed glass case at the movie theater. The idea is to display what you have for sale attractively and enticingly.

Set your popcorn machine on the table opposite the one where Ms. Rainmaker is working her magic. What, you don't own a popcorn maker? Buy one! You can get a good quality popcorn maker for around $100 online. Get one. It's a necessity. It's one of your three secret weapons for increasing your concessions sales. We'll talk about those three secret weapons in the next section, but for now, get a popcorn maker and set it on that table.

Next, you need a work table. The work table should be set up against the wall behind the table serving as the service counter. Here you should set all your equipment for preparing food. A great, easy, and economical way to prepare hotdogs is with – you guessed it – a George Foreman grill! Get one!

Also make sure you have at least two large ice coolers. One cooler is for staging and the other is for selling. To ensure your customers always receive an ice cold soda or bottle of water, fill both coolers with sodas and bottles. Begin selling from your selling cooler. As you run out, restock it from the staging cooler, but as soon as you take drinks from the staging cooler, replace them with the warm drinks you have in reserve. That way your drinks get cold in your staging cooler and you never run the risk of accidentally pulling a drink out before it's had a chance to get ice cold.

Finally, have several price lists professional printed (or done with a computer) with big lettering that lists the price of every item you have for sale and its price. Tape these lists to the tops of your tables so customers can see them easily. It's best to print these in color. Remember to include all those food logos we discussed moments ago.

Your three secret weapons

Now it's time to use some good 'ole subliminal advertising. Ever been to Disney World? If you haven't, when you first enter the Magic Kingdom theme park, the first area you're in is called Main Street USA. It's a theme park unto itself, modeled to look like a small town in turn-of-the-century America. Anyway, the most famous attraction in Main Street USA is its bakery. Every year, millions of guests are drawn to this bakery by the grand aroma of fresh baked cookies wafting through the bakery's open doors.

Sounds good, doesn't it? But guess what? Those aren't real cookies those guests are smelling – it's fragrance spray pumped onto the walking paths of Main Street USA. Yes, it's fake cookie spray. Walt Disney had his engineers install a machine that constantly pumps chocolate chip cookie fragrance outside the bakery because he knew his customers wouldn't be able to resist the awesome aroma.

So we're going to borrow a page from Walt's little black book and increase our concessions profits, too. Your three secret weapons are your popcorn maker, a bottle of cookie scented air spray, and a big fan.

Here's how it works. Your popcorn maker is set on that table away from where the orders are taken. Start popping popcorn well before your doors open to fill your building with the aroma of freshly popped popcorn. Then place that big fan right behind the popcorn maker and aim it right at your audience. The fan will carry that delicious popcorn smell to your fans in the stands, drawing them to your concessions stand like flies.

I've done this many, many times before and trust me, it *works*. People can't resist it. And once they come to the table to take the popcorn bait, your attractive Ms. Rainmaker should be standing ready to do her stuff, selling sodas and hotdogs and nachos to go along with that bag of popcorn!

But that's just half of our subliminal advertising strategy. The second half is a product called, "Your Season Freshly Baked Cookie Scented Room Spray." You can buy it for less than $5 a can from *www.sallybeauty.com*. This spray smells just like freshly baked chocolate chip cookies. Take this and occasionally spray it right into that big fan we talked about and let the fan carry the scent over to your audience. They'll be headed to your concessions stand faster than the Cookie Monster can devour a plate of Oreos.

Just be sure you have plenty of chocolate chip cookies and popcorn ready to sell!

Where to find Ms. Rainmaker?

All right, so you need an attractive young woman to work your concessions stand to sell, sell, sell. Where do you find her? There are a lot of potential places, but probably the best place to look is at chain restaurants like Hard Rock Café, Outback Steakhouse, or TGI Friday's since waitresses there have already been taught the sales techniques we've discussed so far. Plus they have experience interacting with people and selling.

To find her, just keep your eyes open when you go out to eat. Once you find a waitress who's outgoing, warm, and enthusiastic about her job, you've found her. Just offer her the job and make it worth her while by offering an hourly wage, a *commission* (which we discuss next), and tips.

Many young waitresses in places like these are college girls who are eager to make money for school. If your offer sounds fair and attractive, you should have no problem recruiting someone.

How much to charge

I touched on this topic briefly before, but now it's time for us to talk about it in detail. Knowing how much to charge and setting prices aggressively are key to you making money in pro wrestling. It's been my experience that, by and large, concessions stands at indie pro wrestling events *under*charge for what they have to offer. As such, they're losing money.

Oftentimes promoters decide how much to charge for a burger or a hotdog based on how much they cost in "the wild." That is, how much does a burger cost at McDonald's? How much does a hotdog cost at Dairy Queen? Once they've determined that amount, they mistakenly conclude, "Well I can't charge more for a burger than McDonald's does! I'll be ripping my fans off."

The reason why this is a mistaken conclusion is specifically because of that term I just introduced – "the wild." McDonald's, Hardee's, Dairy Queen, KFC, and Burger King are all in the wild. That is, they are in direct competition with

ALAINA BUZAS

Price the Minors: Pay attention to the prices of concessions items at minor league baseball games. This will give you a good idea of how much you should charge at your shows.

one another. In today's world, it is not at all uncommon to see a McDonald's on one side of the street and a Burger King immediately across on the other. It's a dog-eat-dog world in the wild. If customers don't like your food, your service, or your prices, they have plenty of other options available. If customers decide a McDonald's cheeseburger is too expensive, there's a Burger King not far away. So to keep from losing customers, all these fast food joints have to constantly be in a price war with each other. If one guy lowers his prices, the other guys do, too.

That's the beauty of running concessions at wrestling shows – you're not in the wild! You have a complete monopoly over what gets sold in your house. Ever wonder why a Coke at a Major League Baseball game costs $4? Ever wonder why a large tub of popcorn at the movie theater costs $6? It's because once their customers walk through the gate, they can't shop around for a better price. It's a noncompetitive environment.

In order for your promotion to succeed, you must exploit this advantage. Again, my rule of thumb is to charge roughly equivalent to what minor league baseball teams charge for their concessions. For example, at the time of this writing, a plain old hotdog with nothing on it costs between $3.50 and $4 at a minor league game. A regular soda costs $3.50!

If they can charge prices like that, so can you!

For the sake of simplicity and to keep the line moving, I always recommend you charge even fifty cent amounts for things. For example, if you're considering charging $3.25 for a hotdog, just round up to $3.50. This will make making change much easier on Ms. Rainmaker. After all, you want her selling, not doing complicated mathematics.

While on the subject of Ms. Rainmaker, it's time to discuss her compensation. Remember, a person in sales is always much more motivated to sell if there's something in it for them. As such, you should pay her a commission on everything she sells. Pay her 50 cents for everything. If she sells a hotdog, she gets 50 cents of the take. If she sells a soda, same thing. That way it's in her best interest to sell, sell, and sell!

Also allow her to place a tip jar on the table next to where she takes the orders. If she's good at what she does and is warm and friendly the way I described, she's sure to make good tips. So at end of the night, she gets an hourly wage you and she agree to in advance, a commission on everything she sells, and whatever's in the tip jar. This should keep her motivated to keep performing well for you.

Running a gimmick table

Now it's time to turn the discussion to the old gimmick table. Many of the tactics we discussed in the previous sections apply to operating a gimmick table, too, so be sure to apply them. For example, you want a Ms. Rainmaker working your gimmick table as well as your concessions. Let's start the discussion with the cardinal rule – no outside tables.

No outsiders allowed

Now I know this may irritate a lot of vendors out there who like to operate their own tables at local wrestling shows, but it has to be said. Let me be plainly clear about it: Do *not* allow outsiders to set up tables at your show! It doesn't matter what they're selling – it can be Ginsu knives or Chia Pets – do *not* let them in, even if they agree to pay you rent to set up their table.

Why, you ask? Because these jokers will bleed you of cash! Remember, a wrestling fan walks through your doors with a set amount of cash money in his pocket. That means he has a set amount of money he can spend for the night. You want him to spend it on stuff *you* have to sell. If you allow some guy to come in and sell fake Rolex watches or Mexican wrestling masks, the fans who buy that junk will have less money to spend on *you!*

Why would anyone do this? You're letting your competition in your house. It's like a caveman inviting a saber tooth tiger into his cave. He's just going to cut into your profits. Remember, it's your mission to make money in this business. You're the one who's keeping indie pro wrestling alive. These other hangers on, are they doing anything to promote wrestling as a sport and a business? Heck no! They'd set up their junk tables at a ballet performance if they were allowed to. All they care about is having near exclusive access to your customers.

Don't let them. Cut them out. It's your business, not theirs.

Let the children come

I love to see kids at indie pro wrestling events – ones that are safe and family-friendly, that is. Not only are we creating the next generation of pro wrestling fans, we're also dramatically increasing our earning potential by having them there. How, you ask? By offering stuff that kids like.

This is one of the biggest reasons I've been harping so loud about taking out the trash in indie pro wrestling. Quite simply, you don't want guys busting fluorescent light tubes over each other, guys dressed up as transvestites, guys beating up their opponents' girlfriends, or guys mooning the crowd because if you do, *parents won't bring their kids.*

And if parents don't bring their kids, you won't have 9-year-old boys pleading with their fathers to buy them that cool Cena action figure you have for sale on your gimmick table! Children are an awesome source of revenue. When I go to a wrestling show by myself, I might be perfectly content to watch the show without buying a thing. But when I take my nephew with me, you know doggone well I'm buying him a Coke, a hotdog, a Snickers bar, and, more than likely, a toy belt and a wrestling mask.

Parents like to spend money on their kids. Getting the kids souvenirs is all part of the experience. But how are you going to sell those souvenirs and Snickers bars if there aren't kids there to clamor for them?

The moral of the lesson is to keep the show family-friendly. Don't make the show kid-oriented; that's not what I'm saying. I'm saying keep it a sport and keep it clean, like the NFL, MLB, and NBA do. Make your wrestling show something the dads like and dads feel comfortable watching. Don't worry about the kids liking it; kids like what their dads like. If Dad likes NASCAR, junior likes NASCAR. If Dad's a San Diego Chargers fan, junior's a Chargers fan. Likewise, if Dad likes your promotion, his kids will, too.

Where to put the gimmick table

Casinos know all about the importance of traffic flow. Pay a visit to any casino in the United States and you'll notice a commonality amongst all of them – there's only one men's room and one ladies' room. You'll also notice that all the attractions – the craps table, the roulette wheel, the card games, the buffet – are on one side of the casino and the bathrooms are completely on the other. And the only way to get to the bathroom is to walk past rows and rows and rows of slot machines.

You see, casino operators know that the slots are their best money makers. They also know that the temptation for a person to drop a dollar or two in a slot machine on the way to the bathroom is almost irresistible. "Ah, what the heck?" people think. "I might hit." More times than not, they drop a dollar (or twenty) in the slot machine, lose, and continue on their way.

Ka-ching!

We can use this same model in placing our gimmick tables. The goal is to place it strategically where lots of fans will walk past. You could place it by the bathrooms, but I prefer by the concessions stand, particularly if you deploy the three secret weapons we discussed earlier. Those fragrant aromas of fresh baked cookies and just popped popcorn will draw the fans to your concessions stands like flies…and on their way to the cookies, popcorn, and hotdogs, they have to walk past the replica belts, t-shirts, and action figures.

So place your gimmick table smack dab next to your concessions stand. This strategy is even more effective when there's a line in front of the concessions and fans have a chance to take a look at what's on the table as they're waiting to order a large slice of pizza and an icy Mountain Dew.

This is where you put the gimmick table while the show is underway; however, about midway through your main event, have your gimmick table workers move the gimmick table to right next to the exit doors. This way they'll have a second chance to take a look on their way out.

What to sell

What should you sell at your gimmick table? Why, wrestling stuff, of course! First up, you should always have t-shirts with your promotion's logo and catchphrase on them. Use designs that are sharp and leading edge. Look at designs of t-shirts sold by the NFL for inspiration. Try to use bold, dark colors like navy blue and red.

Another great theme for t-shirts is making a statement. For example, you could print a shirt that says, "Damn right I like pro wrestling!" or, "Restore kayfabe!" Shirts like these will surely sell well to the smart marks, especially if you have an attractive young lady wearing one and peddling it.

High quality baseball caps are also a good item. They're a bit more expensive to print, but you can sell them for more money. Again, choose bold, dark colors.

Some of the best stuff you can sell is the big boys' merchandise. Even though you're working to establish your own brand, there's no reason why you can't sell WWE action figures, toy belts, posters, and masks. A great way to build up your stock is through Amazon. Search Amazon for "WWE toys," and a huge selection will be returned. Then browse through the results to find things that you can move. Look for action figures of the big name guys who are getting pushed. On Amazon you'll notice the Amazon price, which is typically the manufacturer's suggested retail price (MSRP), and lower prices offered by vendors selling the same item for much less. For example, a Cena action figure might go for $19.99 at Amazon and Walmart, but you can buy the same action figure from an Amazon partner for, say, $14. Then when you sell it at your show, you just mark it up to MSRP, which is $19.99 ($20).

Thus you stand to make a couple dollars from every figure you sell. While your profit from each individual item might not be great, once you add up everything you've sold for the evening, you'll find that you've made a tidy profit.

Other great options are books and DVDs. For example, you can buy a like new copy of RD Reynolds' excellent book, *The Death of WCW* for less than $5. You could buy that book and mark it up to $10. Then when someone is browsing your table, you say, "Oh, hey, have you read this book? No? Oh, wow. Man, you've *got* to read it. It's hilarious. An excellent read. One of the best wrestling books ever."

Ka-ching! Instant $5 profit.

Same holds true with DVDs. As I type these words, you can buy copies of, "Bloodsport: ECW's Most Violent Matches" for under $5. Mark it up to $10 and sell it hard: "That DVD is gruesome…shocking. The matches on it are unreal…sick…" Saying something like that will surely stoke a fan's curiosity, so it's very probable he'll fork over $10 to see it for himself.

Ka-ching! Instant $5 profit.

The key is to select merchandise that you feel confident will sell. Don't buy obscure or boring merchandise. While you might be interested in seeing a DVD of the most extreme puroresu matches in the history of Japanese pro wrestling, there's not a very good chance it will sell well to others. Pick items that feature big name, well known people and events.

Whatever you do, make sure your gimmick table is well-stocked. You want it to look like a small retail store. There should be lots of things to browse through, lots of things to grab your fans' attention. The longer they stay at your table, the more apt they are to buy something.

Remember, make money

As I said before, making money is good. It's good for the business, it's good for the boys, it's good for fans, and it's good for you. Do not shy away from it. You must pursue all money-making avenues aggressively.

Grow your business! As soon as you start making money on concessions and your gimmicks table, pump that money back into your business to make it better. Buy more advertising, more merchandise for your gimmick table, more food to offer at your concessions stand.

Grow!

It's like this – you don't feel bad about getting a raise at your day job, do you? A raise means more money, more security for your family and yourself. A raise is a good thing, right? Well so is making more money through your wrestling promotion.

It's the only way any of us has a chance at realizing *The Dream*.

9

The Ultimate Pro Wrestling Workout Routine

"No one is going to pay to see you if you look normal."
- Lanny Poffo, leaping genius

Sport is sport

If you've read this far and have been paying attention, you should get by now that I'm a complete stickler about pro wrestlers being in shape and looking the part. Make no mistake: Pro wrestling is a *sport*. Let me say it again: Pro wrestling is a *sport*. Anyone who tells you otherwise is just a nitwit. And because pro wrestling *is* a sport, it is essential that its participants be properly and fully conditioned for it.

Let me put it like this. Football is a sport. There's no question about it. Every sane person will agree that football is a sport. Now, football can be played at many levels, all the way from the NFL pros in the Super Bowl down to ten-year-olds playing touch on a sandlot. Regardless of the level, all people playing the game are participating in a sport. However, the folks at the highest levels of the game are the most in shape. It's a requirement to make the team and play the game. It's what fans pay to see. Sure, you can be a doughy out of shape slob or a scrawny toothpick and organize a pickup game at the local park, but no one is going to pay to come see you.

The same thing holds true about pro wrestling. Sure, a crew of chubby and pencil-necked kids can rent a ring and put on a show at the local VFW hall, but no one other than their friends and family are going to buy a ticket. If you want to be successful as pro wrestler – either by being an indie sensation like Kahagas and Roderick Strong or by winning the Big Gold Belt in WWE – you must get in incredible, Rocky-like shape. Period. End of story. No more arguments.

No more excuses.

And as I hope you can tell by now, I am not one to tell you to do something without telling you how. That's not my style. So because I am so adamant about guys getting in shape for pro wrestling, that's what this chapter is all about – how to get in the best shape of your life for your wrestling career.

My credentials

So you might reasonably be asking yourself at this point, "Wait. What does a wrestling promoter know about exercise? What qualifies Norm to tell me how to work out?" That's a perfectly fair question. Here's my answer: When I was a pro wrestler I paid the bills by working fulltime as a personal trainer. I've held certifications from the American College of Sports Medicine as an Exercise Specialist and a Gold Certification from the American Council on Exercise as a Personal Trainer. I've trained many competitive athletes (many were pro wrestlers) and swimsuit models for over 20 years. So trust me, I know what I'm talking about.

The next six months

The conditioning program I lay out for you is a six month program. Let me be clear about that. You will *not* see results overnight. It took over four years to build the Golden Gate Bridge. It took five years to build Hoover Dam. The Great Pyramid of Egypt took over 20 years. Great things take *time, dedication, persistence,* and *hard work.* These are the essential ingredients to a successful conditioning program. There is no substitute for them.

So I want you to start this program as soon as you've finished reading this chapter. Go buy a calendar and mark the day you start. Grab your camera and take a picture of yourself without your shirt on. Flip forward six months on the calendar and mark the day you will have completed this program. On that day, take another photo and compare them side-by-side. You will be amazed at the difference.

Amazed. You will be looking at two different people. A wave of pure euphoria will wash over you. You will feel a level of success and accomplishment like you've never felt before.

The key to this success is to *stay focused.* Do not give up! Success in anything in life requires constant focus, especially in the face of discouragement, frustration, and tedium. The difference between successful people and average people is successful people finish whatever they start, regardless of the challenges, setbacks, and work it requires.

Think about it. Almost everyone sets out to do great things in life: Get in shape, get a college degree, build a business, learn how to play the electric guitar, become a successful pro wrestler, etc. When they first embark on these missions, they're very enthusiastic and excited. The first few days in, their enthusiasm is contagious and success seems guaranteed, but as the days wear on and the realization that success is going to require lots of time and hard work, their enthusiasm starts to wane. Little by little, they stop trying. They miss workouts or don't study as hard or don't practice as much. Then the excuse making starts. They start making up sorts of excuses as to why they could never achieve the goal they set for themselves. "I'm just too busy," or "This wasn't right for me," or "I need to spend more time with my family..."

Excuses. That's all they are. And here's the bottom line: Successful people do not yield to excuses. Oh, rest assured, they get tempted to give up. They get frustrated and often feel their interest and focus drifting. But the difference between average people and successful people is, successful people don't give in to these temptations! When a successful person starts something, he says to himself, "I don't care what happens. Come hell or high water, I'm finishing this. I am not going to get distracted. I am not going to start something else until I finish this."

That, my friend, is what makes successful people extraordinary. Most people are average. I'd say 95% of people walking around on the street are average. They do just enough to get by and when they attempt something big, they give up in the face of difficulty. The other 5% of the population are the people that are doing things, creating things, accomplishing big things, and making headlines. They do this not because they are super human, but because they refuse to allow themselves to get bored, discouraged, or disinterested. They refuse to give up.

So I ask you right now, are you average or are you extraordinary? It's your choice.

About Sam

Sam was a guy with many God-given talents. He was tall, smart, handsome, and athletic. He was very photogenic and could sing like Elvis Presley. A friend of his named Tom came up to him and said, "Sam, you're so talented. You should be an actor." So Sam took Tom's encouraging advice and started taking acting lessons. Then Bob came to Sam and said, "Sam, you're so athletic. You should play football." So Sam gave up acting and started working out to make the local semi-pro football team. Then Tim came to him and said, "Sam, you're such a great singer. Why are you wasting your time trying out for some semi-pro football team?" So Sam starting taking singing lessons. Then Mike came to Sam and said, "Too many people are trying to be singers nowadays. With your height and looks, you should be a model." So Sam quit the singing lessons and signed up at a model agency…

In the end, Sam tried everything and accomplished *nothing!*

There are several morals to the story about Sam. The first one is about focus. You have to pick something and stick with it. You can't conquer everything in the world. There just aren't enough hours in the day. The second and more consequential moral is this: Many people, all with good intentions, are going to come to you and tell you what you're doing is wrong and that you should be doing something else. And if you listen to them, you will lose your focus and get nowhere.

You probably see a little bit of Sam in your life…or maybe a lot of him. The key to success, however, is to stay on the line.

Such is the case with the workout program I'm laying out for you in this chapter. Once you start it, people in the gym are going to come up to you and say things like, "Why are you doing this exercise? That exercise over there is much better," and, "You shouldn't do that exercise like that. You should do it like this," and, "Why are you doing that workout routine? Don't you know the Ultra Power Reps Routine is far better?"

Ignore these people. They mean well, but if you listen to them, you will get sidetracked. You'll start one workout routine, then another, then another, and then yet another. In the end you'll have gone nowhere. Trust me: The routine I've designed will get you awesome results *if you stick to it and do it religiously.*

It takes dedication

If you want to accomplish anything great in life, you must be dedicated. You must focus like a laser on the task at hand and resolve not to quit until the goal is met and the job is done. Getting in awesome shape for any sport requires tons of dedication, so right now, right this moment, close your eyes and tell yourself, "I am dedicating myself to my workout routine. I *will* get in shape, no matter what happens."

As a personal trainer, I heard excuses all the time: I don't have time…I'm too busy…My work is just so crazy right now…I'm traveling too much…

You know what I'm going to say: That's right, *excuses.*

Think about it. WWE wrestlers are on the road 300 days out of the year. They hop on a plane, land, work a show, go to bed, and the next day, they're on another plane. Yet throughout it all, they all find the time to work out.

When Randy Orton travels, the first thing he tells himself when he's stepping off the plane is, "I need to find a gym." Other people think, "I need to find a bar," or, "I need to get something to eat," but not Orton. He's immediately thinking of getting in the gym. So if guys living the crazy road lifestyle of WWE can make time to get into the gym, so can you. If you work late, get up early in the morning and work out. If you travel a lot, that's fine. Almost every hotel has a workout room. If that workout room is lacking, find a local gym nearby.

In order to get results from any fitness program, your routine must be very regular. Irregular training is no good. If your routine calls for you to work out five days a week, you must work out five days a week. This nonsense you see some posers doing where they train hard on

Monday, skip Tuesday and Wednesday, train on Thursday, skip the weekend, train on Monday, skip Tuesday, etc. just doesn't work. Consistency is key. Do *not* skip workouts!

Think of it this way. There are literally thousands of aspiring indie pro wrestlers in the United States today. Every time you skip a workout, some other wrestler out there is not. And that puts him one step closer to that spot on WWE's roster or one step closer to that gold belt than you. Think of that each time you feel tired and are tempted to skip. It's a great motivator.

Build your house one brick at a time

When construction workers build a house, they don't wave a magic wand and, voila, a house appears. No, they build a house brick-by-brick, board-by-board, shingle-by-shingle. When a bricklayer lays the first couple of bricks that will become a huge wall, if you look at those first lonely three or four bricks lying on the concrete slab, it probably wouldn't occur to you that in due time, those three or four bricks will become a massive twenty foot brick wall. The point here is, the bricklayer keeps laying bricks, one-by-one, day in, day out until the wall is done. It's a slow process, but if he keeps at it, soon enough his job is done and he can step back and admire his impressive work.

Getting in shape – particularly building muscle – is a lot like building a brick wall. If you expect results immediately, you will very quickly become frustrated and will be tempted to quit. Don't fall into that trap. Instead, stay focused. Each time you go to the gym to lift weights, you're putting a few bricks on the house you're building. If you look for results immediately, it won't seem like you're making any progress at all, but if you look at yourself after a month of consistently hitting the gym and hitting it hard, you'll be amazed at how you transform yourself.

The three components of conditioning

There are three components to a pro wrestler's conditioning program: Strength, endurance, and nutrition. All three are essential to performing well in the ring and preventing injury. Strength training involves weights and will get you more muscular and stronger, thus more capable of doing the power moves like suplexes and powerslams. Endurance training is aerobic or cardiovascular training. This is critical so that you're not sucking for air ten minutes into your matches. And last but not least is nutrition. Proper nutrition provides all the essentials your body needs to build muscle.

The routine I'm laying out for you includes all three components of conditioning. Remember, you have to do all three to succeed. You can't do one and not the other two. We'll jump right into it by discussing the strength training component of this routine.

Some basics

If you've ever lifted weights before, you're probably already familiar with what I'm about to cover. Bear with me and read through this section anyway. If you've never really lifted weight before, pay close attention. The terms and fundamentals I introduce here are critical to success.

Weightlifting involves moving a target muscle group through its range of motion against a resistance. That resistance is typically a heavy weight, but it doesn't have to be – elastic bands or your own bodyweight can provide the resistance, too. But for our purposes, we're talking about weights. So, weightlifting involves moving a target muscle group through its full range of motion against a heavy weight.

Each time you move the weight through the range of motion, that's called a repetition or a *rep*, for short. Multiple reps make up a *set*. So for example, if someone says, "I'm going to do four sets of twelve on the bench press," what he's saying is he's going to bench press the barbell twelve times, rest a moment, bench press twelve times, rest, bench press twelve times, rest, and then bench press twelve times a fourth and final time. Got it? Great! Let's move on.

So weight training involves doing multiple sets of multiple repetitions of various exercises for each target muscle group. What's a target muscle group, you ask? Good question. Your body is made up of bone, tissue, and muscles. Your muscles are what move your body. Specifically, each muscle is attached to your bones. When a muscle contracts, it pulls on the bone and effectively moves it. To be able to move in different directions and in different ways, your body has many different muscle groups. Your chest muscles, for example, pull your arms in across your body. When you throw a baseball, for example, you're using your chest muscles.

Every muscle group has an antagonist. That is, for every action a muscle group performs, there's another muscle group that performs exactly the opposite action. For example, your biceps flex your arm, while your triceps straighten it back out again.

It's very important to work all the opposing muscle groups to prevent an imbalance in your joints. For example, if you build up your chest but don't bother working your back, your shoulder joints will be out of balance and serious injury can result. The program I outline here for you works all the muscles in your body evenly and appropriately.

But since there are so many muscles in your body, it would be impractical to work them out all on the same day. Instead, we organize muscle groups into logical pairs and then work those two groups on rotating days. This is referred to as a *split*. Our workout program is a three day split: Chest and triceps, back and biceps, and shoulders and legs. You are going to work out five days each week, so start by doing chest and triceps. The next day you'll do back and biceps. The third day you'll do shoulders and legs. Then you'll rest two days and then start the split all over again, starting again with chest and triceps.

Form is crucial

Every single time I walk in any gym, I see guys doing stupid things. There are guys doing barbell curls with a ridiculous amount of weight on the bar, forcing them to swing their torsos back and forth to get the weight up, which effectively works your lower back more than your arms. There are guys doing bench presses so heavy, they can't lift the weight on their own at all, so they have to have a spotter to lift some of the weight for them. But then they jump off the bench and announce, "Look at that! I just benched 350 pounds!" Then there are still other guys who claim they're doing tricep pushdowns, but they're bent way over the attachment, effectively turning a triceps pushdown into a very sloppy and inefficient chest press.

Don't pay any attention to these guys. They're boneheads, just wasting their time and energy. To get results in the gym, you must pay exceedingly close attention to *form*. By that I mean you must perform every prescribed exercise exactly as it's intended to be. No swinging, no jerking, no cheating, no dropping the weight. Your form must be textbook perfect. Otherwise you end up not working the target muscle at all and instead use muscles totally unrelated to the ones you're trying to work. Don't fall into that trap. You won't get results.

So in just a bit I'm going to explain in detail every exercise you are to perform in this routine. Pay close attention to the form as I describe it and make sure every time you hit the gym, you stick to using that form religiously.

Warming up

Before you start pumping the iron, it's absolutely essential that you thoroughly warm up first. Warming us is just that – you literally warm up your body temperature. Warming up gets your heart really pumping and increases blood flow throughout your entire body, including all your muscles. Blood in your muscles increases their elasticity, which greatly reduces the chance of injury. Never attempt to lift weights without thoroughly warming up first.

You warm up by performing some sort of cardiovascular activity for five to ten minutes. It doesn't matter what it is – bicycle riding, jogging, stair climbing, jumping rope, etc. All that matters is that you break a sweat and start breathing heavily. You should be able to feel your heart thumping away in your chest.

I recommend jumping rope. It's very effective, most convenient, and you don't need any equipment – not even a rope! All you need to do is find a nice open spot and start bouncing on your toes like boxers do right before the start of a fight. Pretend like your actually jumping rope. Do this for a minimum of five minutes. By the time you're done, you should be very warm and sweaty. Then you can hit the iron.

The routine

OK, without further ado, here's the routine you're going to perform:

Chest & Triceps	Back & Biceps	Legs & Shoulders
Bench Press	Pullups	Squats
Incline Press	Close Grip Pulldowns	Leg Curls
Dips	Seated Rows	Leg Extensions
Flyes	Pullovers	Toe Raises
Tricep Extensions	Barbell Curls	Military Press
Tricep Pushdowns	Preacher Curls	Upright Rows
Crunches	Reverse Curls	Lateral Raises

Notice that there are seven exercises per day. You're to do four sets, down pyramid style, which we discuss shortly.

How many days?

The Ultimate Pro Wrestler's Workout Routine is a three on, two off program. That means you work out three days consecutively, rest two days, then work out three days, and so on.

Down pyramiding

One of the most common questions I get asked by new trainees is, "How much weight should I use?" That's an excellent question, and the answer is vital. Determining how much weight you should use requires three things: Trial and error, a repetition range, and record keeping.

When you first start lifting weights, you'll have really no idea how much weight you can lift. As such, you're going to have to make an educated guess and then do some trial and error. For example, if you are about to do the bench press for the first time ever, you want to err on the lighter side. You put maybe 65 total pounds on the bar[4] and then try it out to see how it feels. If it feels way too light, then you increase it some. If it feels too heavy, decrease it.

---

[4] Be aware that a standard Olympic bar, which is used at all gyms today, weighs 45 pounds by itself. So 65 pounds would equal the bar plus a ten pound plate on each side.

The idea is to reach what we call *momentary muscular failure* somewhere between eight and ten repetitions on your first set, using proper form. So let's say you attempt 100 pounds on your first set of the bench press. During this first set, you should be able to perform anywhere between eight and ten repetitions in good form. If you can't do eight – in other words, your muscles give out at six or seven – the weight you've selected is too heavy. On the other hand, if you can do more than ten, the weight you've selected is too light. If, however, your muscles give out on the eighth, ninth, or tenth rep, the weight you chose is just right for you.

Pay no attention to how much weight other people are lifting. Don't even look at them. Put blinders on. Focus on what weight is right for *you*. Don't try to load up the bar with a weight that's too heavy for you just because you want to catch up to your buddy or because you want to impress someone. That leads to bad form, injury, and poor results. Focus on you.

All right, so you've done your first set. You get up off the bench and allow your workout partner to do his set. Once he's done his set, it's time for your second set. Here's where the down pyramiding kicks in. What you do for this set is reduce the amount of weight you did on your first set by ten percent. So if you were bench pressing 100 pounds, reduce the weight to 90 pounds. This time you don't count the reps; you just lift until your muscles give out, which *should* occur before the twelfth rep. But if you can do more than 12, that's fine – keep pressing until your muscles give.

Repeat this process for the third and fourth sets. So on the third set you'd do 80 pounds, and on the fourth set you'd do 70 pounds. That's why this technique is called *down pyraminding* – you start with the heaviest weight you can handle for eight to ten reps while your muscles are fresh. Then you progressively reduce the resistance set-by-set. This method causes the most amount of microtrauma to your muscles, thereby promoting maximum muscle growth.

How much rest?

A lot of new trainees ask this question – how long should I rest in between sets? Simple: Just long enough for your partner to do his set. So do your set, let your partner jump in for his, and as soon as he's done, you should be on that bench, ready to do yours. This holds true for every exercise in the routine.

How fast?

Another common question is, how fast should I perform the exercises? The answer is as easy as 1-2: When you lift the weight, you should take one second to lift it. When you lower the weight, take two seconds. There are two crucial things to remember here. One, when you lift the weight, lift it, don't jerk it or throw it. Two, as you lower the weight, lower under smooth control – don't just drop it and let gravity do the work for you. If you lower the weight properly, it should take about two seconds to return the weight to the starting position. Just remember 1-2.

Keep records!

This, bar none, is the number one mistake I see guys make in the gym – they fail to keep records of their workouts. This is such a waste! Guys don't realize it, but they're robbing themselves of huge gains by simply not carrying a pencil and notebook with them in the gym to record what they do. If you want results in the gym, you *must* keep very detailed and accurate records of what you're doing.

It's not just a good idea, it's a must.

I can't tell you how many times I've had a guy come up to me and say, "Norm, I just don't know what's wrong. I won't grow anymore. I've been lifting every day, I eat right, and I've been training like an animal, but I just won't grow. What's my problem?"

So then I ask the guy, "Let's see your logbook." To which he replies, "Oh, I don't keep one."

Bingo.

That's your problem, knucklehead!

Nothing will sabotage your gains in the gym more than failing to keep records. I hope I've been clear on this point. It's imperative. I can't stress it enough – keep records!

The good news is, keeping records is not very hard. As I mentioned already, all you need is a pencil and a small notebook. Here's an example of a record for a sample chest and triceps workout:

1/19/2013				
Bench Press	225 x 9	200	180	160
Incline Press	165 x 10	145	130	115
Decline Press	205 x 8	185	165	145
Flyes	30 x 10	25	25	20
Tricep Extensions	90 x 10	80	70	60
Tricep Pushdowns	100 x 10	90	80	70
Crunches	Failure			

Now let's look at our sample workout record entry in detail. Notice at the top I wrote the date I did this particular workout. That way I can chart my progress over time. Next, there are five columns. In the first column I write down the name of the exercise I did. In the next column over, I write how much weight I did for my first set. Remember, the first set should be your heaviest set. Consider this set your *benchmark* set. It's the set that sets the standard for the next three sets that follow.

Notice I wrote down the weight I lifted and the number of reps I did at that weight, separated by a little *X*. Here's how you read that notation: On my first set of the bench press I did 225 pounds for nine repetitions. On my first set of the incline press I did 165 pounds for ten repetitions. On my first set of the decline press I did 205 pounds for eight repetitions, and so on. It's crucial that you record the weight and number of repetitions you did for your first set of each and every exercise. I'll explain why in the next section.

In the third, fourth, and fifth columns I wrote the weight I did for each subsequent set. Notice I didn't bother writing down how many reps I did. That's because the number of reps doesn't matter on these sets just so long as you push your muscles to absolute failure on each set. And when I say failure, I mean *failure*. Your muscles give out and you just can't possibly lift the weight again in proper form.

Again, you *must* reach failure on each set!

Finally you might have noticed I didn't write any weight or reps down for my crunches. That's because I don't count reps when I do crunches – I just do them until I can't do any more.

As you can plainly see, this isn't rocket science. It's very basic record keeping, but it will mean the difference between success and failure for you. Read on to learn why.

Constant progression

How do you build a brick house? We said it before: Brick by brick. Each day the bricklayer lays a few more bricks, a few more bricks, a few more bricks until before he knows it, he's built an entire house. The key to his success is *constant progression*. That is, every day he shows up at the job site and adds a bit more to the project until it's finished.

Proper weightlifting follows this same principle – each time you step into the gym, you should attempt to do *more than the last time*. What qualifies as more? Either more weight or more reps. Every time you go to do a workout, you should look back in your logbook for what you did during the last session, then attempt to do more than that amount.

Let's look at an example. Let's say on Monday, May 10, it's your chest and triceps day. So on your first set (remember, that's your *benchmark set*) of the bench press you do eight reps at 225 pounds. So you write that in your log. Remember, the objective is to reach momentary muscular failure on your first set somewhere between eight and ten reps, and on this set you did just that – you failed on eight.

Now suppose it's Saturday, May 15, and it's time to do chest and triceps again. Remembering the principle of constant progression, you tell yourself, "I have to do more than I did last time." So you look in your logbook and see that on Monday you did 225 for eight reps. So today you set a new goal for yourself – 225 for at least *nine* reps. The next time you do chest and triceps after that, you would try to get 225 for ten reps.

OK, so now you can do ten reps; you've hit the upper limit of the target rep range (between eight and ten reps). So what now? Simple: *You increase the weight.* So you can do 225 for 10 reps. You've reached that goal. Now to continue making progress, you add 2½ pounds to each side of the bar and attempt to lift 230 pounds for at least eight repetitions.

It's a very simple principle: Pick a weight where you can do at least eight reps. Keep doing that weight until you can do ten. Once you can do ten reps, increase the weight by a total of five pounds (2½ pounds on each side of the bar) and attempt to do at least eight. You keep doing this religiously, little by little, five pounds at a time, and before you know it, you're benching 300 pounds!

As a personal trainer I have used this principle on my clients with outstanding success. It has *never* failed any of my clients. I've had guys come into the gym who've never lifted weights in their life. I would start them off bench pressing a measly 65 pounds, and they struggled with it. Less than a year later, that same guy would be benching close to 300 pounds. The keys are consistency and steadfast devotion.

No one exemplifies this sort of consistency and devotion more than the legendary Milo of Croton. Milo of Croton was an ancient Greek wrestler who lived in the 6th century BC. He was the Hulk Hogan of his day. He won just about every match he was ever in. Legend has it that Milo one time lifted a four-year-old bull onto his shoulders, carried it to slaughter, cooked it up, and ate the whole thing in one meal. How could any man be able to lift and carry a four-year-old bull, you ask? Simple: Through consistency and devotion. He built up his enormous strength over time by starting when the bull was a tiny newborn calf. He'd hoist the calf onto his shoulders and then run ten miles with it. He'd do this every single day until the calf was a full grown bull. Since the calf grew slowly, Milo was able to make constant gains bit-by-bit until he could hoist a 3,000 pound monster onto his back!

This is the principle of constant progression. As you can see, the only way to do this properly is by keeping good records, which, again, most guys don't do. They just amble into the gym and throw whatever looks good onto the bar and do reps with it. One session they might do 225; the next session they might try 250. Then the next session they go back to 225 because 250 was too heavy. They keep this up ad nausea, stuck in one place, like they're running on a treadmill. Then they wonder why they don't get anywhere.

Don't make this mistake! Remember, keep records and make progress slowly and steadily, like the tortoise that raced – and beat – the hare. You'll be amazed at the progress you'll make.

Stay in order

One important thing to keep in mind is to perform all your exercises in order. Let's use the chest and triceps day as an example again. Notice I have you doing bench press first, followed by incline press, followed by decline press. *Do not change this order!* Do them exactly in the order I've prescribed. If you arrive at the gym and see that all the flat bench press stations are taken, don't try to save time by skipping ahead to incline press with the intent to come back to bench press afterwards.

Don't do this! Muscles must be worked in specific order in order to be effective. The order that I've designed for you is perfect; don't tinker with it.

The exercises

OK, it's time now for us to go over the exercises in our routine. Each exercise is illustrated in the next few pages, demonstrated by indie sensation Colby Godwin. Study each photo carefully. We took special care to demonstrate each exercise precisely as it's to be performed. Remember, the form of each exercise is essential, so study carefully.

You will need a partner to perform most of these exercises safely. When doing exercises like dips and pullups, you may find you're not strong enough when you first start to do even one repetition. That's OK. Just hang from the bar, cross your legs at your ankles, and have your partner grab your ankles and brace them against his knee. Then push up with your feet to assist yourself until you can do reps all on your own.

Bench press

The bench press is the time-tested standard in building muscle. The target muscle group is your pectoral muscles in your chest. To perform this exercise, lie down on the bench and position yourself so that your eyes are directly under the bar. Put your feet flat on the floor and grasp the bar such that when you lower the bar to your chest, your upper arm and lower arm form a 90° angle. With a spotter standing ready, lift the bar off the rack and lower it to the middle of your chest. Touch your chest and then press it back up to the starting position, stopping just before your elbows lock out.

Incline press

The incline press is similar to the bench press, with the difference being that the bench is inclined at about a 30° angle. Inclining the bench changes the lifting angle such that the upper portion of your chest is isolated from the rest of your chest. This places special emphasis on your upper chest to ensure you get full chest development. Perform this exercise very much like the bench press. Using a spotter, lift the bar of the rack and then lower it to your upper chest. Then press it back up to the starting position, again, just before your elbows lock out.

Dips

The dip is as old school as you can get. This exercise works the lower part of your chest to fill out its girth. To do this exercise you need parallel bars. Every decent gym in America has a set of parallel bars somewhere. Start by placing your hands squarely on the bars with your arms bent at a 90° angle. Remove your feet from the foot rests so that you're holding yourself up. Then extend your arms until they're straight. Then lower yourself back down to the starting position. This exercise can be very tough when you first start doing it, so cross your legs at the ankle and have your spotter grab them. Now you can assist yourself by pushing up with your legs. Do this until you can perform the exercise yourself without any assistance.

Flyes

All right, so you've done bench press, incline press, and dip so far. Your chest will be pretty close to exhausted by now. Finish them off with a set of dumbbell flyes. Grasp a dumbbell in each hand and lay on a flat bench with your feet up on the bench. Lift the dumbbells together directly over your chest (not your face). Keep your arms almost perfectly straight with just a very slight bend in your elbows. Do not bend your arms at all while doing this exercise – keep them straight with that slight elbow bend the entire time! Open your

arms until you feel a stretch in your chest, which should be when your arms just pass the mark where they're parallel to the floor. Then return the dumbbells to the starting position.

Tricep Extensions

Once you finish your flyes, you're done working your chest. Time to move on to your triceps. Your triceps is the muscle on the backside of your upper arm, on the opposite side of your biceps. The triceps extension is an excellent old school exercise to build massive triceps. To do this exercise, you lay down on a flat bench. Your partner hands you a barbell, which you hold with your hand about 16 inches apart. Start with your arms fully extended and straight, with the bar hovering over your face. Then, keeping your elbows in tight, lower the bar down to your forehead. Barely touch your forehead and then press the bar back up to the starting position with your arms fully extended. This exercise is often referred to as "skull crushers," for obvious reasons.

Tricep Pushdowns

This exercise will get you a huge pump in your triceps. Find an overhead cable machine and attach a V-shaped attachment to it. Stand close to the machine, and then put your feet together and bend your knees slightly. The key to this exercise is to keep your elbows pinned to your sides throughout the entire movement – don't let your elbows move up as you return the attachment to the starting position. Start the exercise with the attachment at about chest level. Push the attachment straight down, keeping your back erect and straight. Extend your arms fully. Then return the attachment to chest level,

again, keeping your elbows pinned against your sides the entire time.

Crunches

We finish up chest and triceps day by squeezing in your abdominals at the end. The most fundamental and effective ab exercise is still the old fashioned crunch. Lay flat on a mat on the floor. Place your hands against your ears (not behind your head), bend your knees, and then crunch forward to lift your shoulders off the floor. Then lower yourself back down just where your shoulders touch the floor again. As soon as your shoulders touch, crunch back up again. Do four sets to failure.

Pullups

This exercise is another old school muscle builder. It's awesome in building up your lats, the "wings" of your back that, when developed properly, provide that tapered V-shape that all bodybuilders want. The pullup is a simple exercise in concept, but if you've been out of the gym for a while, it can be very daunting. To do a pullup, all you do is find a pullup bar, grab the bar with an overhand grip with your hands a little wider than shoulder width apart, and then pull yourself up to where your chin touches the bar. Then lower yourself back down in control until your arms are fully straight. Problem is, you may not be strong enough to do a full pullup by yourself. If that's the case, don't fret. Just have your spotter help you. Cross your feet at the ankles and ask your spotter to grab them. Then assist yourself up by pushing with your feet. In time you'll be strong enough to be able to do them on your own without any help.

Close grip pulldowns

Close grip pulldowns are done on a lat pulldown machine, which is a simple machine with a high pulley and a seat with a lap pad to keep you anchored down. To do this exercise, you grasp the bar with your hands about eight inches apart. You sit down on the seat and make sure the lap pad is snug against the tops of your thighs. Then push out your chest to create an arch in your lower back and lean slightly backward, away from the high pulley. Remain in that position throughout the entire movement. Then pull the bar down to your upper chest. Return the bar to its starting position, allowing your arms to fully straighten out. Do *not* allow your torso to straighten back up and then lean back to hoist the weight down. That's cheating!

Seated rows

The seated row works your rhomboids and middle trapezius, the muscles in the middle of your back, in between your shoulder blades. Pay special attention to the form of this exercise, as at least 90% of guys in gyms

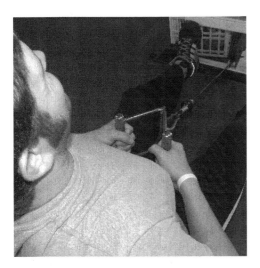

today do it wrong. Start by sitting straight up on the seat. Place your feet on the footpads and straighten your legs out until you have just a slight bend in your legs. The starting position is with your shoulders rounded forward, but with your torso straight up and down. You finish the movement by pulling the attachment in to your stomach and pulling your shoulders back. Imagine someone holding a tennis ball in the middle of your back. The objective is to crush the tennis ball with your shoulder blades. Remember, do not lean your torso back or forward as you do the exercise.

Pullovers

This is my favorite of all exercises. It's intended to work your back, but in reality it works almost every muscle in your upper body. It's a great mass builder. Do this exercise on a simple flat bench. Lay face up on the bench with your head just slightly off the edge. Have your partner hand you an EZ curl bar. Grab the bar using the innermost grips. Lower the bar to your chest and bend your elbows at a 90° angle. Keep your arms bent this way throughout the movement. To perform the pullover, lower the bar behind your head and toward the floor. As soon as you feel a stretch in your back, pull the bar back over and touch your chest.

Barbell curls

This is the one exercise that every guy knows…but few perform correctly. It's great for building up those 22 inch pythons, as the Hulkster would say, but a lot of guys fall into the trap of loading up too much weight on

the bar and end up swinging the weight to get the bar up. Don't do this – it's stupid. Really, to perform this exercise correctly you don't need much weight. Start with a straight barbell with your hands positioned slightly wider than your shoulder width. The bar should be down at your thighs, with your arms straight. Then curl the bar up to your chest. Do *not* lift your elbows away from your sides! Keep them pinned against your body. A lot of guys think they're supposed to curl the bar up to their chin, but this is wrong, as it requires you to lift your elbows to do it. Lifting your elbows is cheating. Also, swinging your torso is big time cheating. Don't do either.

Reverse curls

The preacher curl really isolates your biceps because the preacher bench keeps your arms anchored in place. If you do this exercise right, you should feel an intense burn deep inside your biceps. The key is proper positioning. The preacher bench has an adjustable seat. Adjust the seat such that your arm pits are grounded against the tops of the preacher pad. If your armpits aren't against the pad, the seat is too high. On the other hand, when you do the curl, if your elbows lift off the pad, the seat is too low. Start with your arms straight and then curl the bar up to your chin.

Hammer curls

This exercise is great for your forearms. It's done very much like a barbell curl, except your hands are pronated (pointed down) instead of supinated (pointed up). Start with the bar at your thighs and curl it up to your chest. Again, keep your arms pinned against your sides the entire time.

Squats

This is the single most important exercise in this routine. This is the exercise – far more than any other – that will promote overall muscle growth. Now you may be think, "Wait! I thought squats were for your legs? How do they promote overall growth?" Simple: Squats work the largest muscles in your body – the glutes and the quadriceps – which stimulates the production of muscle building hormones in your body.

More muscle-building hormones from working your legs affects your chest, back, arms, and every other muscle in your body. Make no mistake – if you want to pack on ripped muscle, you *must* do squats.

Here's how. First, find a power cage. Adjust the key bars so that they're low enough for you to squat very deep. Again, you'll see a lot of guys in the gym loading up huge amounts

of weight for their squats, but if you pay attention, you'll see that they don't go down very far. In fact, a lot of those guys barely go a quarter of the way down! Pay no attention to these guys. Instead, you want to go all the way down, to where the top of your calf touches the bottom of your hamstring. At this position, your thighs should be perfectly parallel to the floor. Don't go below parallel, as you risk injuring your knees. Then lift yourself back up into a standing position. This exercise is grueling, but very much worth it.

Leg curls

Leg curls target the backs of your legs, your hamstrings. The leg curl is performed on a leg curl machine where you lay flat on your stomach, hook your ankles behind a roller pad, and then curl the roller pad up to your backside. When you lay down on the bench, your knees should be hanging just off the edge. Remember to keep your entire body flat and stationary on the bench. Do not lift your torso up to generate momentum.

Leg extensions

Leg extensions are the opposite of leg curls – leg curls work the back of your legs, while leg extensions work the front, the quadriceps. Leg extensions are performed on a leg extension machine. Sit on the machine with your lower back firmly pressed against the backrest. Hook your ankles under the roller pads and then extend your legs. Slowly return the weight back to the starting position.

Toe raises

Toe raises build up your calves. A lot of guys neglect their calves – don't be one of them. Nothing looks sillier than muscular thighs and puny calves. Toe raises are done on a toe raise machine. Position the balls of your feet on the machine's step, with your heels hanging off the end. Start by pointing your heels down toward the floor until you feel a deep stretch in your calves. Then stand up as high as you can on your toes. Lower back down to where you feel the stretch again in your calves.

Military presses

The military press is a fantastic exercise for building up your shoulders. It's also great for building up strength for power moves like body slams and suplexes. Sit on a military press bench and press your lower back completely against the backrest. With your spotter standing ready, lift the bar off the rack and extend your arms so that the weight is pressed over your head. Lower the weight in control down to the very top of your chest. At this position, check your hand positioning. Your hands should be wide enough on the bar such that in this lowered position, your upper arm and forearm form a 90° angle. Touch and press the weight back up over your head again.

Upright rows

This exercise targets your upper trapezius, the muscle in between your shoulder and your neck. To perform an upright row, grab a barbell with an overhand grip and your hands centered on the bar, about eight inches apart. Stand perfectly upright with your feet together and your knees slightly bent. Pull the bar up under your chin, focusing on pulling your elbows up high. Your elbows should be pointing up at the ceiling in the finished position. Lower the bar back down until your arms are fully straight. Do not swing your torso to generate momentum.

Lateral raises

The lateral raise isolates your deltoids and gives your shoulders a very muscular, rounded shape. This exercise is done with dumbbells. Grab a dumbbell in each hand and stand with your feet together and your knees slightly bent. Hold your arms 95% straight – that is, throughout the entire movement, your arms should be locked almost perfectly straight. You should have just a tiny bend at the elbows. Once you've positioned your arms this way, do not allow your elbows to bend anymore as you lift the weight. Perform the exercise by lifting both arms out from your sides until they are perfectly parallel to the floor. Then lower them back down to your sides and repeat.

BENCH PRESS Grasp the bar such that when you lower the bar to your chest, your upper arm and lower arm form a 90° angle. With a spotter standing ready, lift the bar off the rack and lower it to the middle of your chest. Touch your chest and then press it back up.

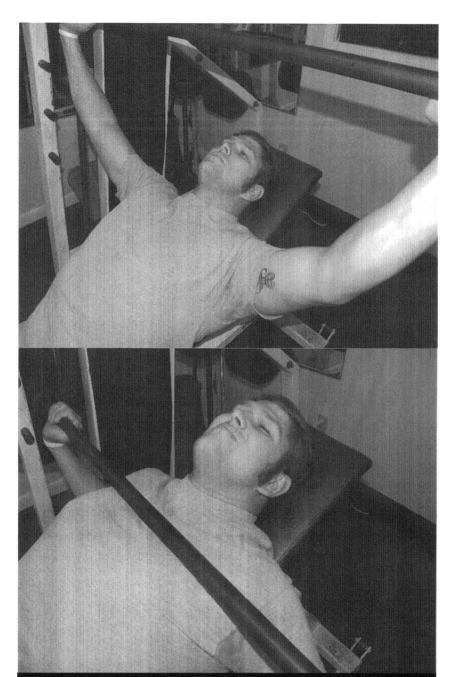

INCLINE PRESS The incline press is done almost exactly as the bench press, with the difference being that the bench is inclined at about a 30° angle. Touch the bar to your upper chest and then press it back up to the starting position.

DIPS Lift yourself up on parallel bars. Tuck your chin to your chest and then lower yourself until your arms are at a 90° angle. Then press yourself back up to the starting position.

FLYES   Grab a set of dumbbells and lay on a flat bench. Lift the dumbbells directly over your chest. Open your arms until you feel a stretch across your chest and then return the dumbbells to the starting position. Keep your arms 90% straight throughout.

TRICEP EXTENSIONS Start with your arms fully extended and straight. Then, keeping your elbows in tight, lower the bar down to your forehead. Barely touch your forehead and then press the bar back up to the starting position with your arms fully extended.

TRICEP PUSHDOWNS Pin your elbows in tight against your sides. Grab a V-shaped attachment and start with it at chest level. Press the attachment down until your arms are straight and locked. Return to the start and repeat. Don't let your elbows move at all throughout!

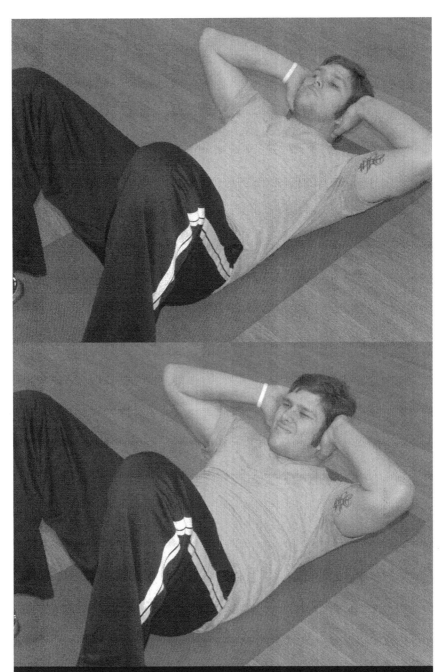

CRUNCHES Lay flat on a mat on the floor. Place your hands against your ears (not behind your head), bend your knees, and then crunch forward to lift your shoulders off the floor. Then lower yourself just to where your shoulders touch the floor again.

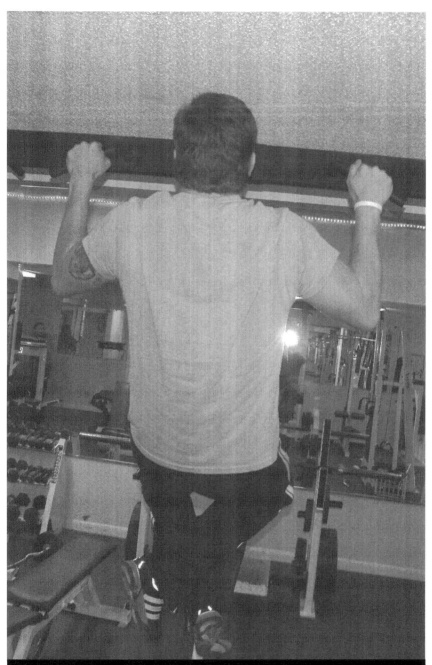

PULLUPS Find a pullup bar, grab the bar with an overhand grip with your hands a little wider than shoulder width apart, and then pull yourself up to where your chin touches the bar. Then lower yourself back down in control until your arms are fully straight.

326

CLOSE PULLDOWNS Do this exercise on a lat pulldown machine. Grasp the bar with your hands eight inches apart. Lean back and arch your lower back. Pull the bar down to your chest and repeat. Do not straighten back up when you return the bar to the starting position.

327

SEATED ROWS Use a low pulley to do this exercise. Sit up straight and pull the attachment into your stomach, pulling your shoulder blades together. Do not lean back; do not lean forward – stay upright.

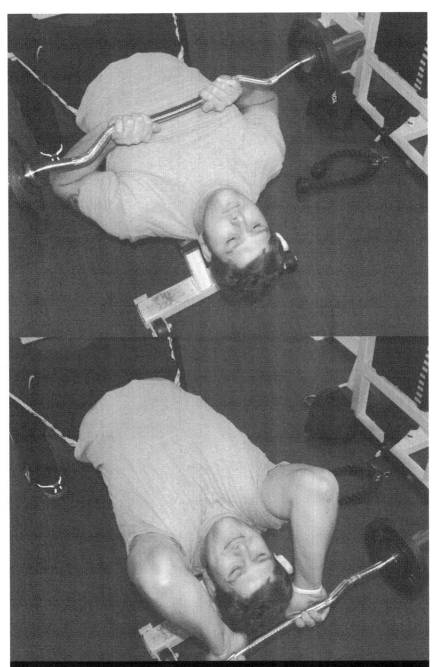

PULLOVERS Use an EZ curl bar to do this exercise. Lie flat on a bench. Hold the bar using the inside grips. Keeping arms completely bent at the elbow, lower the bar behind your head until you feel a stretch. Then pull the back over to touch your chest.

BARBELL CURLS Use a straight bar for this exercise. Hold the bar slightly wider than shoulder width. Start with your arms straight and then curl the bar up to your chest. Keep your elbows pinned to your sides. Do not raise your elbows up from your sides and do not swing.

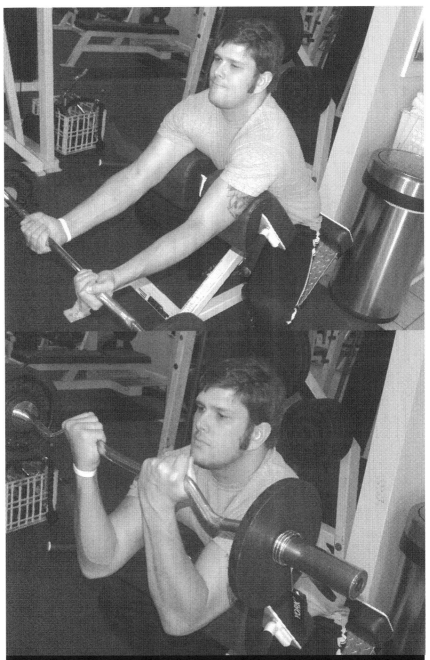

PREACHER CURLS This exercise is done on a preacher curl bench. Grasp the bar slightly wider than your elbows. Point your elbows in towards each other on the pad. Curl the bar up to your chin and then repeat. Keep your upper arms immobile throughout.

REVERSE CURLS This exercise will thicken your forearms. Grab a straight bar with your hands *over* (not under) the bar. Curl the bar up to chest level and then return it to the starting position. As with the barbell curl, keep your elbows pinned against you sides throughout.

SQUATS This is the single most important exercise in this routine. Position a straight bar on your shoulders. Keeping your torso erect and your chin up, squat down until the bottoms of your hamstrings touch your calves. Then return to the standing position and repeat.

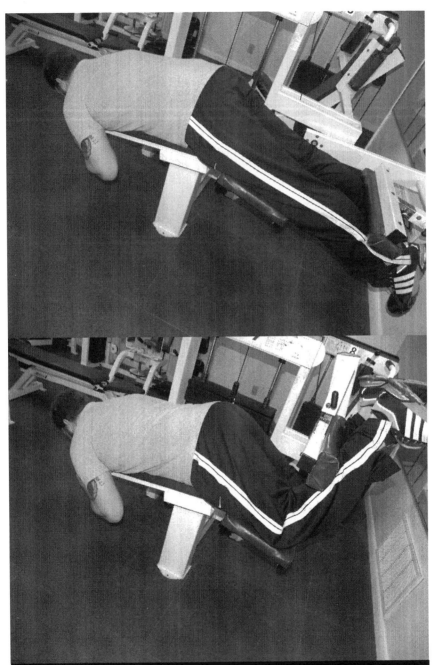

LEG CURL This exercise works your hamstrings, the backs of your legs. Lie face down on a leg curl machine and hook your legs under the leg pad. The pad should be just above your ankles. Then curl the pad all the way up to your backside. Lower the weight and repeat.

LEG EXTENSIONS Sit on the machine with your lower back firmly pressed against the backrest. Hook your ankles under the roller pads and then extend your legs. Slowly return the weight back to the starting position.

TOE RAISES Don't neglect your calves! Stand on a platform with one leg tucked behind the other. Hold a dumbbell in your hand and raise up on your toes. Lower back down to wear you feel a stretch in your calf. Then switch legs.

MILITARY PRESS This exercise is great for building big shoulders. Grab an Olympic bar slightly wider than shoulder width. Start with the bar under your chin and then press it up over your head. Lower and repeat. Your partner can put his knee in your back as a support.

UPRIGHT ROWS Do this exercise to build your trapezius muscles. Grab a barbell with your hands six inches apart. Pull the bar up under your chin. Lower and repeat. Make sure to lift your elbows high in the finished position.

338

LAT RAISES This exercise will put a cap on your deltoids. Grab two dumbbells. Bend your elbow very slightly and then keep them that way throughout the movement. Raise your arms until they are parallel to the floor. Lower and repeat.

HIIT

OK, so now you know your weightlifting routine. Next up for us to discuss is your cardio training. Cardio training will burn fat off your body and strengthen your heart and lungs so you can perform better and longer in the ring.

When you mention cardio, most guys think of long, boring, grueling jogging sessions that take an hour or more to do. Or maybe you envision long, dull bouts on a stationary bike. If that's what you're thinking, rejoice! You won't be spending long, taxing hours on a treadmill, bike, or stair climbing machine.

You're going to spend 20 minutes.

You read that right – 20 minutes total. No more, no less.

You're going to be doing something called *High Intensity Interval Training*, or HIIT for short. HIIT is a revolutionary exercise methodology that will dramatically improve your cardiovascular conditioning in just a fraction of the time of traditional long duration cardio training. You can get the benefits of five hours of jogging in less than one hour using HIIT.

It's true. It's scientifically proven. Guys who get up on a treadmill and run for an hour every day are literally wasting their time. You can better results in just 20 minutes. Not only will your heart and lungs get in better shape, you'll burn way more fat.

It sounds too good to be true, but it's not. It's extremely effective and the ideal conditioning strategy for pro wrestlers. That's because HIIT involves all out, maximal exertion for a short duration of time, followed by a rest period. This lines up perfectly with pro wrestling's demands that you run the ropes full tilt for a few seconds and then drop into a rest hold. Wrestlers need to be able to perform explosively in short bursts, and that's exactly what you do in HIIT.

Here's how it works. You pick any form of cardio exercise you want – running (either on a treadmill or outdoors), stair climbing, elliptical training, etc. For the sake of the example, let's use running. You start out for three minutes warming up – do a good light jog to get your body temperature up and your joints loose. Then you sprint.

I mean, *sprint.*

I mean, all out run…as fast as you can! Imagine a grizzly bear is chasing you, and you're running for your life. You should be pushing yourself to your absolute limit. Full tilt. You do this for one full minute. After one full minute you slow your pace down to a walk and walk for a minute. Then you start sprinting again.

You repeat this sprint/walk cycle seven times. One minute sprint, one minute walk, one minute sprint, one minute walk…and so on for seven times. That's a total of 14 minutes of sprinting/walking. Be aware that after a little bit of sprinting you'll be so gassed you won't be able to sprint very fast. That's OK, so long as you're pushing yourself to 100% of your capacity.

Once you've completed the cycle seven times, cool down by walking/jogging for three minutes.

And that's it. You're done. Don't do any more cardio exercise beyond this. Think I'm crazy? That's fine. Just try this method for three months. Watch the fat just fall off of you and your muscles get really, really ripped.

I guarantee it.

Feeding the machine

All right, so we've covered two of the legs of the three-legged stool – weightlifting and cardio training (HIIT). Now it's time to discuss the third – nutrition. Nutrition will make or break you. It's essential that you commit to good nutrition in order to realize the results you're after.

What I'm about to describe is not a diet – a diet is something temporary. No, what I'm about to describe is a *lifestyle.* You are about to change your entire life…dramatically…for the better. This is not something you do until you reach some arbitrary goal. It's something you do for life. And by adopting this lifestyle, you will probably add 20 years or more onto your life. So don't think diet and don't think temporary. Think lifestyle change. Think forever.

Let's get started.

The banned list

Let's start the discussion off with what *not* to eat. This is the banned list. These are the foods that you are to avoid at all costs. Brace yourself, because this may come as a shock.

- Fast food (McDonald's, Hardees, Taco Bell, etc.)
- Pizza
- White bread
- White rice
- White potatoes (including baked potatoes)
- Regular (white) pasta
- Whole milk
- Butter and margarine
- Sauces (cream sauces, meat sauces, etc.)
- Ice cream
- Candies
- Fried food (fried chicken, fried vegetables, etc.)
- French fries
- Fatty meats (salami, pepperoni, hot dogs, etc.)
- Regular soda (diet soda is OK)
- Snack chips (potato chips, cheese puffs, corn chips, etc.)
- Fake cheese (nacho cheese, American cheese, Cheese Whiz)
- Sugary breakfast cereals
- Waffles, pancakes, and pastries
- Donuts
- Cakes and pies
- Fatty salad dressings (Caesar, Ranch, creamy anything)
- Alcohol

So, I take it you may not be too pleased with me right now. You might be saying to yourself, "What?! I can't eat pizza ever again?" Here's the deal – these foods both make you fat and, um, oh yeah – kill you. Again, avoid them at all costs.

However, I realize that you are human and life is meant to be enjoyed, so as such you're permitted one cheat day per week, where you're allowed to eat anything on this list. But you can only do this on your designated cheat day, which I recommend be Friday or Saturday. Every other day of the week you must eat healthy. No exceptions. And don't go overboard on your cheat day. You don't want to sabotage all the hard work you did during the week with one trip to Golden Corral.

The OK list

So now that you've learned what *not* to eat, let's take a look at what's OK:

- Whole wheat bread
- Whole wheat pasta
- Skim or 1% milk
- Cheese (in moderation)
- Sweet potatoes or yams
- Chicken
- Fish
- Lean beef
- Lean pork
- Fruits and vegetables, preferably raw
- Oatmeal
- Healthy breakfast cereals (Life, Raisin Bran, etc.)
- Whole eggs
- Nuts
- Beans

If you modify your diet to include only these foods, you'll be amazed by how much fat you'll lose, how much muscle you'll build, and how much better you'll feel. Let's talk about these foods in more detail.

Carbs, protein, & fat – the building blocks of food

Everything you eat – and I mean everything, from a raw carrot to a McDonald's Big Mac to a King Size Snickers bar – is made up of one or more of the three building blocks of food: Carbohydrates, protein, and fat.

Carbohydrates (or carbs for short) are sugars. Your body uses carbohydrates for energy. Carbs can be either simple or complex. Generally speaking, simple carbs are bad and complex carbs are good. Examples of simple carbs include sugar, candy, white potatoes, white bread, and white rice. Simple carbs cause a sudden spike of sugar in your blood and promote diabetes. They also burn up quickly, meaning you can get a sugar high, followed by a sugar crash. Complex carbs, on the other hand, burn much slower. Examples include sweet potatoes, yams, whole wheat bread, whole wheat pasta, fruits, and vegetables. You want the bulk of your daily calories to come from complex carbs.

Protein is a component of all living organisms and is used by your body to build tissues, organs, and – lo and behold – muscle. As such, you need lots and lots of protein to build muscle. Good sources of protein include eggs, low fat milk, lean meats, fish, poultry, nuts, and beans. You can also get protein from protein powder, which we'll discuss shortly.

Fat is concentrated energy. Contrary to what a lot of people believe, fat is an essential part of a healthy diet. The key is to eat healthy fats and avoid the unhealthy ones. Healthy fats are the *unsaturated fats* that are found in plants and fish. Good sources include fresh fish, nuts, olive oil, safflower oil, avocados, peanut butter, and homemade salad dressings (oil & vinegar based). Examples of foods high in saturated fats include ice cream, butter, hot dogs, hamburgers, tacos, potato chips, French fries, and whole milk. Now, if you've been paying attention, you've probably noticed that these examples of foods containing saturated fat are also many of the foods on the banned list! There's a reason why certain foods make the banned list, and being high in saturated fat ranks right at the top!

So to sum up, there are three basic nutrients in food – carbs, protein, and fat. You want the bulk of your calories to come from complex carbs. You want lots of protein to build muscle. And you want to eat plenty of *un*saturated fats to stay healthy. How much, you ask? Read on.

How much and how often?

So how much food should you eat? And how often should you eat it? Good question! First of all, realize that muscle is built from food. Remember my analogy of the bricklayer? Food is like bricks and lumber when building a house. No bricks and lumber, no house. Not enough good food, no muscle. It's that simple.

So, how much should you eat? Well, it depends on where you are now. If you've got a spare tire around your stomach (or worse), you need to reduce your calorie intake to burn the fat off. But you don't want to reduce your calories so much that you don't build muscle. So the rule of thumb for guys wanting to shed fat is 15 calories per pound of bodyweight. So if you weigh 250 pounds, you should be eating no more than 3,750 calories per day.

Now, what if you're a beanpole? If you're skinny and need to pack on mass, you want to eat 22 calories per pound of bodyweight. So if you weigh 150, you need to eat no fewer than 3,300 calories per day.

What if you're not overly skinny and not fat? In that case you want to eat 20 calories per pound of body fat. So if you weigh 180, you want to eat 3,600 calories per day.

With that said, where should the calories come from? Here's a very simple rule of thumb. Eat one gram of protein per pound of bodyweight every day. So if you weigh 200 pounds, you need 200 grams of protein. Each gram of protein is equal to four calories, so that's 800 total calories from protein. For the sake of this example, let's suppose you're one of those guys who's not too fat and not too skinny. So you need 4,000 total calories per day. Subtract 800 from 4,000 and you're left with 3,200 calories. So that means you want to get 3,200 calories from complex carbs and unsaturated fats – whole wheat bread, oatmeal, nuts, whole wheat pasta, lowfat milk, and tons and tons of fruits and vegetables.

Now you don't want to eat all this food in one sitting. Instead you want to spread it out throughout the day so your body has a steady stream of nutrients. Instead of eating three big meals, you should eat five or six smaller meals throughout the day.

Protein, protein, protein!

Like I said, you need lots of protein to build muscle, especially when you're training hard. Again, the rule of thumb is one gram of protein per pound of bodyweight. So if you weigh 200 pounds, you need 200 grams of protein every day.

If you're not used to eating this much protein, you might be surprised by how difficult it is to do. For example, let's say you're current daily breakfast is a glass of orange juice and a bowl of Raisin Bran cereal with milk. That's only 11 grams of protein...you'd have to find somehow to eat 189 more grams later on in the day! So you'd need to add some protein to your breakfast to get this number up. You could do that by adding in a couple of hard boiled eggs and a full glass of skim milk. If you ate your Raisin Bran with skim milk over it, ate two hard boiled eggs, and washed it all down with a full glass of skim milk and a full glass of orange juice, you'd bring your protein total up to 31 grams. Now we're getting somewhere. But you'd still have to eat 169 grams of protein later in the day. This can get expensive!

That's where protein powder comes in very handy. One heaping scoop of whey protein powder gives you 30 grams of protein at a very good price. You can buy whey protein pretty much anywhere these days – at health food stores, online, and even at Walmart. You just mix the protein up in water, milk, or juice and boom! You get an instant thirty grams of protein. I recommend you drink a protein shake at least twice a day to supplement your food intake so that you'll be sure you're getting enough protein. Again, if you don't get enough protein, you'll rob yourself of potential muscle gains.

Protein before and after working out

To maximize your muscle gains, you want to eat at least 30 grams of protein immediately before and immediately after working out. And when I say immediately, I mean *immediately*. An excellent way to do this is to carry a plastic shaker bottle filled with whey protein shake. That way you glug down high quality protein right before you enter the gym to fuel your workout and immediately afterwards, when you're in the locker room changing clothes.

You have a 30 minute window of opportunity immediately after working out during which if you eat extra protein, your muscles absorb the protein more readily that normal. Don't miss this window! As soon as you're finished lifting weights and are headed out to do your HIIT training, drink down some protein!

Cooking the right way

Remember, don't ever fry anything. Frying foods loads them up with saturated fat. You also don't ever want to boil your vegetables. Boiling vegetables leaches all the valuable nutrients from them. Instead, bake, broil, grill, steam, or microwave all your foods to preserve their nutritional value.

Fruits and vegetables

You want to eat fruits and vegetables at every one of your five or six daily meals. Citrus, apples, grapes, raisins, bananas, pears, and peaches make great snacks. And you can't eat too many vegetables. I recommend you eat at least one fresh green salad per day. Make your own dressings out of extra virgin olive oil, vinegar, citrus, garlic, and ginger. Avoid store bought dressings whenever possible. Toss in tomatoes, cucumbers, baby greens, sprouts, raw spinach, carrots, onions, and olives.

That's it!

That's all there is to the Ultimate Pro Wrestling Training Program! It's really not very complex at all. Remember, consistency and dedication are key. Don't skip workouts. Don't procrastinate. Don't make up excuses to miss workouts. Don't tell yourself you're too tired, too busy, too sick, too sore, too overworked, or too overtrained. Those are all just excuses. Success comes to those who put forth the necessary effort.

Be one of those people!

Conclusion

I love pro wrestling; I hate what it's become. I started this book by describing *The Dream*. And I was serious about it. Let's not let others dictate to us how we can achieve the dream of our lifetime – let's achieve it ourselves. We can do that by remaking our sport. We can make it fun and appealing to the masses again. We can convince good folks to buy tickets and come see what we have to offer. Pro wrestling, when done right, is like a live action movie, unfolding in person right in front of the audience.

Who wouldn't enjoy that?

As I said throughout this book, we have to raise our standards. We have to improve our product. We have to exceed our fans' expectations. We have to do it right.

If you follow the advice I've given you in this book, you *will* do it right. It will take time, effort, and hard work, but they will come. They will fill your seats and buy your concessions.

So make it happen. Start right now.

I want to hear about your success! Send me an email at *norm@fixingtheindies* and tell me how you're doing! Got a question or need advice? I'm here for you. Just drop me a line.

Made in the USA
Lexington, KY
24 February 2014